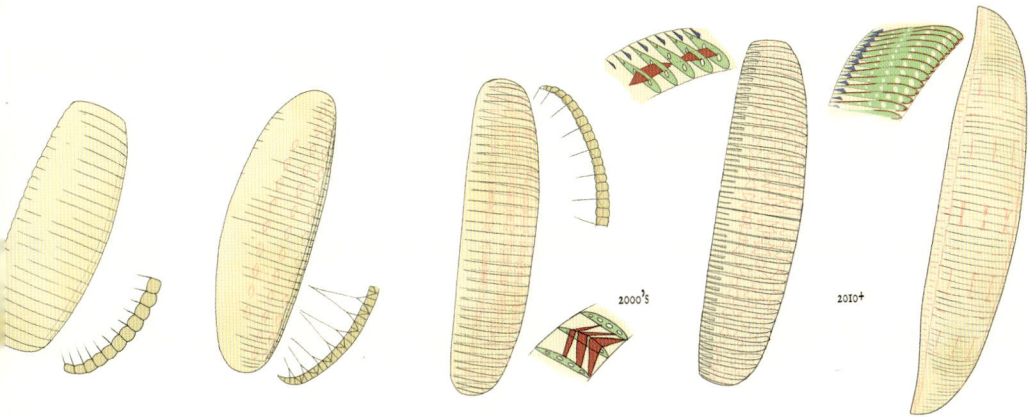

Early 1990's : The introduction of elipsoid shaping.
The nose of the glider also becomes more of an aerofoil
section with the cell openings moving downwards.

Miniribs on trailing edge and some internal plastic
battens in cell openings replacing Mylar

Refinements of internal
structure.
H-Ribs.

2000's

2010+

Diagonal ribs developed by Hannes Papesh for the
Xenon. Austria 1995

Internal battens across the chord and
Shark Nose profile (Ozone R&D 2015)

Steve Ham 2019

PARAGLIDING
THE BEGINNER'S GUIDE

By Bastienne Wentzel
and Ed Ewing

Cross Country

In the core, since 1988

About this book

This book started life when Bastienne Wentzel combined her love of flying and teaching with her background as a science writer to publish a paragliding book for pilots in her native Netherlands. It quickly sold out and was re-printed. The idea to publish an English version aimed at pilots worldwide was then born and she approached us at Cross Country Magazine. We loved the idea, and after a meeting at the famous Coupe Icare, the world's biggest free-flight festival in France, we got started. The result is what you have in your hands. More than 300 pages dedicated to helping you become a better pilot. As well as the basics, you'll find a wealth of information in here about the development of the sport, the latest equipment, techniques to help you fly better, and knowledge about the weather, air law and more. There is theory, yes, but it is under-pinned by real-world experience and know-how. We hope you enjoy it! The Cross Country team

About Cross Country magazine

Cross Country was established in 1988 by Sherry Thevenot, an artist who married into the hang gliding scene and wanted to reflect the spirit of free flight through magazines. The magazine somehow just slotted right in, and it has grown ever since – it is now read by pilots around the world in both digital and print. It has always been edited and owned by pilots, and always will be. Find us on online at www.xcmag.com and join us on social media @xcmag

Publisher's info

Cross Country International
Tollgate, Beddingham
Lewes
BN8 6JZ, UK
www.xcmag.com

Authors: Bastienne Wentzel and Ed Ewing
Editors: Ed Ewing and Andrew Craig
Designer: Marcus King
Illustrations: Charlie King and Bastienne Wentzel
Cover photo: Adi Geisegger (adigeisegger.com)
End-papers illustrations: Steve Ham (flypiedrahita.com)
Subeditor: Charlie King
Test pilot: Russell Ogden
Sales: Verity Sowden
Publisher: Hugh Miller
ISBN: 978-1-8380173-3-0

> "The Guide says there is an art to flying," said Ford, "or rather a knack. The knack lies in learning how to throw yourself at the ground and miss."
>
> Douglas Adams, Life, the Universe and Everything

▲ **GET READY TO FLY**
Bastienne Wentzel will be your guide
Photo: Ingrid van Gemert

▶ WELCOME TO PARAGLIDING!

Since you've picked up this book, the chances are that you've already tasted free flight on a paraglider. You may be an experienced pilot looking for more information. You've come to the right place! Or you may be a new pilot, just started on a paragliding course. In any case, I need to warn you: paragliding is addictive! So now you know what you're getting into if you decide to read on.

Who is it for?

This book is for all pilots, new and experienced. It contains everything from the basic concept of a paraglider to the answer to the question: "Why does it fly?" It gives you all the background and knowledge you need to progress as a pilot, all the way to thermalling and flying cross country.

After reading this book, you will be able to understand the more advanced literature and information that is out there, because you will have a good grasp of the basics.

It's definitely not a do-it-yourself flying course. Taking a course with an accredited paragliding school will ensure that you'll learn to fly faster and more safely than from a book – and you'll have more fun, too.

How to read this book

We start at the beginning – with a bit of history and everything about the paraglider. Then we keep going, through basic and advanced flying techniques, weather and aerodynamics, until we reach the end: navigating your way through your first cross-country flights.

Throughout the text, you'll find words printed in bold. These are important concepts which you'll also find in the index at the back of the book for easy reference.

Next to the main text, you'll find many illustrations and boxes. Take a good look at these as well, they clarify difficult concepts and expand on interesting subjects.

Finally, you'll find Learn More boxes at the end of each chapter. These contain a list of links, websites and books where you can find still more information on the topics covered in the chapter.

I hope you have lots of fun reading this book!

Bastienne Wentzel

CONTENTS

#7
RULES & REGULATIONS

Rules of the air, 249

Air law and airspace, 253

Licences and associations, 263

#8
NAVIGATION

Planet Earth, 277

Direction and course, 280

Maps, 281

Navigating using instruments, 287

Electronic visibility, 294

Choosing a flight instrument, 297

Index, 302

Meet the team, 316

Contributors, 318

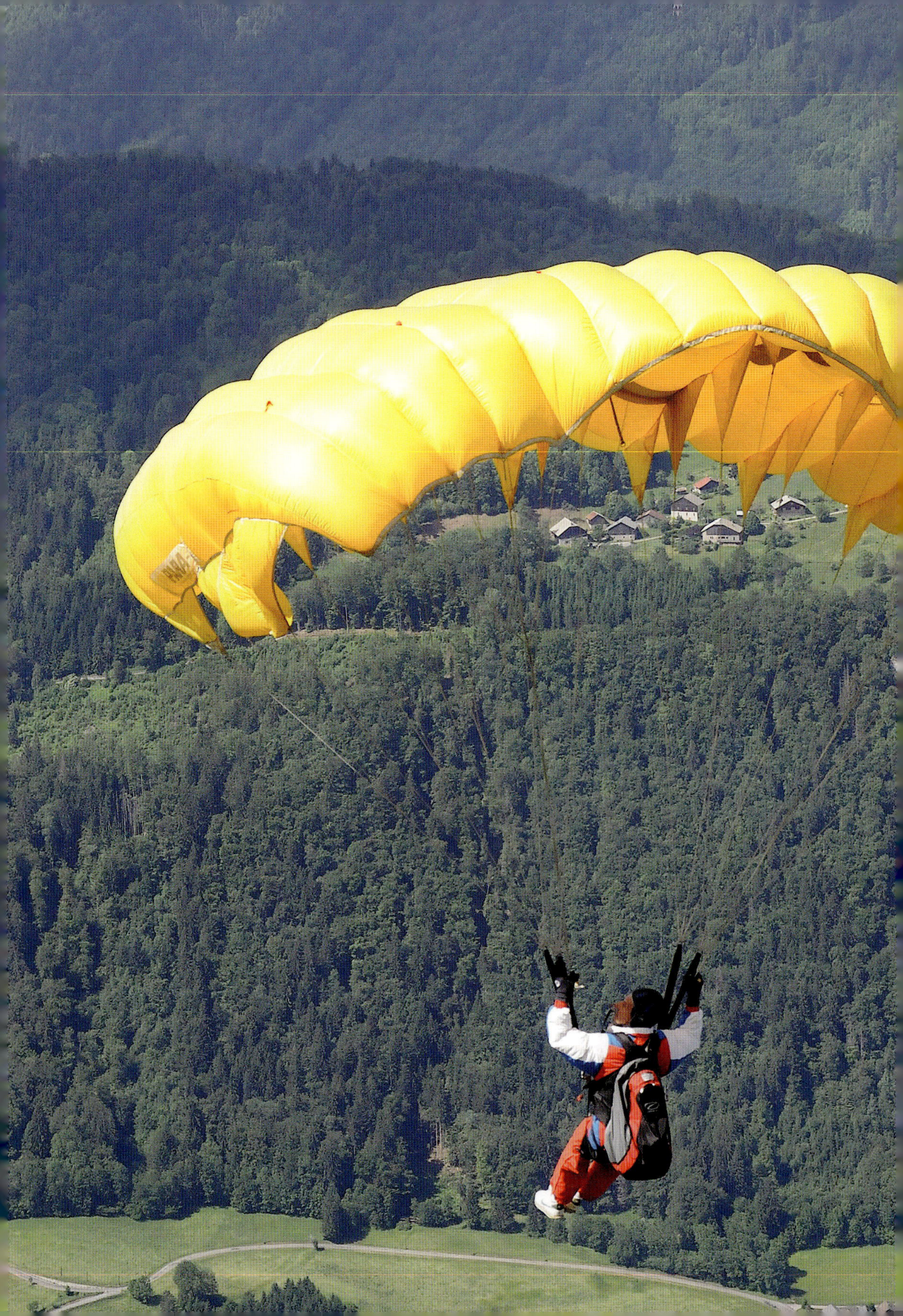

HISTORY #1

- ▶ HOW IT ALL BEGAN
- ▶ PARAGLIDING PIONEERS
- ▶ THE EVOLUTION OF THE SPORT

▲ IN THE BEGINNING
Groundhandling a replica of the Sailwing. Developed in 1965 it was a predecessor to the modern paraglider.

◄ ◄ PIONEERS
In 1978 three French pioneers flew their parachutes down from a mountain near Mieussy, France for the very first time. It was the start of modern 'parapente'. In 2013 Jean-Claude Bétemps, pictured, flew a replica Jalbert Para-Foil from the same hill to mark the sport's 35th anniversary.
Photos: Michel Ferrer

How it all began

Not many sports can boast a real birthday, but paragliding can. On 27 June 1978, three French friends – **Jean-Claude Bétemps**, **André Bohn** and **Gerard Bosson** – took their makeshift wings and flew them down from a hill near Mieussy in the French Alps. The three men had invited the press to see them launch their adapted, steerable parachutes, which were later called 'parapentes', or paragliders.

The event was a great success. They demonstrated for the first time that it was possible to launch a steerable parachute from a slope and fly down. Parachutes aren't designed to fly from a hill. They're supposed to slow down a fall from an aeroplane. Today, this 1978 experiment is regarded as the start of modern paragliding, which is still called parapente in its country of birth. And Mieussy remains a popular (and beautiful) flying spot. France was marked as the birthplace of modern paragliding by this event, and the sport is still very popular there. From France it spread quickly to many other countries around the world.

The first paragliders

Decades earlier, several precursors of the paraglider were developed. **Francis Rogallo**, an American Nasa engineer, wanted to develop steerable parachutes for his employer in the 1950s. When the capsule of a spacecraft returns to earth, it hangs from three round parachutes. These descend through the air with no control, meaning that Nasa capsules had to make water landings. Using steerable parachutes, such as those that Rogallo was developing, would enable Nasa to touch down the valuable spacecraft on land.

The parachutes that Rogallo developed were never used for spacecraft, but he has no regrets. "One of our goals was to make it possible for anybody to fly," said Rogallo in a documentary. "I wanted to fly. I tried to get into the army and the navy air corps and none of them wanted me. And I didn't have the money to do it on my own, it was so expensive. So I had to find some way that anybody could do it with almost no money, and I did."

Together with his wife, Gertrude, Rogallo designed a triangular cloth, suspended on thin lines. This so-called **flexible wing** had the aerodynamics of a fixed wing such as an aeroplane, but the structure of a parachute. "This combination of a parachute structure and aeroplane aerodynamics makes this wing unique," said Rogallo.

Not only was the flexible wing the first steerable parachute and predecessor of the paraglider; the Rogallo wing, as it became known, was also the foundation upon which hang gliders were designed. What's more, a type of emergency parachute for paragliders is still based on Rogallo's design.

▲ DESIGN AND DEVELOPMENT
After the slow early years of development the sport started to take off in the late 1980s. By the 1990s design and development was booming – the paragliders above are from 1989 and 2007
Photos: Nova / Bastienne Wentzel

During the 1960s, interest in flying parachute-like devices increased. A Canadian, **Domina Jalbert**, developed the **ram air parachute** in 1964. It was the first parachute with a canopy made of an upper and a lower surface with cell openings. Like Rogallo's flexible wing, the ram air parachute had an aerofoil shape and was steerable. It was the precursor of square parachutes, also known as mattress parachutes.

A year later, **David Barish**, another Nasa employee, flew his Sailwing for the first time near New York. This wing looks somewhat like a modern paraglider: wide in the middle with tapering wingtips. The **Sailwing** may qualify Barish as the inventor of the modern paraglider. However, the canopy of his Sailwing had only an upper surface. It had no cells sealed at the back and open at the front, like the ram air parachute and modern paragliders. But the Sailwing was certainly ahead of its time. Since 2012, single-skin paragliders have been gaining ground again. These modern, very lightweight constructions also have only an upper surface but perform in many ways like conventional double-surface paragliders.

In the early 1970s, the German **Dieter Strasilla** and the Swiss **Andréa Kühn** flew their home-made **Skywings** from the Jungfraujoch, high in the Swiss Alps. The Skywings looked much like Jalbert's parachutes, having a double surface and cells open at the front. They experimented, flying with skis on and playing around on surfboards with their Skywings. Like Barish, Strasilla and Kühn were also pioneers: speedriding

▶THE EVOLUTION OF OUR WINGS

1948 Francis Rogallo filed a patent in which he described a triangle-shaped flexible wing made from cloth and lines, the predecessor of the modern paraglider

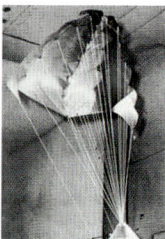

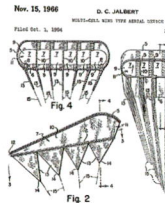

1964 Domina Jalbert developed and patented the ram air parachute. It had an upper and lower canopy and cells with openings at the front: the 'Jalbert parafoil'

1965 David Barish flew his Sailwing for the first time. Made of one surface of cloth it was wide in the middle and tapered toward the wingtips

1978 On 27 June three friends flew down from a mountain in Mieussy in the French Alps. The event caught imaginations and marked the start of 'parapente'

1985 The first theory book for paragliding was written by Bertrand Dubuis and Patrick Gilligan. It followed several hang gliding books from the 1970s

with skis and snow kiting have become very popular nowadays.

The sport takes off

As we mentioned, the three French friends Bétemps, Bohn and Bosson flew from Mieussy for the first time in 1978. In the following years, the sport of paragliding grew quickly. More and more adventurers trekked into the mountains with parachutes to fly down from the top, saving them the tough descent on foot.

The first paragliding school was established in 1979 in – where else – France. The same year, paragliding was introduced at the world championships for hang gliding, a sport which was some years ahead in its development.

In 1985, a book of theory was published which mentioned the English

▲ **MODERN DAY**
Today's wings offer safety, ease of use and performance
Photo: Advance Paragliders

1989 As the sport took off, the first FAI Paragliding World Championships were held in Kössen in Austria. Pilots flew wings like this Nova CXC

1990s The sport started to boom, with new schools, glider manufacturers and clubs. What started in the Alps soon spread all around the world

2000s Better wings, capable of being flown all day for hundreds of kilometres, saw the distance record pushed from 335km to 505km in a decade

2010s Ozone's two-line BBHPP revolutionised design. Sharknose, 3D-shaping and light materials improved performance and safety

2020s Today's 125,000 pilots can choose from single-skin gliders that weigh 1kg, to competition wings that can fly all day. The dream of unpowered flight is reality

15

expression **paragliding** for the first time. While 'paragliding' is mostly used in the English language part of the world, '**parapente**' is still the preferred expression in the French-speaking parts. The latter word is a contraction of 'parachute', which in French means 'against falling', and 'vol de pente', which means 'flight from a slope'.

In 1989, the first FAI **Paragliding World Championships** took place at Kössen, in Austria. Even today, Kössen hosts a popular paragliding festival each year.

From the 1990s onwards, there have been many technological advances in the construction of paragliders. The aim of flying a paraglider shifted quickly from flying down a slope to staying up as long as possible, and flying a long way.

Paraglider canopies became ever more aerofoil-shaped, dramatically improving the flight characteristics compared to the early parachute-like structures. As early as 1991, **Urs Haari** flew 200km measured in a straight line.

In 2008, the 500km mark was broken for the first time by **Nevil Hulett**, flying in South Africa. In 2019, the world record for the longest straight-distance stood at 588km, set by a Brazilian team consisting of **Marcelo Prieto**, **Rafael Saladini** and **Rafael de Moraes Barros**, flying in Brazil. Also flying in Brazil, Swiss paraglider pilot **Yael Margelisch** became the first woman to fly more than 500km in October 2019.

Modern materials, better knowledge and more advanced design software are still being used to improve the flight characteristics of paragliders, resulting in ever better, higher-performing and safer wings. The wings of today are the best there have ever been. The wings of tomorrow promise to be even better still.

▶**FIRST STEPS**
Pioneer David Barish (1921-2009) testing his Sailwing in the Catskills, USA, 15 October 1965. He flew about 70m. The paragliding distance record today is nearer 600km

▶**LEARN MORE**

- **Francis Rogallo obituary, LA Times,** tinyurl.com/RogalloObituary

- **David Barish obituary, New York Times,** tinyurl.com/BarishObituary

- **Domina Jalbert biography,** tinyurl.com/dominajalbert

- **Memories from paragliding pioneer Dieter Strasilla,** strasilla.de

- **Interview with Francis Rogallo,** tinyurl.com/RogalloInterview

- **The history of paragliding, from 1987,** tinyurl.com/Parasailing1987

- **Flying from Everest in 1988,** tinyurl.com/FlyingEverest1988

- **Teaching in the early days,** tinyurl.com/paragliding80s

- **The Super Max video series, classic comedy by Philippe Bernard,** tinyurl.com/Supermax1

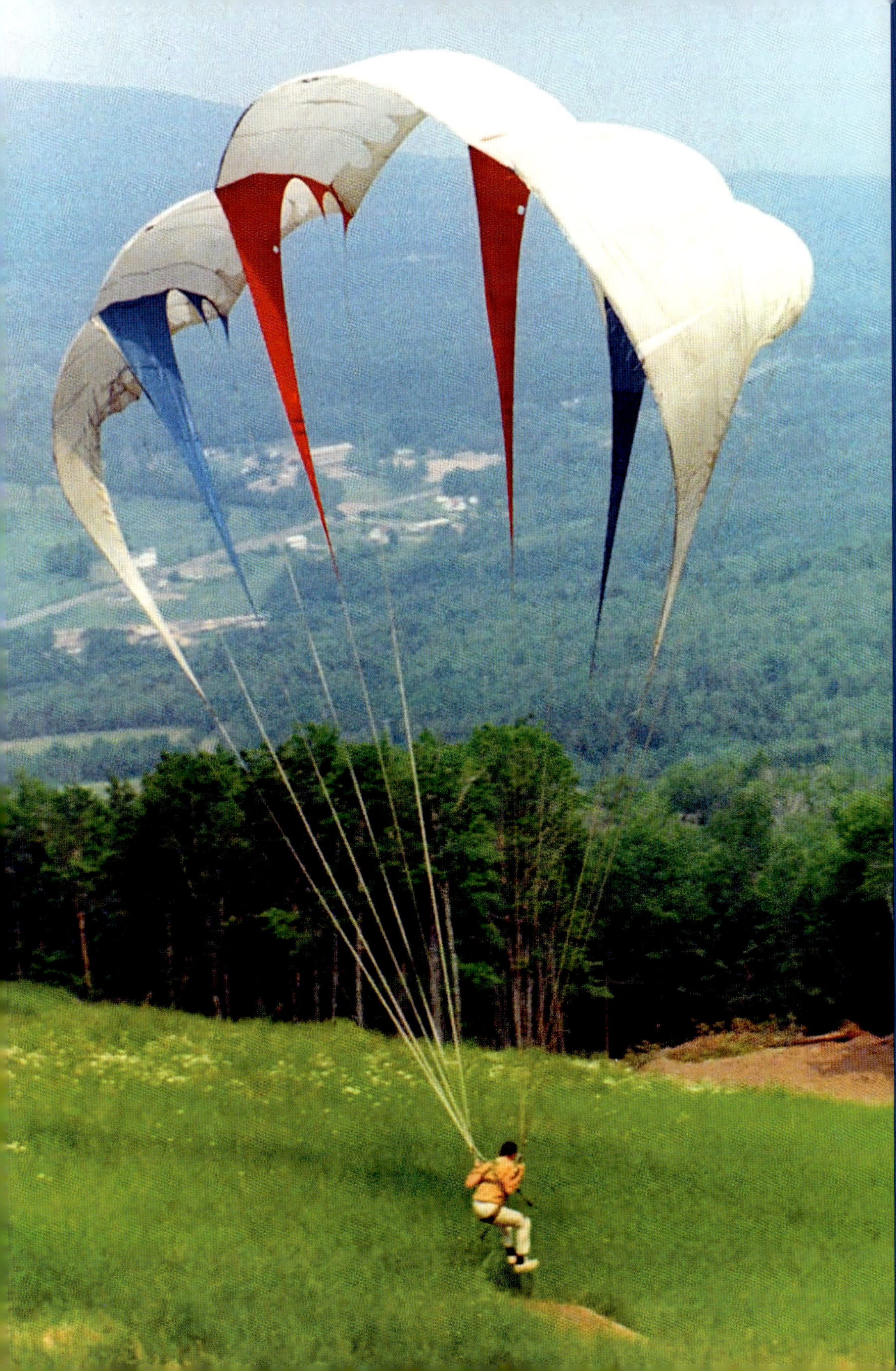

EQUIPMENT #2

The magic of your paraglider

We've chosen to take to the skies suspended on strings under an aircraft made of fabric. It's amazing that such a thing will actually lift us and carry us upwards. The reason is the shape of the canopy. When the fabric fills with air, it forms an aerofoil, a wing-like shape that can generate lift.

Before we examine how this works in the chapter about Aerodynamics, let's look at the equipment itself. The nature of the equipment and materials that carry us into the air is crucial to many aspects of paragliding. Knowledge of it is essential for flying well, but also for making a sound choice when you buy your own glider. And proper maintenance of your glider is very important to keep you flying safely. That's the purpose of this chapter.

Our aircraft is the paraglider, a special type of glider. It's an unpowered aircraft that can be foot-launched by the pilot. It's heavier than air, in contrast to a hot air balloon. Unlike a hang glider, it has no rigid main structure. Let's take a closer look.

▲ **READY TO FLY**
The basic parts of a paraglider are the canopy, lines and risers. The harness is separate and is attached to the paraglider by strong karabiners or maillons
Photo: Jérôme Maupoint

▶ THE PARAGLIDER

Construction

The **canopy** of a paraglider consists of two layers of fabric sewn together. At the front of the canopy, the **leading edge**, are **cell openings** or cell entries allowing air to flow in. The rear of the canopy, the **trailing edge**, is closed, keeping the air inside the canopy. This is how the canopy obtains its **aerofoil** (wing-like) shape.

At the leading edge, there's a point where the stream of air around the canopy divides into one part that flows along the upper side and another that flows along the bottom. This is called the **stagnation point**. It's the point where the highest pressure on the profile of the canopy is found. The stagnation point is found towards the lower surface of the canopy profile in most normal flying conditions, just behind the nose. This is where the cell openings are placed.

The space between the upper and lower surfaces is divided into **cells** which are separated by **ribs**. The cells and ribs maintain the aerofoil shape of the canopy, and ensure that the forces transmitted through the lines are evenly distributed. In the cell openings you may find reinforcements such as small **rods**. These help to keep the cell openings open.

In the ribs of the cells there are openings, the **cross-ports**. These allow air to flow from one cell to another, distributing the pressure evenly over all the cells. After any deformation of the canopy, the cross-ports make sure that the pressure is quickly restored, allowing the canopy to regain its shape and fly on.

SIDE VIEW

A Upper surface	F Cell opening
B Lower surface	G Lines
C Leading edge	H Brake line
D Trailing edge	I Riser
E Cross-port	

FRONT VIEW

A Cell	E Upper lines
B Rib	F Main lines
C Diagonal rib	G Stabilo line
D Stabilo	

airflow

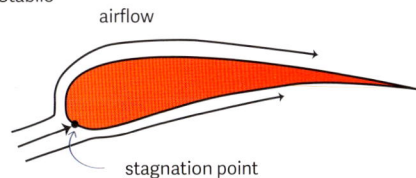

stagnation point

STAGNATION POINT
The stagnation point is where the highest pressure on the profile of the canopy is found

Between cells you'll also find **diagonal ribs**. These connect the upper corner of one cell with the lower corner of another. Some diagonal ribs even span two or more cells. These diagonal connections allow the use of fewer lines, reducing the weight and drag of the paraglider. Without diagonal ribs, each cell would have to be suspended from a line.

At the two tips of the canopy you'll find a stabilisation panel or **stabilo**. These keep the wing stable and stop it rolling excessively to the left or right during flight.

Materials

The fabric of a paraglider canopy is made from woven **polyamide** (**nylon**). This fabric is lightweight and very strong. It's woven in a **ripstop-pattern**, which is visible as small squares. This ensures that a small tear does not rip further. You'll also find ripstop material in tents and sails (spinnaker cloth). The fabric is coated, making it airtight and protecting it against UV radiation. The **coating** may for example be polyurethane or silicone.

Paraglider fabric weighs on average 30 to 35 grams per square metre. A quick calculation reveals that a $25m^2$ canopy uses less than 2 kilograms of fabric. Adding the weight of ribs, lines and risers, you end up with an average canopy weight of about 5kg.

Lightweight canopies sometimes weigh as little as 2kg because they're made with lighter materials. Competition gliders may have many more cells, using up more material and weighing 6 or 7kg.

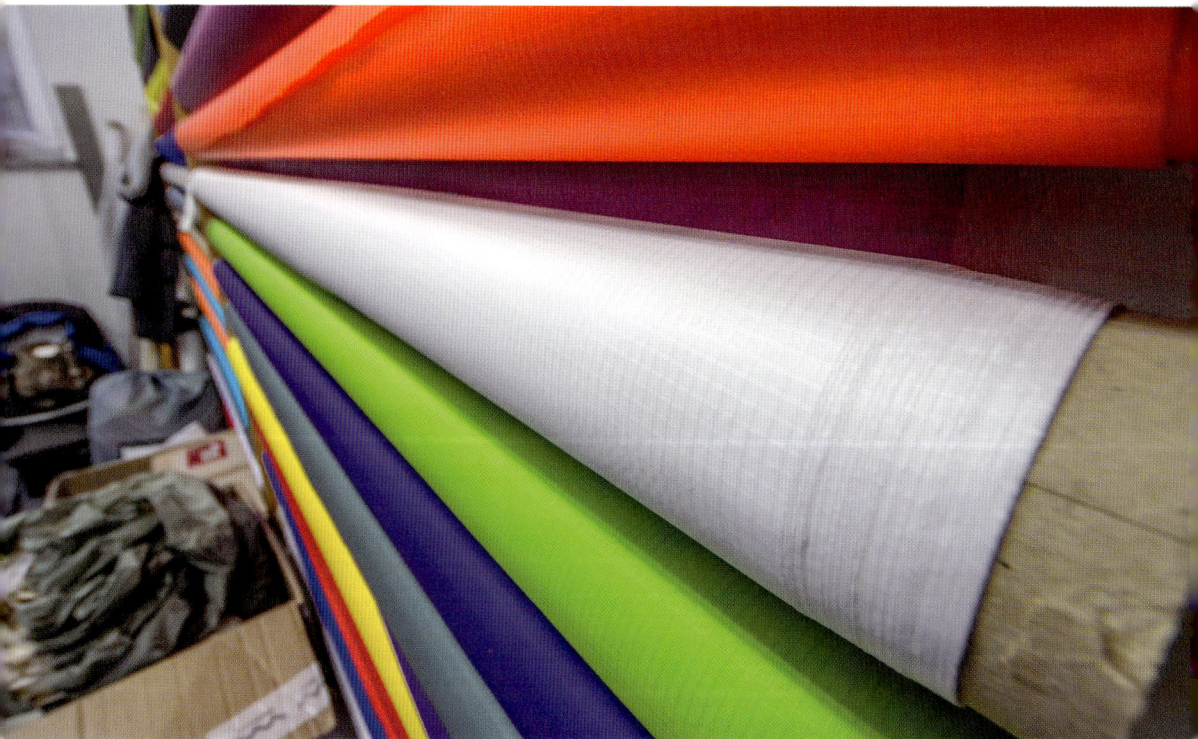

Properties

The width of a paraglider canopy from wingtip to wingtip is called its **span**. The length measured from the leading edge to the trailing edge is called the **chord**. A paraglider in stable flight always flies down with respect to the air. The airflow therefore comes from below at an angle, and the cell openings are placed on the lower side of the profile to catch as much as possible of this airflow.

The ratio between the span and the chord is different for each canopy. Some are more oblong than others. This ratio is called the **aspect ratio**, abbreviated **A/R**, and it determines many of the flight characteristics of the glider. Slim canopies are less affected by the drag that the vortex from each tip causes (see the chapter on Aerodynamics). This reduction of drag comes at a price: high-aspect ratio gliders are more difficult to fly. They're more sensitive to pilot error, and thus require more experience.

Size and weight

The weight that a canopy can carry depends on its surface area. That is why gliders come in different sizes. Regular solo gliders usually have a canopy with a **surface area** between 20 and 30m². A tandem glider may be 40m² or more.

There are several ways to define the surface area of a canopy. One is the **projected area** (the 'shadow' that an inflated canopy casts). The other is the actual or **flat area** of the canopy spread out flat on the ground. These have different values, and it is important that you know which one is being quoted when discussing the surface area.

▶ ASPECT RATIO

Aspect ratio is an important concept to understand in paragliding. It's the ratio of span (length) to chord (width). Beginner gliders have low aspect ratios, advanced gliders have higher aspect ratios and therefore higher performance. Gliders with higher A/R require a more skilled pilot.

Beginner wing: aspect ratio of 4.5 to 5

Intermediate wing: aspect ratio of 5 to 6

Sports wing: aspect ratio of 6 to 7

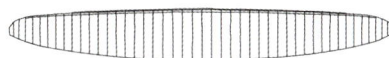

Competition wing: aspect ratio > 7

▶ CALCULATING PROPERTIES

It's useful to know the aspect ratio of a glider because it helps to determine its flight characteristics. The aspect ratio can be calculated by dividing the span by the chord. But the canopy is oval in shape, with a different chord at the tips and in the centre. In calculations we therefore use the average chord. The aspect ratio equals the span divided by the average chord.

If you don't know the average chord, you can calculate the aspect ratio by taking the span squared and dividing by the surface area of the canopy. These are usually given by the manufacturer in their manual or technical data sheet.

By playing around with these two formulas you can calculate other properties of the canopy. You get the surface area by multiplying the average chord by the span. If you want to calculate the average chord, divide the surface area by the span.

Finally, the wing load is the all-up weight (glider plus pilot and all equipment) divided by the surface area.

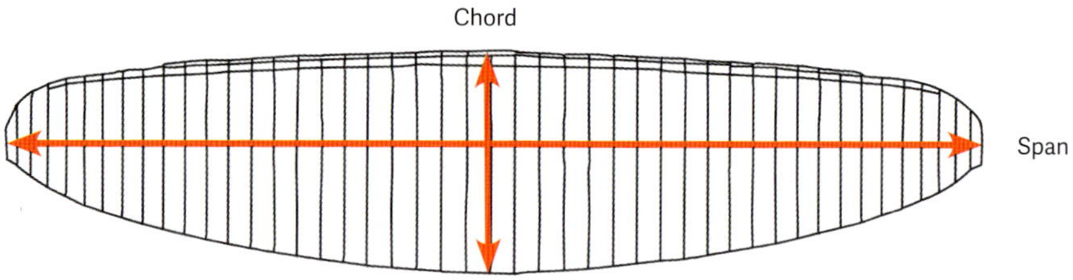

Chord

Span

$$\text{Aspect ratio} = \frac{\text{Span}}{\text{Average chord}} \qquad A = \frac{W}{K}$$

$$\text{Aspect ratio} = \frac{(\text{Span})^2}{\text{Surface area}} \qquad A = \frac{W^2}{S}$$

$$\text{Span} \times \text{Average chord} = \text{Surface area} \qquad W \times K = S$$

$$\text{Average chord} = \frac{\text{Surface area}}{\text{Span}} \qquad K = \frac{S}{W}$$

$$\text{Wing load} = \frac{\text{All-up weight}}{\text{Surface area}}$$

A = Aspect ratio
K = Average chord
W = Span
S = Surface area

The flight characteristics of a glider depend on the **wing load**. That's the weight of the glider plus the pilot divided by the surface area. Regular solo gliders have a wing load of 3 to 4kg per square metre. With a much higher wing load, the glider will fly faster and react more dynamically. If the wing load is too low, the canopy will fly slower and may collapse more easily.

It's therefore sensible to choose a glider size that fits your weight. The weight range indicated for a particular canopy is called the **all-up weight** or **take-off weight** (**TOW**). This means the weight of the pilot, their gear and the glider together. You can estimate your all-up weight by adding 15kg to 20kg to your naked body weight. Or, to get the exact figure, simply step on to your scales with all your gear and the glider – everything that will leave the ground with you.

Depending on the wing load an average paraglider flies at a speed of about 38km/h. This is called **trim speed**. A typical paraglider has a minimum **descent rate** of about one metre per second (1m/s).

Different classes

A glider with a higher aspect ratio places a higher demand on the pilot's skills than one with a lower aspect ratio. But many other properties also have an impact on the flight characteristics, such as the number of cells, the size of the cell openings, the amount of curvature of the canopy (the **arc**) and the shape of the wing.

The many different gliders on the market are not all equally easy to fly. It's like driving a car: the average Volkswagen Golf has easy and predictable driving behaviour for most drivers; but get behind the wheel of a Ferrari racing car, step on the gas and if you do not have the necessary experience the chances are that you won't even make it through the first corner.

To make sure an inexperienced pilot does not inadvertently launch with a high-performance racing glider, most paragliders are certified and classified according to set rules. Developed in Europe and used worldwide these are known as the **EN** (**European Norm**) classifications. They go from A to D.

EN-A denotes a safe, easy-to-fly glider, while an EN-D is a glider that places high demands on the pilot's skills. These EN-classified wings are sometimes referred to as **serial wings**. Beyond EN-D, there is a CCC class for competition gliders. This class contains demanding gliders which would otherwise not be allowed in official competitions because they would fail the tests for EN-D.

▶ EN CLASSIFICATION

EN-A	Suitable for everyone, including beginners
EN-B	Intermediate and above. The most popular category
EN-C	Advanced, for sports pilots who fly regularly
EN-D	High performance gliders for expert pilots who fly regularly
CCC	A special class of wing for competition gliders

▲ BEGINNERS VS EXPERTS
The glider on the left is a beginner's paraglider certified EN-A, with an aspect ratio of 5.3 and about 40 cells. The one on the right is a CCC competition wing with aspect ratio of 7.1 and about 100 cells.
Photo: Jérôme Maupoint / Marcus King

EN-A and some EN-B classified gliders are suitable for training. When qualified, pilots are advised to fly only a glider that has at least passed an EN load test. This certifies that the canopy, lines and risers are able to withstand all the forces that they'll be subjected to during the flight.

The German **DHV** (Deutsche Hängegleiter Verband) has similar classifications for paragliders, called the **LTF** requirements.

German pilots can fly only with equipment that satisfies these demands. The DHV also classifies gliders according to their ease of piloting and safety from LTF-A through LTF-D.

To classify a glider, tests are performed according to the EN regulations. The main issue is **passive safety**. In these tests, a test pilot induces an incident and then waits to see what happens without intervening.

For example, the test pilot induces a collapse in which two thirds of the canopy loses pressure and folds back. The canopy will start to turn or dive forward, but in most cases the wing fills up with air and pressure is restored automatically. The glider recovers on its own and flies straight again without the pilot needing to do anything.

During the test it's observed how far the glider rotates and how long it takes before it resumes normal flight. A small turn of less than 90° and no large dive or roll will earn the glider an 'A'. A turn of more than 360° plus a dive or roll will mark a 'D' on this test, indicating extreme behaviour by this particular glider. In this way, more than 20 different situations are assessed.

The result of the classification is based on the highest score in this series of tests. If a glider receives an A on all tests but one, in which it gets a D, it's still classified as an EN-D glider. Most gliders that are used in schools for students are EN-A classified. These gliders have scored an A on each and every test.

You may hear pilots talk of a 'low B' or 'high B'. The EN-B category is very broad, and this is an informal way of further classifying that category.

Maintenance and checks

The fabric of the canopy and in particular the air-tight coating are sensitive to **UV light**. The glider therefore ages most when left in direct sunlight. Manufacturers say that 500 hours of sunlight causes such an increase in **air permeability** that the canopy is too porous to fly safely. The flight characteristics deteriorate and the glider will reach a deep stall more easily. That means the glider will descend straight down like a parachute.

When flying, the canopy is inevitably exposed to sunlight. You can protect your glider from direct sunlight when you're not flying by covering it up or leaving it in the shade.

The coating on the fabric also gets worn by being pulled over rough surfaces. During take-off, the upper side of the canopy drags over the ground, causing

▶ ANNUAL INSPECTION

Wear and tear makes a **periodic inspection** necessary to establish whether the glider is still fit to fly. This needs to be done by the manufacturer or by a qualified glider repair workshop. Among other things they'll measure the **porosity** of the fabric (that is, how fast the air permeates through the cloth) and they'll determine the **tensile strength** of the lines by pulling one until it snaps.

A glider should be checked according to the manufacturer's instructions. If these are unavailable, a guideline is to check at least every two years or after flying for 150 hours. A glider that does not pass the checks should not be flown until it is repaired and certified airworthy. If it can't be, then it should be retired.

wear. But you can take care not to scrape it across the ground more than necessary.

There are many methods of folding and packing a glider and each has pros and cons. Whichever method you choose, make sure that you don't bend stiff parts, such as rods or ribs. This causes the wing to lose some of its shape. Instead, stack the rods in the leading edge together in the so-called **concertina packing method**. Never kneel on top of the glider for a tighter fold or to press the air out. This wears the fabric quickly.

Make sure you remove any loose dirt from the glider, inside and outside, before folding it. If you must, you can remove stains from the fabric with clean water and let it dry thoroughly. But this is purely for cosmetic purposes, and it wears the air-tight coating. Never use soap or solvents on a glider.

If you're not going to use the glider for a while, take it out of its inner bag and loosen the folds a bit so that all of the material can dry out. Store the glider in a dry place at room temperature. Too cold will cause moisture to condense on the material, helping mould to grow. Too hot will cause the polyamide fabric to age more quickly.

The polyamide fabric is a plastic, and will melt with heat, for example if hot ash falls on it from a cigarette. Don't smoke close to gliders!

If you notice a small rip in the fabric of up to about 5cm, you can fix it with a piece of **ripstop tape** on the inside and another on the outside of the wing. A large tear needs to be repaired by a certified repair shop or the manufacturer.

▶ LINES AND RISERS

Materials

There are about 200 to 300 metres of **line** used in a single paraglider. These come together at the **risers**, which are in turn connected to the harness. Lines are made of **aramid** or **polyethylene**, which are fibres with a tensile strength two to three times higher than steel wire. Brand names of these fibres include **Kevlar**, **Technora** or **Twaron** for aramid, and **Dyneema** or **Spectra** for polyethylene.

The properties of these two materials are slightly different, and each has its own pros and cons. Aramid (Kevlar) is sensitive to bending, reducing the tensile strength notably. Polyethylene (Dyneema) is more sensitive to temperature fluctuations and moisture, causing stretching and shrinking with uneven line lengths as a result.

Most paraglider lines are 1mm to 2.5mm in diameter and have a **tensile strength** of 75kg to 150kg, depending on the thickness and type of material. This means you can suspend a maximum of this weight from a single line before it breaks. A different indication of the strength of a material is the **Working Load Limit** or **WLL** (an older term is Safe Working Load or SWL). This is the load you can safely place on a material to be sure it will not break. The WLL varies, but is normally one fifth of the tensile strength. The WLL of a line with a tensile strength of 100kg is 20kg.

Lines made of these fibres are generally covered by sheathing. The main purpose of the sheath is to protect the fibre from ultraviolet light and from sharp objects which might tear or weaken the lines. **Sheathed lines** are also easier to detangle

▲ SHEATHED AND UNSHEATHED LINES
Sheathed lines have an outer sheath around the woven core. They are easy to handle and are used on beginner and intermediate wings. Unsheathed lines offer performance gains (less drag) and are used on more advanced wings
Photos: Bastienne Wentzel and Marcus King

and sort. Gliders for more advanced pilots may not have sheathing on all or part of the lines to reduce weight and drag, but this increases the chances of damaging the lines or launching with knots or tangles.

Before a glider is introduced to the market, it is first submitted to a **shock test** and a **load test**. The shock test determines the resistance of the entire construction, canopy, lines, risers and karabiners, to a sudden pull, usually of 1,000kg.

The load test assesses whether the glider can endure a prolonged load, normally of eight times the maximum take-off weight. The entire glider must pass this test. There's an additional test for the suspension lines. These are folded 5,000 times, and then they must all pass a load test of about 14 times the maximum take-off weight. The precise specifications of all these tests vary between inspection bodies.

Line layout

Connected to the canopy and carrying the weight of the pilot are the **suspension lines**, often simply called 'lines'. The short lines directly connected to the canopy form the top line cascade on each side. Three or four top lines in a row come together at the middle line cascade, and again two or three meet at the lower line cascade. These connect to the piece of webbing called the riser. Each of the three lower line cascades has its own riser. The **control lines** or **brake lines** are connected to the trailing edge of the canopy. These do not carry any weight.

At the lower end of the brake line you'll find a **brake handle** – sometimes called the control or **toggle** – for you to grasp and take control of the glider.

Finally, the **stabilo line** runs from one of the risers to the stabilisation panel at the tip of the paraglider.

The designer of the glider determines how long the lines should be. The tuning of the line lengths is called the **trimming** of the wing. The lengths and the way all lines are connected to the canopy and the risers are called the **line layout**. The line layout drawing can usually be found on the manufacturer's website, and is useful for finding the part number of a damaged or broken line that you want to replace.

Line lengths determine the flying characteristics of the glider. You should not tie a knot in a line or otherwise shorten it: knots decrease line strength.

▶ LINE LAYOUT DIAGRAMS

This is an example of a line layout. The top represents the leading edge of the canopy with the A-lines, the bottom is the trailing edge with the brake lines attached. The two most frequently used line materials are aramide and polyethylene. Both have their pros and cons:

Aramid (Kevlar, Technora and Twaron)
- Heavier
- Sensitive to bending
- Sensitive to UV radiation

Polyethylene (Dyneema and Spectra)
- Lighter and easier to make knots
- Sensitive to temperature changes
- Propensity for stretching and shrinking

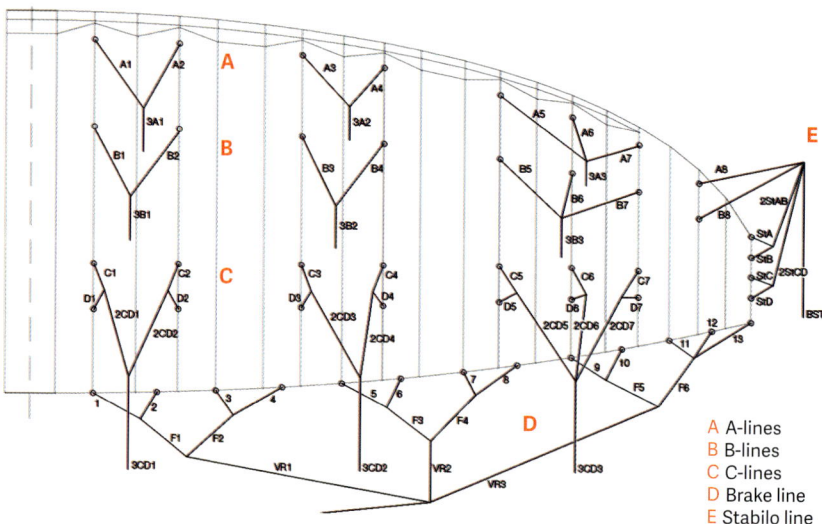

A A-lines
B B-lines
C C-lines
D Brake line
E Stabilo line

If one is broken, it should be replaced by a line that is exactly the same material, length, diameter and tensile strength as the original. A replacement can usually be ordered from the manufacturer, or you can have it replaced by your dealer or a repair workshop.

During the glider's periodic inspection, the lengths of all lines are precisely measured. If the length is off by more than a few millimetres, the line is replaced. The maximum allowance for line lengths varies between lines and gliders. Also during the inspection, one or two lines are tested for tensile strength. They're pulled with an increasing load until they break. If they break at too low a load, all lines are replaced, or the glider fails the inspection.

Risers and speed system

Lines come together at the risers. Most paragliders nowadays have three pairs of risers labelled from A to C. Older gliders may also have D-risers.

The **A-risers** connect to the A-lines that are attached to the front part of the canopy, the Bs attach a bit further toward the trailing edge, and so on. The A and B lines take the most weight: together, they bear two-thirds to three-quarters of the total.

On some gliders each A-riser is divided into an inner and an outer A-riser. Pulling down on the outer A-line on the A-riser is how pilots pull in **big ears**. Big ears is a descent technique that we'll describe in more detail later in the book.

Connected to the A-risers is the **speed system**. This is a pulley system on each side with a line running through and

▲ **THE RISERS**

A Split A-riser and A-lines	E Maillon
	F Brake-line pulley
B B-riser and B-lines	G Speed system
C C-riser and C-lines	H Brake handle
D Brake line	I Attachment loop

▼ **SPEED SYSTEM**
Brummel hooks connect the speed bar to the risers

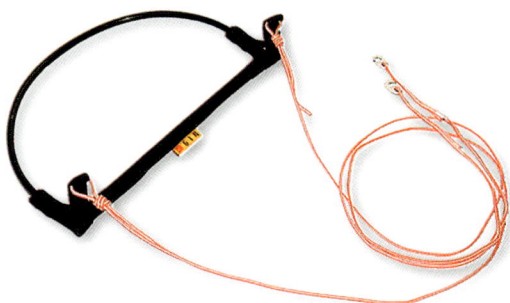

31

a **brummel hook** attached to it. This is attached to the **speed bar** which is connected to the harness. Pushing the speed bar with your feet changes the length of the risers slightly. The wing tilts down a bit, thereby increasing the airspeed of the paraglider. The speed system needs to be adjusted for the individual pilot. The speed bar should be set up so that you can depress it fully with stretched legs. That will draw the pulleys of the speed system together until they touch each other and the glider is fully accelerated.

A different method of altering the flying speed of the paraglider is **trimmers** or **trim tabs**. These are clamps on the rear risers of some gliders with webbing running through. To operate them you pull on the loop of the webbing ('trimmers closed') to slow down the speed. Opening the clamps ('trimmers open') will slide the webbing up and speed up the glider. Once the trim tabs are set evenly, you don't have to hold them on like you do the speed bar. But it's harder to adjust the flying speed with trimmers than with a speed bar, since your hands are usually occupied with the controls. Trimmers are useful for soaring in high winds, especially in smooth coastal air. Trimmers are also often used on tandem paragliders to increase the speed, since it would be difficult for the pilot, sitting behind the passenger who is in front, to use a speed bar.

▶ THE HARNESS

Construction

A paraglider pilot sits in a **harness**, which is attached to the risers and wing. Most harnesses are comfortable seats in which you can sit effortlessly for

hours on a long-distance flight. However, lightweight versions used for hike-and-fly trips may be less comfortable; some of them resemble a climbing harness. When you buy a harness choose the right size and fit for your body. This is based on a pilot's weight and height.

A harness is built around the **main webbing** that carries and distributes the pilot's weight. It's the framework of the harness, and attaches it to the risers. A certified harness is load tested to carry several times the pilot's weight in a normal flying position, in landing position and during towing. A guideline for the load applied during this test is nine times the pilot's weight, with a minimum of 900kg.

Around the main webbing is a seat made of fabric and foam. Older types of harnesses had **cross bracing** integrated into the main webbing, which ensured a stable position for the pilot in turbulent air. Modern harnesses are equipped with an **anti-balancing system** (**ABS**) instead. This system facilitates steering by weight shifting but at the same time helps to provide a stable seat in turbulence.

Behind the main webbing, some form of **back protection** is required. During a hard or crash landing, this protection should absorb the forces of the impact to stop or minimise harm to the pilot. In most tests, a pass require the forces transmitted to be below 20G, which is equal to an impact with a force of 20 times your bodyweight. Usually, the back protector absorbs these forces with a thick layer of foam of 15cm or more.

A different form of back protection is an **airbag**, a much lighter construction than

Clip in

Karabiners connect the harness to the paraglider. These are extremely strong and usually rated to 2,200kg

Straps

Straps hold the pilot safely and also distribute the weight evenly. Adjust before you fly so the harness fits

Bump

Thick foam back protection in the back of a harness is there to protect the pilot in case of a bumpy landing

Throw!

Reserve parachutes can be mounted on the left, right or in front of the pilot. They are only deployed in emergency

Size

Harnesses can come in several sizes, usually based on pilot height and weight. Choose the right size to be comfortable

a foam protector. The airbag usually fills itself after take-off, and hence starts to provide full protection a few seconds after launch. A combination of foam and airbag is often found, providing the advantage of protection during launch, combined with a lighter weight. Some harnesses have protection on the sides for the hips, usually a layer of foam.

Most harnesses, but not all, have a rigid **seatplate**, usually made from carbon fibre because this is light and strong. Some pilots use a foot rest known as a **stirrup**. This is a long, partly elastic strap attached to the bottom of the harness to put your feet in. Stretching and locking your knees now provides a comfortable sitting position without your legs dangling down. The stirrup can also help you settle snugly into your harness after take-off. Most harnesses made for cross-country flying are also equipped with a **pod**. This is a piece of stretchy fabric that encloses the legs during flying. It improves the aerodynamics, and is also a lot warmer during long flights at high altitude or in winter. Be aware that a pod harness can change the flying characteristics of a wing. The certification of you glider is not applicable anymore. Talk to your instructor before flying with one.

Connected to the harness are two strong webbing loops, the **attachment loops**. The position at which these are attached to the harness varies from 35cm to 65cm above the seatplate. High attachment points ensure a stable pilot position during flying, but steering by weight shifting is reduced. Lower attachment loops facilitate steering by weightshifting, but the pilot will feel more movement in turbulent air.

▲ TYPES OF HARNESS
Top is a lightweight harness for hike-and-fly trips. In the middle is an all-round harness. Bottom is an advanced supine harness with a pod
Photos: Advance, Gin and Woody Valley

Karabiners

Karabiners are metal connectors with a hinge system with a spring-loaded gate. Commonly used in climbing where they are oval-shaped, **karabiners** in paragliding tend to be squarer, with flat bottoms. This allows for the webbing of a harness or riser to lie flat. They're not multi-directional and should be loaded in the direction they are designed for – try not to cross-load them across the gate. The most common ones used in paragliding are **twistlock karabiners**. Another frequently used type are **autolock karabiners** (without a twist lock). The important thing with a karabiner is that the gate is shut properly. Once it's shut it is structurally sound.

Maillons rapides

The small metal connectors between lines and risers are called **maillons rapides**, or simply **maillons.** They come in many different shapes and sizes. They

have a threaded sleeve, which tightens over a thread. When they're properly fitted, no thread should be visible. Maillons rapides (literally 'quick links' in French) are strong when screwed closed but should be loaded only along the major axis. They will bend when open and under load. It's therefore important to make sure they are closed tightly.

Many manufacturers close them and insert a **small plastic keeper** inside the maillon – this is to keep the lines in place. If you lose this plastic keeper it's not a structural issue, simply keep the maillon properly closed. But these inserts

don't necessarily stop the maillons from coming undone, so even if they're present, the maillons must be checked as part of your daily inspection. Many systems also use a small rubber band to keep the lines in place. It is good practice to occasionally lift this rubber band up and knock out any dirt. The band will roll back into place quite neatly.

There is always some debate about how tightly you should keep your maillons closed. Should you use a spanner? Finger tight is enough for maillons – you don't want to over-tighten them. However, if you are concerned that your finger tightness is not enough, then a one-quarter turn with a spanner will do it. Maillons should not be opened or closed under load – take the load off before tightening or opening, or their integrity may be damaged.

Soft links

Some lightweight paragliders use fabric connectors called **soft links** instead of metal. These are very strong, but check them visually each time you fly.

Rating

Karabiners and maillons are all rated as technical safety equipment and must meet stringent safety standards, including high minimum breaking strength and maximum working load. Keep karabiners clean, dry and free from dirt, and avoid using them for things they are not designed for (towing cars, for example). Aluminium alloy karabiners have a limited lifespan, which is usually less than that of stainless steel versions.

35

Strapping in

The harness is worn over the shoulders like a rucksack with two shoulder straps. The pilot is secured in the harness via two leg straps and a chest strap. In most cases, the leg straps fasten with separate buckles, but sometimes they connect directly to the chest strap. Most harnesses have an additional small strap to keep the shoulder straps from sliding off your shoulders.

The **leg straps** are the most essential straps. It's vital to remember to fasten these securely, and not to unbuckle them once you've closed them, unless you're about to take the harness off and put it down. If you forget to fasten the leg straps it's still possible to take off, but you may slowly slide out of the harness after launch. With harnesses without a safety device, you're only held in initially by the chest strap, and you can fly quite some way from launch before falling, possibly from a high altitude. Unfortunately, this still causes fatal accidents.

Set the leg straps as loose as you find comfortable, and as tight as you need to let you get into your seat after launch. This has no influence on the flight characteristics of the glider.

The length of the **chest strap**, however, does influence the glider's behaviour. The glider manufacturer will specify the optimum length of the chest strap, which is given as the distance between the two karabiners.

This distance depends on the size of the glider and the pilot, but is typically 42cm. A rule of thumb is that your lower arm from fist to elbow should fit between the karabiners in the flight position.

Tightening the chest strap by more than about 4cm will dampen the movements that you feel in turbulent air, but will also mean you can't use weightshift so effectively. The glider will be more sensitive to twisting, which happens when the risers entwine around each other after a sudden quick turn such as a partial collapse of the canopy.

Loosening the chest strap by more than 4cm from the standard length will cause the glider to react sensitively towards weightshift. A turn may happen too fast. The pilot will feel more movement in turbulent air.

▶ SAFE-T-BAR

A safety device seen in many harnesses is the Safe-T-Bar. This is a strap with a T-buckle at the end which runs from one of the leg straps to the chest strap. The latter can't be fastened without the Safe-T-Bar. It means if you launch without the leg straps fastened (but with a closed chest strap), you can not fall out of the harness. It will not be a comfortable ride, but at least you'll reach your landing place alive. If you forget to fasten both leg straps and the chest strap, the glider will fly away without you.

All these differences are also dependent on the height of the attachment loops and the type of harness.

Reserve parachute

For all flights that take you more than a few metres from the ground, it's worth flying with a **reserve parachute**, also called an **emergency parachute** or **rescue parachute**. In practice this means that you'll always carry one, except when groundhandling, on the practice hill or soaring low dunes.

Even at low altitudes it pays to carry one. Modern reserves open so quickly that even from about 30m they'll slow your fall enough to prevent or reduce injury. Reserves, like wings, are chosen according to your all-up take-off weight.

There are several types of reserves. The most common are **round parachutes** known as **pulled-down apex** parachutes. There are also **square** parachutes and **Rogallo-type** parachutes.

All certified parachutes used in paragliding must be certified and open quickly – in seconds. They come in different sizes, for different pilot weights. Most of them will bring you down wherever the wind blows you. However, some parachutes, like the

▲ TYPES OF RESERVE
A pulled-down apex round parachute; a square parachute; and a steerable Rogallo parachute. Round are most popular, while steerable Rogallo parachutes are for more experienced pilots
Photos: Andy Busslinger, Gin, High Adventure

Rogallo-type, can be steered. **Steerable reserves** enable you to choose your landing spot (within reason).

Whatever the type, a reserve is connected to the harness by a **bridle**. The harness connection is usually behind the pilot, so that they hang forward out of the harness after they deploy the reserve. This means they will land on their feet and prevents a big impact on the lower back. According to guidelines, the bridle should have a breaking strength of at least 2,400kg.

The parachute should be packed properly and wrapped in the **inner container**. This package is placed in the **outer container**, which is usually integrated into the harness. This container may have a plastic window or holes through which you can see that the **parachute closing pins** (metal or plastic wire) are still securely in their places, passing through the loops that hold the parachute in the container.

This **pin check** should be done before every flight and form part of your pre-flight checks. If the pins are not in place, the reserve could accidentally fall out of the container and inflate during take-off or flight.

Most outer containers are under the seat of the harness or behind the lower back. Some harnesses have a separate parachute **front container**, which is connected to the karabiners before the flight. Since this system does not connect to a bridle in the back of the harness, the pilot may still be seated after a reserve deployment.

However, some reserves in front containers are connected to the attachment points behind the pilot's shoulders, as with a conventional reserve system. Which system you choose is down to harness choice and personal preference. Competition and acro harnesses have space for two reserves.

On the outer container you'll find a brightly coloured **reserve handle**. If you need to throw your reserve, you grab this handle and pull firmly in the opposite direction to the way the parachute was put in, pulling out the inner container. Then you throw this package, including the handle, as far as possible, away from the canopy into clear air and let go of it.

The parachute should open and start to fly. You then bring in your paraglider by pulling on the brake lines or rear risers, to prevent it from re-inflating or tangling with the parachute.

The reserve should be taken out of its container every six months. It should be inflated, aired and dried to prevent the fabric from becoming stuck to itself by dirt or moisture.

The parachute then needs to be repacked by a qualified packer according to the manufacturer's instructions. Reserve parachutes must be folded and packed in a specific way: you can train to do this, or use a specialist packer to do it for you.

Finally, any Velcro closures and attachment points on the harness should be checked regularly. Dirt can make them loose. On the other hand, a little-used Velcro closure may attach too tightly over time because the hooks and loops will get more and more tangled. It's good to undo the Velcro strips once in a while and re-attach them. Try not to sit on your reserve, get it damp or full of sand. Take care of your reserve parachute and it will take care of you.

▶ RESERVE TESTING

Regulations specify that the descent rate of a reserve parachute must be less than 5.5m/s to be certified. That feels similar to jumping off a 1.5m wall. Older reserves may have a descent rate of up to 6.8 m/s. But a reserve should not descend too slowly. A very slow rate may give a comfortable landing, but if you find yourself in rising air under your reserve, you may actually go up. To pass certification a reserve parachute must also open in less than five seconds.

Any reserve parachute you use must be EN-certified and should not be more than 10 years old. After this it must be examined by the manufacturer or replaced, even if it's never been deployed. Cheap secondhand rescues might be old, worn out or used a lot. You can never know what has happened to them, which means they may not be dependable.

▲ ▼ **PARACHUTE PACKING**
Below is a parachute in its container bag, ready to be packed into the harness. Once in the harness, the metal closing pins (above) or plastic wires should be checked every time you fly. The pin should be centred, not pushed to the end of the loop.

▶ **THE PILOT**

Helmet

In most countries a helmet is mandatory for flying, but wearing one is highly recommended in any case – since you have only one head. You will need a helmet that's suitable for paragliding, ideally with an **EN-966** airsports certification.

The main choice is between a **full-face helmet** and an **open-face helmet**. The first protects your face in case of a head-on impact, but the downside is more limited visibility and hearing compared to an open-face helmet. A full-face helmet may be harder to remove after an accident, and will of course take up more space.

Boots and clothes

You need to dress to stay warm in the air and to stay protected on the ground. Clothing that covers your arms and legs will protect you from scratches after a less successful launch or landing in prickly bushes.

Lightweight and windproof one-piece **flying suits** are available for pilots, some equipped with pockets for radios and maps. **Gloves** not only keep your hands warm, but also stop the lines from cutting into your hands if the glider is suddenly pulled by an unexpected gust of wind.

It's a good idea to wear **boots** that protect your ankles and provide a solid grip on take-off and landing.

Radio

Pilots should be in contact with their instructors during training. The most convenient way is by **radio**. A radio can also be useful during free-flying to contact other pilots, listen to weather reports or check the emergency frequency for incidents.

Not everyone can use any frequency for transmitting. Some countries require radio users to have a licence. The so-called **LPD** and **PMR frequencies** are usually free for individuals to use without restriction.

Using **two-metre-band** radios is illegal without a licence in many countries, but they have a much longer range and are less sensitive to interference. Find out what is and isn't legal before you buy a radio. In practice, many pilots use radios where it is not strictly legal. Before each flight you should check with your fellow pilots that your radios are set to the same frequency, and that you can hear each other.

Altimeter

An **altimeter** shows you how high you are. They are mandatory in some countries when flying above a certain altitude or with other air traffic. Altimeters work on changes in air pressure and can be very sensitive. Using an altimeter in an outdoor-style watch is fine, provided that the measurement interval is one second or less and the altitude indicated is accurate to within one metre.

Clothes

Protect yourself against the wind, sunburn and cold. Wear a base layer with more outer layers

Radio

Your instructor may give you a radio. This should be kept clean and dry. Switch off when not in use

Instruments

Flight instruments range from simple variometers to full-blown flight computers

Helmet

Compulsory and necessary. The choice is open-face or full-face

Footwear

Wear boots or sports shoes with a good sole and ankle support. Avoid or cover hooks with tape

It should also be possible to calibrate it. **Calibration** is a procedure in which you check your instrument against another instrument, or a map or known height, to see whether the displayed altitude is still correct. If not, you should be able to correct it. If the altimeter is connected to a sensor that measures speed, it can indicate your airspeed – that is, the speed at which you're moving through the air.

Vario

Most pilots use a **variometer** or **vario** which indicates rate of ascent or descent. The vario also works by sensing air pressure. Many are combined with an altimeter and other options.

The most basic varios are solar powered and indicate with beeps whether you're going up or down. At the other end of the spectrum are **flight computers** with GPS, altimeter, thermal indicators, airspeed readings and more. These store all your flight data for analysis.

GPS

A **GPS** determines your exact location on Earth using a fleet of orbiting satellites. Your car navigation system works in the same way. A GPS can also determine your altitude, but uses the satellites for this measurement as well, not air pressure. A GPS therefore tends to be too slow and inaccurate to use as an altimeter when thermalling or soaring. But it can tell you your groundspeed (as opposed to your airspeed), and the direction in which you're flying.

That's useful when your visibility is temporarily restricted because you're in cloud, but mostly the groundspeed reading is used to determine the speed and direction of the wind. Your groundspeed can be very different from your airspeed because of strong wind, including headwind and crosswind.

Compass

A magnetic **compass** can help to determine and maintain your course on long glides or in low visibility. Compasses must be attached carefully to your harness, since they're very sensitive to the influence of metal and other instruments close by, and may give a false reading.

Cockpit

If you're carrying a lot of instruments during your flight, a **cockpit** can be handy. This is a bag that attaches to the karabiners and sits in front of you.

A disadvantage of a cockpit is that it may prevent you from seeing your leg straps and chest strap. This means that pre-flight checks are even more important; you should never attach the cockpit before fastening your leg straps.

▶ **STAYING SIMPLE**

Some pilots love their instruments; others can take them or leave them. They can be a distraction, so at the start of your flying career it can be better to keep it simple and to fly with only a single, basic model. Small solar-powered varios are enough to tell you whether you are going up or down and are perfect for learning to soar and thermal.

▶ SPECIALIST KIT

Towing

Tow launching is a different method of taking off with a paraglider, in which you're attached to a line and winched into the air. It's usually done in areas where there's no slope to take off from.

There are several ways of pulling a paraglider up into the air. A common method is a **static winch**. This includes a motorised drum on to which the tow line is drawn in. The static winch stays in one place during the towing, with the winch operator setting the tension on the line according to the take-off weight of the glider. Using the throttle of the motor, the operator keeps the tension on the cable even during the tow.

A different method used for paragliders is a **pay-out winch**, where the drum with the tow line is mounted on a vehicle. The vehicle drives along at a speed just higher than the airspeed of the paraglider. At the same time the tow line is paid out to keep the tension level.

An **aerotow tug** (a light aircraft used to pull a glider into the air) is not normally used with paragliders. Flying with a fixed-line tow (also known as static kiting – kiting up in the wind on a rope tied to a vehicle's tow-bar, for example), can be extremely dangerous and is no longer practised.

fixed-line tow (also known as static kiting – kiting up in the wind on a rope tied to a vehicle's tow-bar, for example), can be extremely dangerous and is no longer practised.

Every winch has an emergency cutaway system with which the tow line can be cut quickly. This is necessary if the line gets stuck or the paraglider is in trouble and needs to disconnect.

Winches must be inspected regularly, especially when they're used for training or in clubs. Most countries have inspection regulations. An inspection will include the cutaway system, line tension indicators, and so on; it will also check whether the controls are within reach of the winch operator, and whether moving parts could cause danger.

The **tow line** is a Dyneema cable, often over a kilometre long, with a breaking strength of at least 600kg. The winch installation and all of its parts should have a combined breaking strength of at least 300kg, according to a German guideline.

At the pilot's end of the tow line is a small parachute called a **drogue parachute.**

▼ TOW RELEASE
Two different types of tow release systems. On the left is a flexible SK2 tow bridle with a towing aid which activates the speed system during towing. On the right is a rigid tow release for step towing.

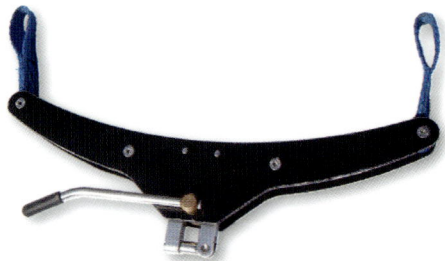

This makes sure that the cable descends straight down after it's disconnected from the pilot, and is visible in the air.

The tow line is attached to the paraglider by the karabiners on the harness, using a **tow release** system. This allows the pilot to release the cable with a simple tug on the handle.

During **step towing** (covered later) a special release is used that has a weak link when pulled sideways. While flying back with the towline paying out, you could be pulled sideways from under the canopy if the line gets stuck. This would cause a dangerous situation. If this happens, the release opens automatically.

Finally, a **towing aid** activates the glider's speed system during towing. While towing, the canopy falls behind the pilot and is more sensitive to deep stall in that situation. Applying the speed system causes the glider to fly faster during towing, diminishing the risk of a stall.

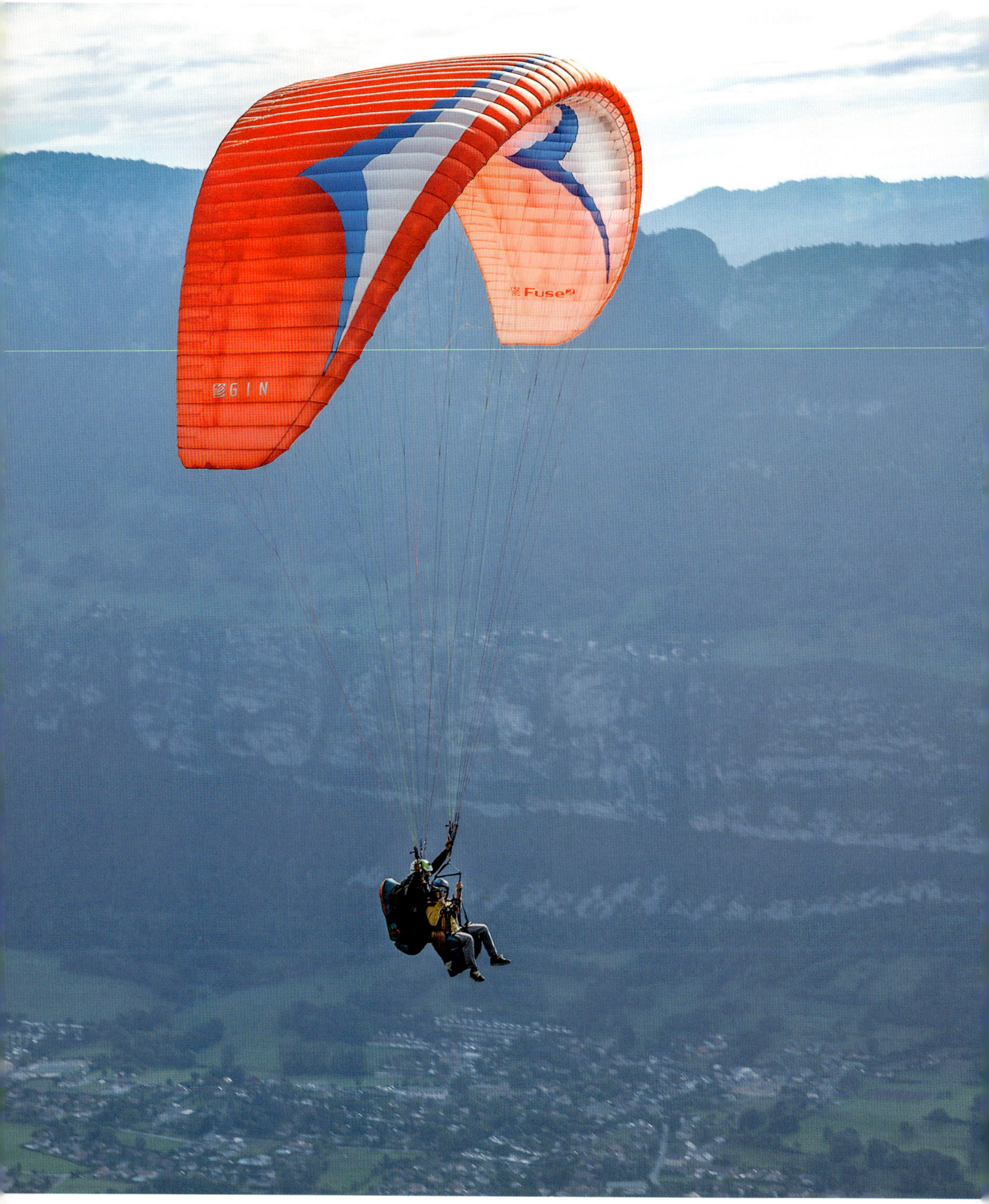
GIN
Fuse

Tandem flying

Tandem paragliding is the perfect way to let others who don't fly themselves discover the beauty of flying. And some people simply enjoy flying together even if both are pilots. The pilot sits at the back and operates the paraglider, with the passenger sitting in front. To fly a tandem glider you must be an experienced solo pilot first and then complete extra training.

You also need a larger wing to carry the extra load. **Tandem paragliders** are usually between 38m² and 42m², although some can be as small as 34m². Note that this is less than twice the size of a solo glider. That means the wing loading and therefore the trim speed of most tandem gliders is faster than similar solo gliders. Tandem wings do not have speed bars, because the pilot would not be able to push one with their feet (the passenger is in the way). Instead, all tandem wings have trimmers to regulate the trim speed.

Many of the factors important in choosing a solo paraglider apply to tandem wings as well. It's recommended that you fly an EN-certified glider. Most tandems have an EN classification as well (often EN-B). The all-up weight with the pilot and passenger must be within the manufacturer's certified weight range. This means you must recalculate the take-off weight with each new passenger.

Both pilot and passenger sit in their own harnesses. These are usually different from solo harnesses: the passenger harness has protection on the bottom, but usually no bulky back protection, as this would get in the way of the pilot. The pilot's harness usually contains the large **tandem reserve parachute**, which is connected to the main karabiners.

To hook up both the pilot and the passenger to the wing, you need **spreaders**. These are extra pieces of webbing, connected to the risers, which split in an upside-down Y shape. The passenger is connected to one pair of the front loops of the spreader. Depending on the passenger's weight, the first or second loop is used to obtain the right balance. The pilot hooks into the rear pair of loops. The risers are connected to the middle loops on the spreaders.

Finally, when towing, a tandem needs to use a special **tandem release** which is suitable for the extra load.

◄ ▼ TANDEM SET-UP
Pilot and passenger harnesses are connected with spreader bars. These are usually hard, but soft spreaders are good if flying children or smaller passengers. Photos: Marcus King

High-wind soaring

Soaring low dunes or hills has attracted much interest in recent years from licensed pilots and new pilots alike. There's a substantial group of pilots who don't fly in the mountains nor from a tow launch. Countries like Denmark, the Netherlands, Belgium, France and Portugal have numerous options for **dune soaring**, and pilots use the strong winds blowing against the low dunes to soar for many hours and miles. Since these dunes may be as low as 15m, ranging up to about 100m, paragliders need fairly strong winds to soar them. With winds under 15km/h you won't get very far.

It's fine to use the same glider for thermal flying and soaring. But if you fly sand dunes like those at Dune du Pyla in France, you're sure to get sand in your glider. And sometimes you'll be flying at such a low altitude that you won't need a reserve parachute. This offers the chance to fly with a different, lighter harness, keeping your main gear clean.

When the wind increases, there may be a point where your 'big' glider will not offer enough forward speed anymore. An option in these conditions is to fly a smaller wing – because if the wing loading is higher, the glider will fly faster.

Many small, fast **mini wings** are available. These are suited for flying in strong winds because they have a higher trim speed, mostly above 40km/h. Many of them come with trimmers as well as a speed system, to make it even easier to adapt the airspeed to the wind speed.

They're available in many sizes from $10m^2$ to $21m^2$ or more. They have shorter lines than serial paragliders, influencing the handling. Some of the larger sizes are EN-classified, so you can get an idea of their flying characteristics. Choose a mini wing that fits your take-off weight, your experience (smaller gliders are more difficult to fly) and the wind speed that you want to fly in.

A STRONG WIND
Marcus King high-wind soaring on the north coast of Jersey in the Channel Islands
Photo: Nick Bisson

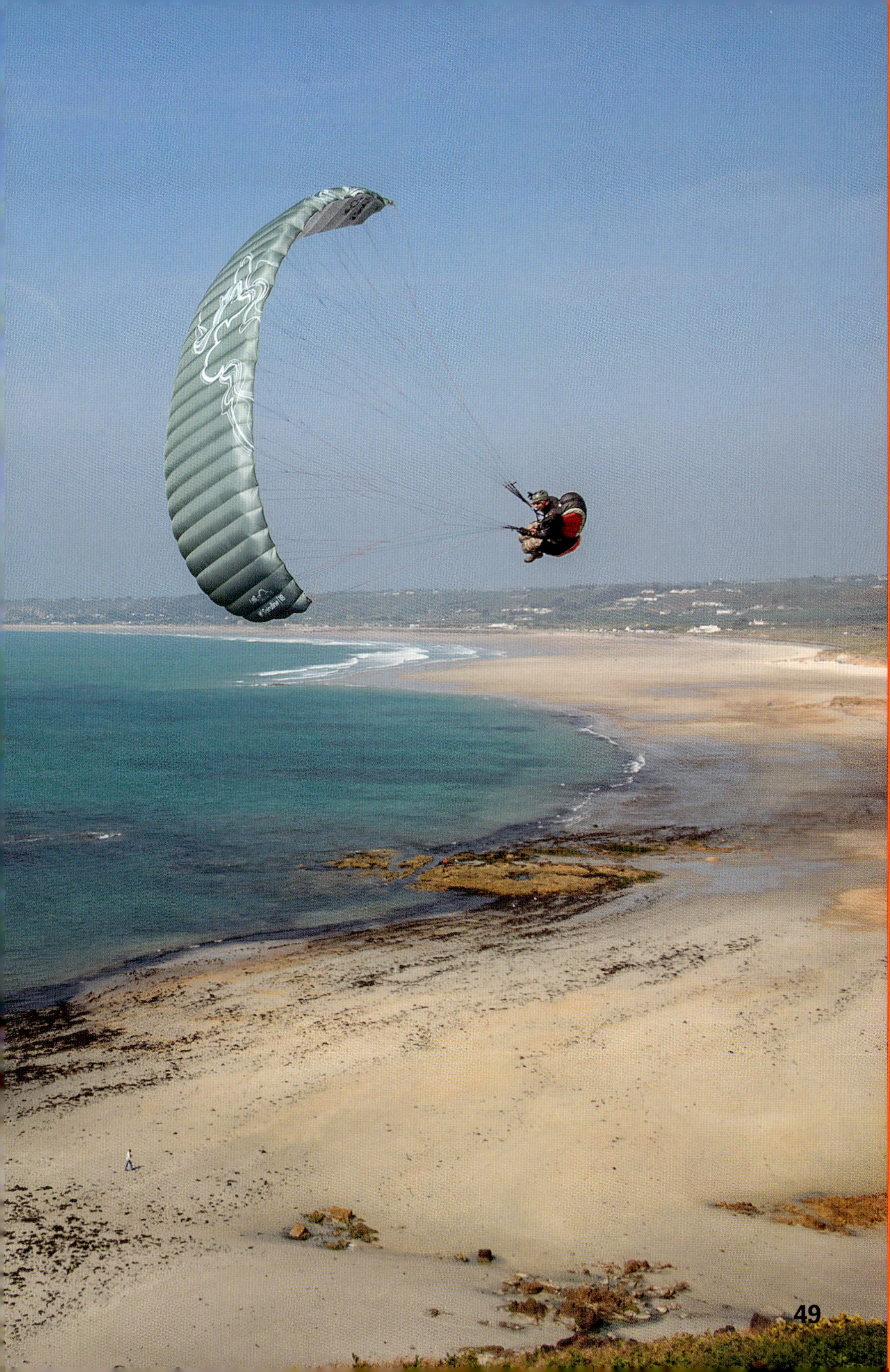

▲ LIGHT IS RIGHT
Enjoying a lightweight harness and glider
combination that weighs less than 3kg
Photo: Marcus King

Hike-and-fly

In the early days of the sport the attraction of paragliding for many was as an easy way to descend after hiking up a hill. But early equipment proved too heavy, and as the sport developed gear got heavier still. In the late 1990s it was normal to have a kit bag weighing 20kg.

At the turn of the millennium, a small revolution started in lightweight equipment. Using lighter cloth, lighter lines, and better design, usable **lightweight paragliders** started to appear on the market. Harnesses and reserves also got the lightweight treatment, and suddenly the 10kg glider plus harness with a reserve package was a reality.

In recent years equipment has got even lighter, and it's now possible to have a harness and paraglider combination that weighs less than 3kg. You really can take that sort of equipment up mountains and fly off the summit. **Hike-and-fly** was born – and lots of pilots do nothing but. The attraction is obvious: hike up a mountain before breakfast and fly back down before most people have set off for work. Or link a series of hikes and flights together to travel long distances, called **vol bivouac**. Pilots have flown the length of the Himalayas using lightweight paragliding equipment.

Now, **lightweight harnesses** come in all forms. Some are reversible: the rucksack converts into a harness with an airbag. Others are taken to the extreme, being no more than Dyneema string as thin as bootlaces with a minimum of cloth to support the pilot's weight. Not all of these are comfortable enough for long flights. As with all equipment, it pays to try them out. The disadvantage of some of these ultra-lightweight harnesses is that they offer little or no back protection.

Regular wings with an upper and a lower surface are now made from such light materials that they can weigh less than 3kg. This has been made possible with the use of not only lighter cloth, but also lighter lines and risers, and soft links (pieces of Dyneema string) instead of karabiners.

Single-skin canopies are even lighter. They can be made of standard materials or light materials, in which case they can weigh as little as 1kg and pack down to the size of a water bottle. Many of these light wings have easy handling and an EN-A or EN-B classification. That's a bonus when you're at the top of a mountain in strong wind on a less-than-ideal take-off.

Recently, the hike-and-fly trend has seen the development of competitions in which adventure pilots race each other to complete a circuit as quickly as possible, over a day or more.

For these adventure races, of which the **Red Bull X-Alps** is the most well-known and extreme, lightweight wings with a high performance have been developed. Whereas competition wings used to weigh as much as 7kg, the latest lightweight performance gliders weigh less than 4kg.

▶ LIGHT HARNESSES

Ultralight string harnesses can weigh less than 400g, but sacrifice comfort

Lightweight reversible harnesses offer a degree of comfort. Weight < 2kg including bag

Reversible harnesses are more robust still and can be used every day. Weight 2-4kg

Lightweight pods are for pilots who want maximum performance. Weight 1.5-4kg.

Single-skin wings

Single-skin paragliders are for pilots who want the ultimate in simplicity and light weight – less than 1kg in some instances. Instead of the traditional double-layered cell structure, **single-skin** paragliders use just one layer of material. This saves a lot of weight, while the risers and lines are also pared back for weight.

Single-skins are light and compact, and can easily fit into a day pack when hiking or in the mountains. They are also simple to launch. In the air they have a different, more direct feel than traditional paragliders, which can be unsettling for pilots at first. They are also slower than standard paragliders and some don't have a speed system. Not all single-skins are classified under the EN system but most are load and strength tested.

Some manufacturers use a mix of single-skin technology and traditional cells to make **hybrid paragliders**. The technology and design is still developing, with regular new ideas and concepts appearing. Note that some schools offer to teach on single-skin gliders. If you do this, you will need extra tuition to learn to fly a standard paraglider.

▲ STAYING CLOSE
Photo: Charlie King

Speedriding

Speed wings are even smaller and faster than mini wings, and are mainly used for **speedriding** with skis. These small gliders were initially developed by improving the glide ratio of parachutes that were used by skiers to descend.

Speed wings are as small as 7m² to 14m² and have large cells, short lines and trimmers to easily change their speed and glide ratio. The design ensures that these gliders stay overhead at all times, so they're easy to launch. They're designed to launch with skis and to make short hops, but nowadays there are speed gliders available with better glide ratios that are used for thrilling foot-launched flights, called **speedflying**.

The harnesses used for speedriding must be light and non-bulky, so as not to hinder the pilot while skiing. They usually have no protection, and there is no reserve parachute needed because the shorts flights are too low to successfully deploy one. There are even harnesses which integrate with a ski suit, with only the karabiners sticking out.

▲ STEEP AND DEEP
Photo: Jérôme Maupoint

Freestyle and acro flying

Aerobatic flying, or **acro** for short, requires a very high level of technical skill from the pilot, and is also visually appealing to spectators.

Although it is perfectly possible and even sensible to learn the first acro skills with a standard paraglider, there is a wide range of specialised equipment available for acro. A dedicated **acro wing** is smaller and more dynamic, and has longer lines than a standard paraglider. This means it can retain energy, for example from a fast spiral dive, and convert it for the next manoeuvre, whereas a standard glider would dampen the movement and fly straight ahead. Acro wings are designed for speed and agility. They typically have a flat area of 16m^2 to 22m^2. They are often only EN load- and shock-tested but not EN-classified.

An intermediate wing for the aspiring acro pilot who also wants to thermal is a **freestyle wing**. These are slightly larger than acro wings and slightly less energetic, and sometimes have a better glide ratio. Some have an EN-C or EN-D classification.

When testing the limits in extreme manoeuvres, things are more likely to go wrong; acro pilots therefore carry two reserve parachutes. A front container with a second reserve will do, but most acro pilots buy a specialised **acro harness**. In addition to two reserve pockets, these harnesses have a more upright sitting position and lower hangpoints to facilitate weightshifting. A harness with airbag protection is not ideal for acro as the airbag deflates during manoeuvres, increasing drag and offering no protection in case of an emergency landing.

▲ **SPIRALLING IN**
Professional acro pilots at the annual Coupe Icare flying
festival in St Hilaire du Touvet, France
Photo: Marcus King

Accuracy

Paraglider pilots are first introduced to the idea of accuracy flying when they have to land on a target or spot at their local hill. They may even take part in a spot-landing competition at club level, where the task might be to crack an egg under their heel and the prize is a beer or two later that evening.

But **accuracy paragliding** is a discipline in its own right, and has many fans around the world as well as a vibrant international competition circuit. The techniques needed to do well in accuracy competitions are ones that pilots often neglect: perfect launches; instrument-free flying; perfect approaches; and centimetre-accurate landings in a variety of conditions. It's easy to overshoot or undershoot.

Most accuracy pilots fly standard paragliders in the EN-A or EN-B class. They use a sit-up harness, or a lightweight harness with back protection, that allows lots of leg movement. They usually fly without instruments, relying on eye alone to approach the target. They may wear lightweight trainers or trail shoes that allow precision landings. Some will adopt shoes from parachuting accuracy – these have a small stud on the tip of the toe to register pinpoint landings.

The aim of an accuracy competition is to land '**dead centre**'. A 30cm pressure pad is used to record exactly how close to the centre a pilot gets. Rings around the pad radiate out to 10m. The best score is zero – the middle of the pad. Each extra centimetre is then worth one point. Land 10m away and you score 1,000 points. Pilots must also land on their feet.

Each competition takes place over several rounds – six is typical – with pilots launching from a low hill or tow. Tow launching above a frozen lake in winter is a perfect way to run an accuracy competition.

On days when there's no wind, or zero thermals, **spot landing** is a useful skill to practise for all pilots.

Scenes from an international accuracy competition in Dubai. Launch is by tow from the beach, allowing a quick turnaround of pilots. Each competitor must land as close to the very centre of the target as possible
Photos: Marcus King

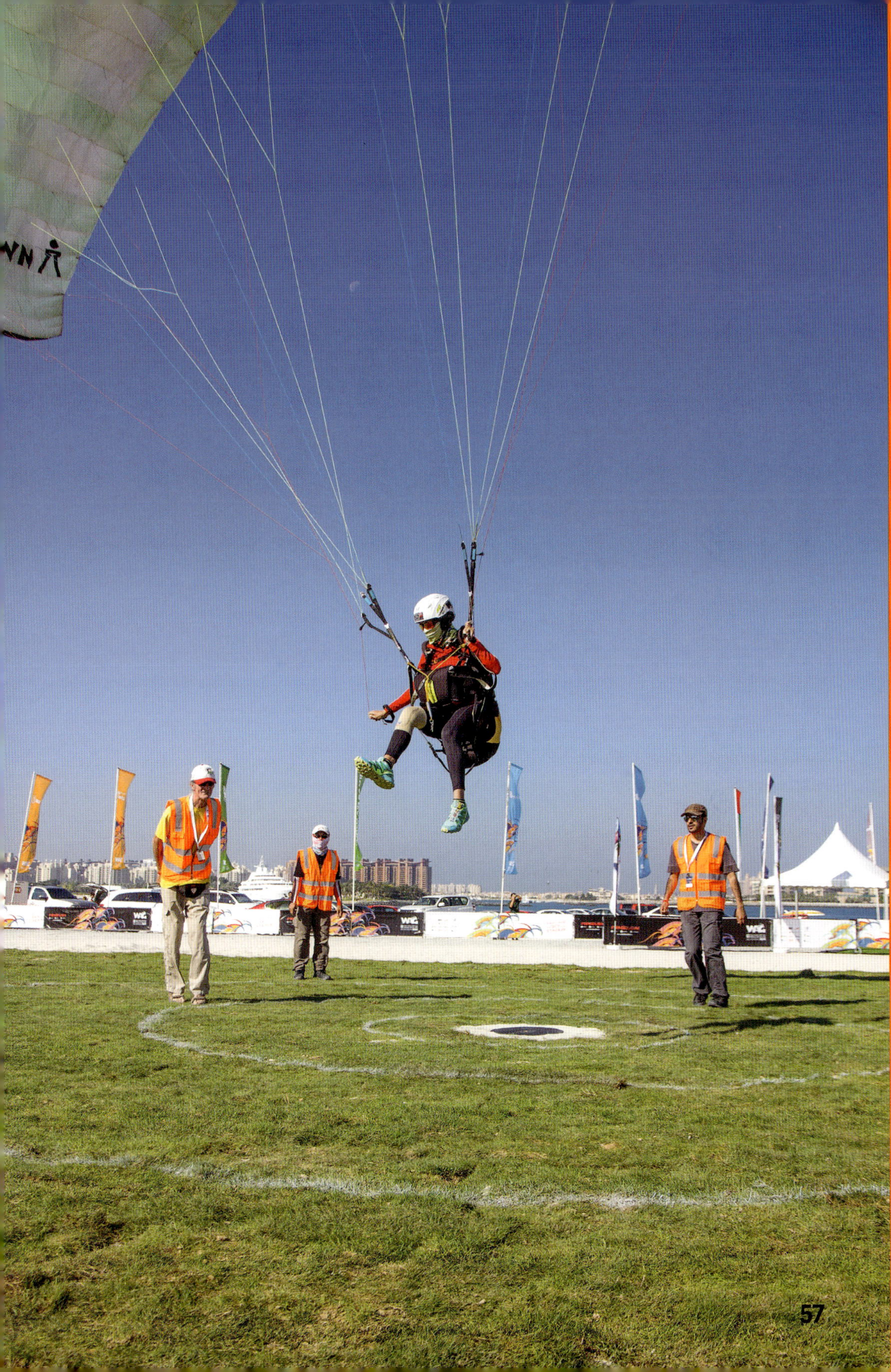

Paramotoring

A motorised paraglider or **powered paraglider** (**PPG**), usually called a **paramotor**, is arguably the lightest, simplest powered aircraft. Paramotoring is paragliding's motorised cousin. You fly a paraglider while sitting in a harness with an engine and a spinning propeller on your back. One advantage is that the paramotor pilot can take off and fly in conditions that free-flight pilots can't. Early morning when all is still and in the calm air of late evening are perfect times to paramotor. Despite many differences, the similarities between paragliding and paramotoring are obvious. We fly with similar canopies and need to learn to control them on the ground and in the air in a similar way.

Paramotor equipment consists of: the paraglider; a special paramotor harness; a two-stroke engine with fuel tank (or, in rare and expensive cases, an electric-powered unit); a wooden or carbon-fibre propeller; a specialist helmet with push-to-talk radio; a flying suit; and various electronic devices like GPS or a flight instrument.

You can use your free-flight paraglider for paramotoring as long as it's also certified for paramotor use. There are also specialist wings that are different to fly and demand different techniques. These **reflex gliders** use a special design that adds pitch stability. The faster you go, the more reflex works to make the wing stable. The trade-off is a slightly different take-off technique and extremely demanding post-collapse behaviour (although collapses are rarer). Advanced wings feature complex speed systems and specialist **tip-steering systems** to facilitate steering in accelerated flight.

A **paramotoring harness** is different from a harness for free-flight paragliding, and is attached to the frame of the paramotor. Once in the air the extra weight of the engine is held by the wing. Different designs have low, mid or high hangpoints. This can affect the way the wing feels in flight, and there are pros and cons to each system, but your instructor will advise what is best for you.

The **propeller**, which has a net or cage around it for safety, is powered by an **engine** of 80 up to 300cc, which typically uses up to four litres of fuel per hour. The engine is started and operated with a hand-held **throttle**. You can carry a maximum of 10 litres of fuel, which limits the range of powered flight. All the equipment combined may add 25 to 40kg extra to the all-up weight, so the right size of glider must be chosen.

▲ A PARAMOTOR
Carrying 10-litres of fuel in the white tank this Parajet paramotor can fly for about two-and-a-half hours
Photo: Parajet

Wing
You can use a paraglider wing, but most pilots fly a specialist paramotor wing

Harness
Special paramotor harnesses are used. These have different hangpoints to free-flight harnesses

Engine
Paramotors weigh 20kg-30kg and are mainly petrol-driven. Some electric paramotors exist too

Photo: Marcus King

▲ BEACH LIFE
Having a motor allows you to launch in places where you might otherwise not be able to. Paramotoring on the coast is popular as there is lots of space to launch and land, and the air is smooth. Photo: Jeff Hamann

For pilots who want to paramotor, learning to fly the glider can feel like a bit of a chore – they want to get on with revving the engine. But most dedicated paramotor instructors say you must be able to fly a paraglider in free flight before adding an engine. Thus most paramotor courses start with several days of glider control and learning to fly the wing. The second week will be dedicated to learning to fly with a motor attached.

Managing the glider on the ground is very important in paramotoring, and as a beginner you will spend many hours groundhandling, until your instructor is happy that you have the wing under full control. Only then will the instructor add an engine to your harness. You will familiarise yourself on the ground with the motor switched off, before getting to practise with the motor running.

From there, you will be talked through your first take-offs and landings. Once you've perfected those, the sky is yours and the exciting new discipline of powered paragliding opens up.

▶ LEARN MORE

- **Understanding EN testing**
  tinyurl.com/ENtestingprocedures

- **EN certification shock and load test**
  tinyurl.com/shockandloadtest

- **EN certification testing centre**
  para-test.com

Paragliding is an evolving discipline and is part of aviation, which is also always evolving. Every year paraglider manufacturers develop new technology and release new wings, harnesses and instruments. As a pilot it is important to stay up to date with these developments. Not only so you know what's new, but for your own safety. Get into the habit of reading the magazines, websites and forums. Sign up to any email newsletters available and check in with the manufacturer of your glider: they will publish updates and any safety notices prominently.

Examples of new developments in paraglider design from recent years include:

Sharknose

Developed commercially by Ozone in 2012 and since adopted by many, a **sharknose** is a specific shape of the cell openings where the lower fabric is set back. The cross section looks like a shark nose. The design is proven and gives better flying characteristics at both low and high speeds. Different manufacturers call it different things, eg air scoop or back-positioned intake.

3D-shaping

The upper cloth of a glider should have as few wrinkles as possible. That is a problem when you are trying to sew a straight piece of cloth into an arc. The fabric will bulge once the air flows in.

To help solve this manufacturers developed **3D shaping.** The fabric is cut into specific shapes and stitched together to give the glider the best possible profile.

Rods

Plastic or metal **rods** inserted into the leading edge of the canopy are present in almost all new gliders. The rods help keep the cells open and keep the profile in shape during take-off and in flight. You need to be careful how you pack wings with plastic rods so you don't bend them.

Two-liners

Instead of three line groups, a **two-line paraglider** has only two: A-lines and B-lines. This reduces the total line length drastically, but the shape of the glider is more difficult to retain without the support of the lines. These gliders are mainly found in the EN-D and competition CCC classes.

Mini-ribs

Extra ribs at the trailing edge of the canopy ensure a cleaner shape, meaning the wing will glide more efficiently. Lots of wings have **mini-ribs**.

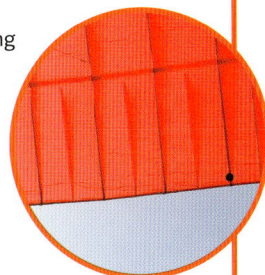

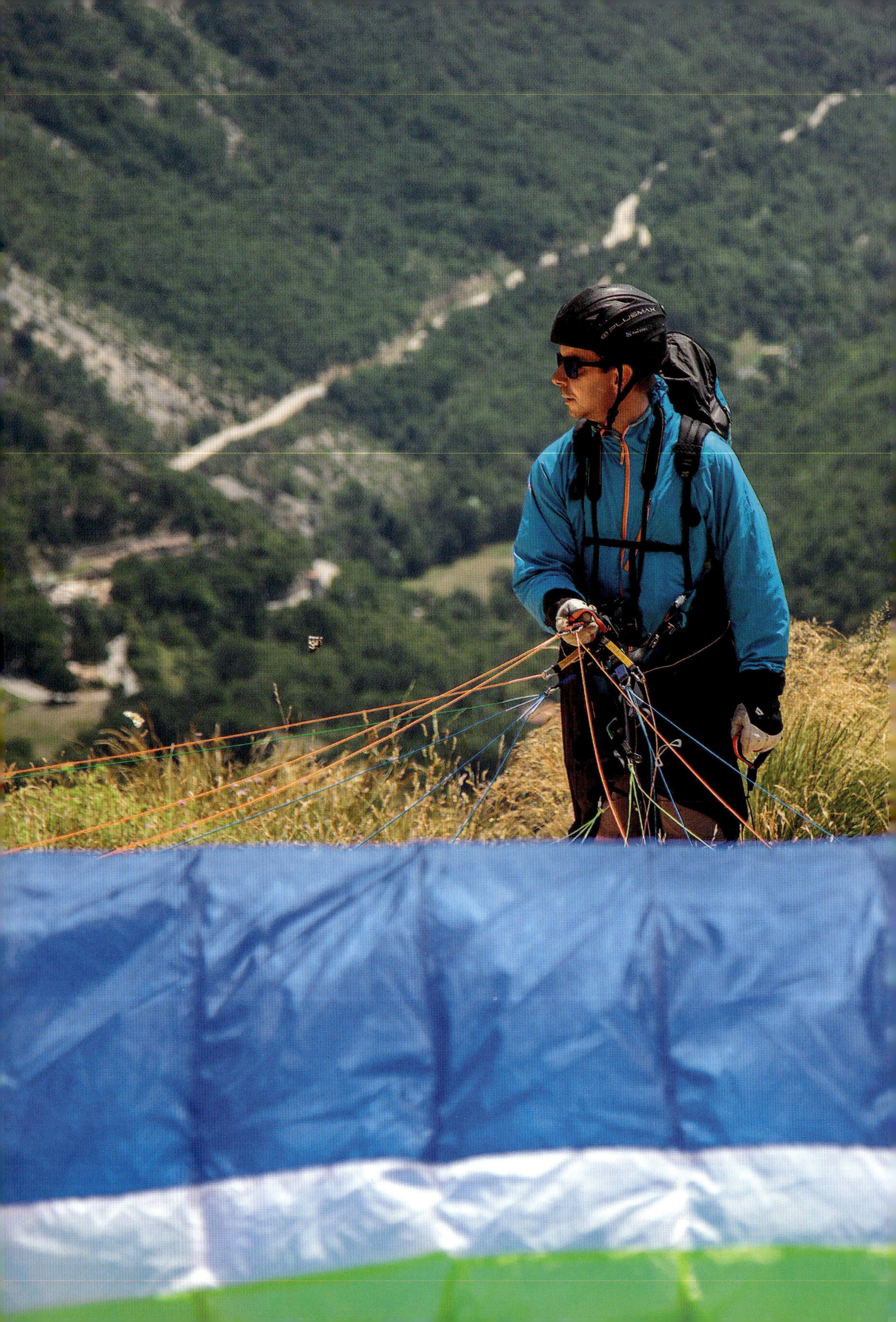

BASIC #3
TECHNIQUES

Your first flights

The only sensible way to learn paragliding is to join a school that's certified by your national paragliding association. On day one you'll start with some basic theory before moving on to understanding and handling the equipment. Following that you will learn how to groundhandle and kite the paraglider, then be told how to launch, steer and land.

With these basics sorted, you'll make your first short flights from the training hill. When you've gathered enough experience, you'll move on to bigger hills and longer flights. You are on your way to becoming a pilot.

In this chapter we discuss the theory that you'll need during your first training sessions. It's meant only as a reference point for what your instructors tell you, and to complement what they say and the instructional materials that they give you. If you have any questions during your paragliding training, ask your instructor. That's what they're there for. Remember, there's no such thing as a stupid question in paragliding – if you're unsure, ask!

► BEFORE YOU FLY

Are you fit to fly?

Although paragliding is not a very physically demanding sport once you're up in the air and gliding, it can require a decent level of **physical fitness** when you're on the ground, especially if you have to hike up and down hills while you learn.

Perhaps more importantly, being a pilot requires a good degree of **mental fitness**. We fly in three-dimensional space, which requires more concentration and sometimes quicker responses than, for example, driving a car. Therefore, before you go paragliding, assess yourself, starting with your physical condition.

Of course you don't fly when you're ill. But when are you too ill to fly? Or when are you too tired to concentrate enough to fly safely? The answers are different for every individual, but here are some points to take into account.

It goes without saying that you don't fly or train to fly under the influence of alcohol, drugs or medicines. International air law states that the blood alcohol content of a pilot may not exceed 0.2 parts per thousand. That's less than the maximum for a car driver in most countries. In the ten hours before you pilot an aircraft it's unwise to consume any alcohol, and in some countries it's illegal to do so.

If you have a cold, consider that nasal congestion will be aggravated at higher altitudes. You may get a severe headache, earache or respiratory problems while flying, just as you will in an airliner. It's best not to fly with a cold if you know you're sensitive to this.

► I'M SAFE

To check whether you're fit to pilot an aircraft, the abbreviation **IMSAFE** is used in aviation. The letters indicate the following:

- **Illness** – Do you feel sick or do you have the symptoms of an illness?

- **Medication** – Are you using medicines?

- **Stress** – Are you worried about matters outside flying?

- **Alcohol** – Have you consumed alcohol less than ten hours ago?

- **Fatigue** – Have you taken too little rest, food or fluids?

- **Emotion** – Have you recently suffered an emotionally upsetting event?

If the answer is 'yes' to any of these questions, you must ask yourself whether you're fit to fly. If in doubt, don't. If you have a pre-existing medical condition that you think might affect you, it makes sense to talk to your instructor and ask your doctor for advice before you sign up for a course.

Next, assess your mental condition. If you're tired, or distracted by matters at home or work, or simply not in the mood to fly – don't. You'll be unable to concentrate. More than with driving, you need all your senses to fly safely.

When and where to fly

Once you've established that you're in proper shape to fly, it's time to decide whether it's a good day to go flying. The main factor here is the **weather**: wind, precipitation and clouds.

Once you start paragliding your interest in the weather will only increase, because there's so much to learn. It's one of the aspects of the sport that makes it so engaging, and at times frustrating.

A paraglider has a built-in flying speed with respect to the air flowing around it. This is known as the **trim speed**, and is about 35-38km/h (22-24mph). When it's accelerated using the speed system, a typical paraglider's top speed is about 45-55km/h. This means strong wind makes a day unsuitable for flying. The exact limit depends on the site, your equipment and your capabilities as a pilot, but most pilots would think twice before trying to launch in winds stronger than 25km/h.

Secondly, a paraglider does not fly well in rain or snow. The drops disrupt the airflow around the canopy, and can ultimately cause the paraglider to stop flying. Additionally, rain and especially thunderstorms are often accompanied by strong winds. A day when these are forecast is therefore not a good flying day. Thirdly, we need to see where we're

---

▶ HEART RATE

Research done by the **Free Flight Physiology Project**, led by Dr Matt Wilkes from the University of Portsmouth Extreme Environments Laboratory, shows that the physical exertion involved in paragliding is about as strenuous as walking. Whatever sort of pilot you are, and however much experience you have, your heart rate increases in anticipation of and during launch; but after about 10 minutes in the air it's back to where it would be if you were simply walking. This graph uses data collected from Flymaster varios, a pilot flying at extreme high altitude in the Karakoram and pilots at the Ozone Chabre Open competition in France.

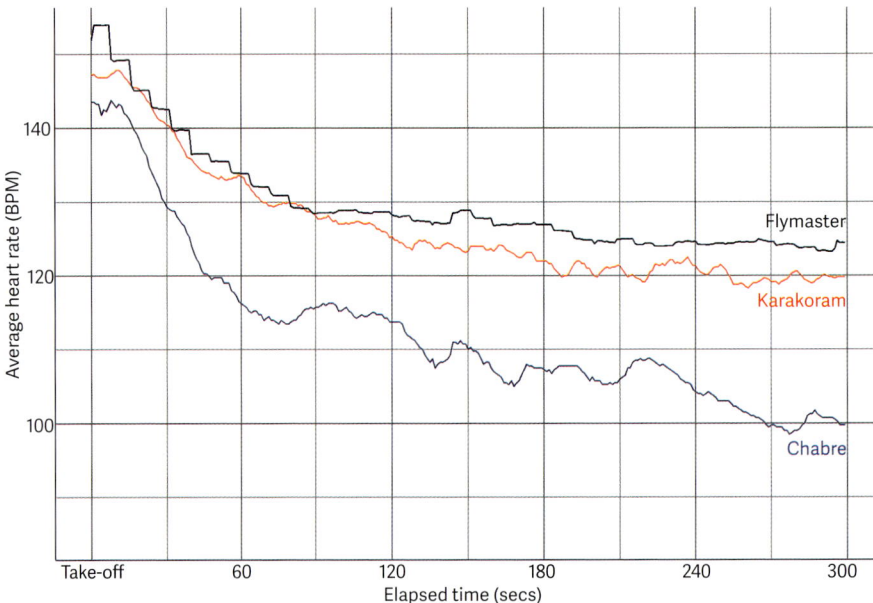

flying. Low cloud blocks visibility and can therefore spoil your flying day.

When you're training, it's a good idea to speak to your instructor about the weather. When you're qualified, always try to speak with local pilots. They'll know best the secrets and dangers of the area. And they'll know the special quirks of the region, as well as the best way to get the most out of the site.

To be able to judge a completely new flying arena requires a lot of experience and knowledge of terrain and meteorology. In the Weather for Pilots and Advanced Flying chapters, we'll go into detail about these subjects.

Theory lessons

All paragliding courses have a theory element and exams. **Theory lessons** help keep the learning process structured and safe, and mean you progress incrementally and smoothly, without missing important steps. At the start theory is simple, but as you progress it gets deeper and more involved.

Your instructor will provide you with the training materials you need as part of your course. Get into the habit of taking notes during theory lessons, or recording them on your phone.

There are also plenty of books that cover theory, including this one; a few good YouTube channels feature qualified instructors and explain the theory well; and online forums also have a wealth of information. Finally, your association magazine will have a training section, while Cross Country magazine, first published in 1988, has been a key source of learning for many pilots for decades.

▶ ACCESSIBILITY

If you're disabled, older, or in need of extra support, don't be put off. Under the right conditions with the right support, paragliding is accessible for most people. Almost anyone can fly tandem with an instructor or tandem pilot, regardless of physical ability. There are qualified solo pilots who use specially adapted wheelchairs, dedicated wheelchair instructors, amputee national champions and 80-year-old cross-country pilots.

Several small but dedicated charities in countries around the world help disabled pilots get trained and into the air. They welcome all pilots, including those with invisible conditions, for example post-traumatic stress disorder.
Photo: Joe Stone, by Julie Tickel

▶ LEARN MORE

- **Project Airtime, USA**
  projectairtime.org

- **Flyability, UK**
  flyability.org.uk

- **Handi-Fly, France**
  federation.ffvl.fr/pages/handi-parapente

Site assessment

Site assessment is a key skill in learning to become an independent pilot. In school the site assessment is done by an instructor: they look at the weather forecast for the day, and the actual weather where they are, and they know the local rules and regulations for each site. They put all of that together at the beginning of the day and decide: "This morning we will train and fly here."

They won't always get it right! And this is because site assessment is a difficult job. The key to it is to have read and understood the **weather forecast** for the day and the area. Look at it the day before you plan to fly, and again in the morning. Make your decision on where to fly based on the most up-to-date information that you have. Be prepared to change your decision if conditions change or you get new information ("It's raining inland but they're flying at the coast", for example.)

To make a good site assessment you need to apply what you know about the weather, and what you know about the local paragliding sites. If you live in a region with established clubs and schools, lots of information will be available. Look at the '**Sites Guide**' part of the club website, for example, and read about all the different sites. Some sites have webcams or weather stations on or near launch. These can give you real-time information about what's happening. Sometimes non-flying related issues can impact a site – for example sites can be closed when protected birds are breeding.

If you live somewhere without established sites, or you plan to fly somewhere off the beaten track, then you need to know how to make a good site assessment on your own. To do this you need to look at the shape of the site (**topography**), the direction of the wind, and the **aspect** of the terrain in relation to the sun. By learning to read these elements of the environment, you'll be able to imagine and then predict the airflow around the site.

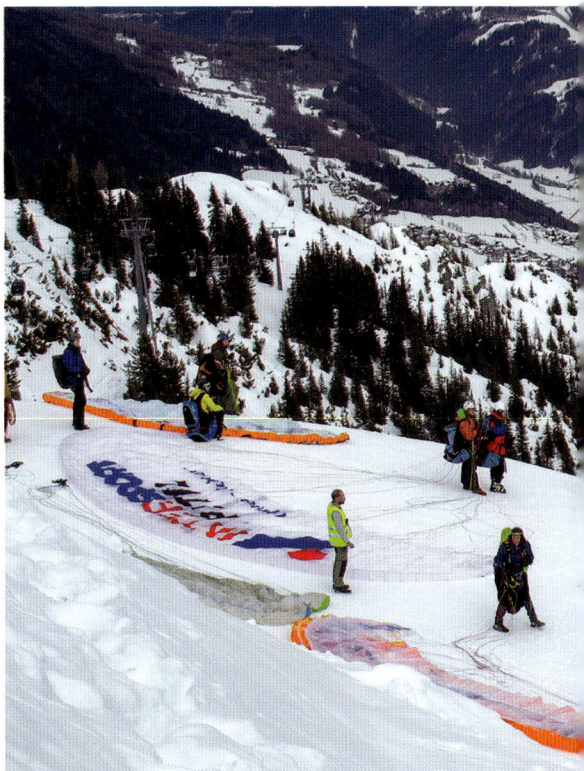

Topography is important because we want clean airflow where we fly. That means in general we look for open slopes and broad valleys. Having something in front of our flying site that can disrupt the airflow is not a good idea – for example another high mountain close by, or a row of high trees or buildings. Is the slope in front of you steep, shallow, or like a cliff? Are there trees, houses, wind turbines or any other potential obstacles in the way? All these affect the shape of the terrain and the airflow over it.

Direction of the wind is important because, like any aircraft, paragliders take off into wind. So this is one of your main considerations when looking at a potential site. Is the wind flowing up the hill towards you, or is it coming from behind (a **backwind**)? For the easiest, safest launch we need to have a smooth, steady wind in our face when we launch.

Understanding aspect – which way a slope faces with regards to the sun – is an important part of site assessment in the mountains. This is because the sun has a big effect on what the air does. East-facing slopes get the sun in the morning, and west-facing slopes get it in the evening. In the northern hemisphere the sun moves through the south, so south-facing slopes get the sun at midday; while in the southern hemisphere the sun moves through the north, so north-facing slopes get the sun at midday.

Learning about which slope gets the sun and when – and therefore how thermals will be affected – is crucial to mountain flying.

We'll look at how to interpret the factors that affect a flying site in more detail in the chapter about Advanced Flying Techniques.

69

▲ ▶ THE LANDING FIELD
Landing fields can look very different from above. These two photos show the same landing field – from the ground and from take-off. That's why it's good practice to check out the landing field from the ground before you fly
Photos: Marcus King

Check out the landing field

Before you go to launch at any new site, visit the landing field first. Even if you fly a site regularly it's a good idea to look again at places that you think you know, especially if you haven't been there in a while. Things change often.

Get out of the car and feel the wind. Have a look around and note the location of obstacles: houses, trees, electricity pylons, wires, livestock, fences, car parks, cable cars and so on.

Note the windsock or wind streamers, if any. You need to land into wind, so finding and remembering where the windsock is on the ground will help you avoid spending time searching for it from the air as you make your final approach.

Spend some time working out how you would approach the landing field in different wind directions. It might seem obvious if the wind is blowing from one direction, but what if it switches? Is it still so obvious, or are there different obstacles? Talk through the landing approaches with your instructor or other pilots – there might be one that is recommended or obligatory, so it's good to spend a few minutes discussing it now, down here, rather than up on launch when everyone is busy getting ready.

Note landmarks and obstacles that you'll be able to see from the air and orientate yourself by. At large sites especially, things can look very different once in the air and that big landing field can in fact be hard to spot.

Look beyond the landing field to see if you have any options for a plan B. Can you land in the next field for example, or is it full of livestock, crops or rocks? Is it busy in the air or on the ground? Are there many other paragliders or hang gliders? Will the approach be crowded or restricted if there are lots of pilots flying?

Finally, consider the best way to get to take-off. Are cars allowed? Is there a bus, chairlift or can you car-share? Can you walk up? It's good practice to have as little impact on the environment of the flying site as possible.

▶ READ THE BOARD

At established sites there is often an information board explaining the site, including launches, landing zones and any restrictions. It will tell you whether you need permission to fly, and usually include contact details for the local club or warden. The recommended landing approach may be indicated. One tip after you have read the board is to take a photo and store it on your phone for reference.

▲ MOUNTAIN LAUNCH
Depending on where you fly, launch sites can be large and established, with astroturf and dedicated windsocks, or they can simply be patches of cleared ground on a hillside. Always take a few minutes to familiarise yourself with a new take-off, including walking to the front to look down the front of the hill. Photo: Marcus King

On take-off

Once you arrive on take-off, have a look around and assess the situation. If you're with an instructor they will be helpful, but it's important to get into the habit of making your own assessment of what's happening and why.

Ask yourself where is the wind coming from? Is it weak or strong, or does it come in gusts, which may indicate thermals? Is the wind direction as you expected, or is something else happening?

Does the weather that you see match the forecast that you've read and what you therefore expect? What types of clouds do you see, and what do they mean?

Look at the sky in the near, middle and far distance. Try to work out what those signs in the sky tell you about the flying conditions as they are now, and what that might mean for the future. Note any clouds building and keep an eye on them as you prepare over the next 30 minutes. Keep an eye on conditions as you get ready.

What does the actual launch look like? Is it steep or shallow? Do you see obstacles such as roads, buildings, trees or cables? What does your launch path look like? Is it covered in stones, or are there holes in the ground that you might trip over? Are there loose branches lying around that could tangle in your lines? If there's snow, how deep and how loose is it, or is it icy and slippery? Can you prepare a flat surface to walk on during take-off?

What's behind the spot where you plan to lay out your glider? What happens if you're dragged back? Will you land in trees, trip over a bench or tree trunk, or will you be blown over the top of the hill? Can you diminish these risks in any way? How?

Importantly, can you safely abort your launch? Where is the last point that you can abort after you've started to run? If there's no wind, you'll need to run further. What happens after that point? Is it a cliff, trees, a road, a ski lift or a gently-sloping grass-covered hillside? Make a mental note of where your point of no return is and make sure that if you have to, you abort your launch before that point.

Radio instruction

During a paragliding course you'll often get instructions over the **radio**. Your radio is usually attached to your harness or held in a holster strapped to your body. Wearing it on a cord hanging around your neck is not great practice. It could get caught on something. If the cord doesn't break, it could cut off your breath.

Some pilots prefer to use an earpiece. The advantage is you can hear your instructor more clearly. The disadvantage is you hear your surroundings less. Additionally, earpieces have sensitive connections, which may malfunction. If you don't hear anything over the radio for a long time as you fly, consider the possibility that the radio has failed. In that case, don't wait for instructions but fly independently, stick to the instructor's initial brief and land safely on your own.

▶ SITE ETIQUETTE

Like all outdoor sports, it's good practice to remember that you're a guest in the area, often on common or even private land. Except for the biggest flying sites, where clubs might own the take-off, in most countries paragliding clubs work with local landowners to allow pilots to fly.

If you follow the local rules that you've discovered during your site assessment, there are likely to be no complaints. You won't want to be the one who ruins things for other pilots. Unfortunately it's not uncommon for sites to be closed or lost because local rules have been repeatedly violated. As the saying goes: take only photographs and leave only footprints.

On launch, it's good practice not to hinder anyone who's ready to take off. If you're alone on a launch or there's plenty of space, you can prepare yourself at the exact spot where you want to take off. Usually, however, it's better to prepare your equipment in a quiet place off to the side and then bundle the glider in a **field pack** or **mushroom** by making large loops of the lines while walking toward the canopy. Swing the field pack over your shoulder and walk to the take-off when you're ready.

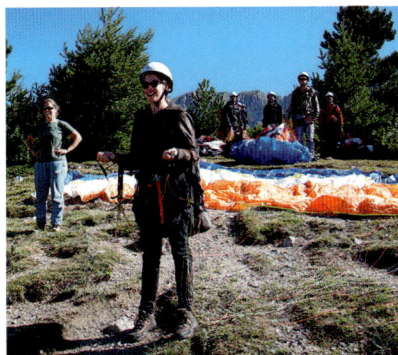

▶ HOW TO USE THE RADIO

▶ **Keep it brief.** Even when flying with friends general **radio etiquette** dictates that you exchange only necessary information over the radio and don't just chat. This is because using the radio uses up the battery, and can also be a nuisance for other pilots. If pilots are irritated listening to the radio, they tend to switch it off, which can then become a safety problem.

▶ **Keep it charged**. If you fly with a radio, it's a good habit to charge it every night. Even if you don't use it during the day, radios have a habit of switching on in the bag or simply mysteriously running flat.

▶ **Do a radio check**. On launch, make sure you check it before you take off. You can do this by asking once for a radio check. For example:
Pilot A: "This is Joanna, radio check please."
Pilot B: "Copy that Joanna, loud and clear."
If you don't hear the reply, but know that someone has spoken, check your volume and connections before checking again.

▶ **Slow down.** When planning to transmit – to talk into the radio – remember to slow down a bit, think about what you want to say, then:
1. Press-and-hold
2. Speak
3. Release.

▶ **Press, then talk.** A common mistake is to start to talk before pressing the transmit button. That way only half the message is transmitted.

▶ **Know your location**. In the air, a typical good radio transmission between pilots will be succinct and will include location by distance and height. For example: "This is Joanna. I am 10km east of launch at 1,200m. Crossing the lake now with Jim."

▶ **Know the shorthand**. If you cannot reply, a quick double-click is the internationally understood signal for "I understand" or "yes" or "received". A single-click means "no" or "negative" or "did not receive".

▶ **Don't be that person**. Make sure your radio is not in a place where you can accidentally push the transmit button. Flying with a group of pilots while one is constantly transmitting without knowing is irritating, and can become a safety matter if the radio is needed for an emergency.

▶ **Practice**. Use the radio on the ground and get to know it before you use it in the air. Know how to operate it, including setting volume and switching channels. You'll avoid all the classic errors of radio communication.

While a radio allows two-way talk, during early instruction you're not expected to talk back. Better to focus on flying. Besides, the radio may be used for several students, which means if you talk the instructor can't guide others.

Flight plan

Before you take off you should have thought about what you intend to do in the air. This is called a **flight plan**. Having a flight plan means that you're aware of your surroundings and circumstances, and you've considered possible risks and ways to avoid them. The simplest flight plan includes deciding what you'll do after you've launched. For example: "After take-off I will turn left, where I expect to find a thermal. If there's no thermal there and I sink below a certain height, I will head for landing."

It also means knowing what to do when you climb out. "If I do find a thermal and climb higher, then I will fly to the right and continue searching for thermals over the spine out front. I will get as much height as I can before heading downwind on XC."

And it definitely means understanding and giving thought to your landing approach before you take off. "To land in the landing field down there I will land into the wind, which is coming from left to right along the lake at the moment. That means I need to have enough height to clear that crane and that church steeple before making my final turn and approach into wind."

A flight plan can also include watching the weather develop, for example when thunderstorms are forecast later in the day. Finally, the plan may include practising techniques and manoeuvres such as soaring for a set period of time or number of beats, big ears, figures of eight, 360-degree turns or steep turns.

▼ FLIGHT PLAN
Before you launch it is important to have a plan for what you will do in the air. This can be as simple as knowing you will glide directly to the landing field for a good landing, or be more complex and involve flying cross country
Photo: Andy Busslinger

▲ GET READY TO FLY
Whether you are launching from a hill or towing, also known as winch launching, having a set routine to check your equipment is flight-worthy is important. This routine is known as the daily inspections
Photo: Erwin Voogt

▶ BEFORE LAUNCHING

Daily inspections

It's a good idea to get into the habit of preparing your equipment shortly after you arrive at launch. This means you can take your time, as you wait for the day's conditions to develop. If you keep everything in your bag until the conditions to fly are perfect, you'll then have to rush to set up your glider and harness, which is never helpful.

Before clipping in to your harness or inflating your glider, you need to carry out systematic **daily inspections** on your glider and your harness. This is an important part of flying, and is part of aviation across all its disciplines. You should aim to be disciplined about it too: because of the simple nature of paragliding it is unfortunately too easy to miss these or get complacent. Try not to. The best pilots in the world are absolutely rigorous in completing their daily inspections – before every take-off. In flying the smallest mistake can have the biggest consequences.

Your actual daily inspections may differ depending on equipment and location, but the general principle remains the same: you're checking your equipment to make sure it's fit to fly.

The glider

Lay out the wing and untangle the lines. Make sure there are no knots or twigs in the lines or canopy. Check the fabric surface visually for any tears or holes, top and bottom. Look at the seams and visually check the visible threads.

If the glider has been packed away for a while, walk along the leading edge looking down and into the cells. The internal structure of a paraglider is complex and could be damaged if mistreated or if you drop the wing on its nose.

If you fly at the beach, check for sand in the cells. This can damage the wing, and also affect its flight characteristics. Many wings have small Velcro openings on the trailing edge at the wingtips designed to empty sand or dirt.

Lightweight cloth can be scuffed or marked if dragged. Try not to drag your wing around the take-off or continually pull it up and drop it back down on rocky terrain. Try to avoid folding it on tarmac or grit.

Check the plastic reinforcements inside the wing – these can wear through the fabric at the point of highest tension, if not treated well.

In general give it a good look-over, especially if you had a difficult launch or landing the last time you flew.

Lines and brakes

Untangle all the lines and lay them out. Rather than pulling at the A-riser to untangle them, a neat trick is to hold up all the risers and untangle the brake line at the bottom first. The others tend to follow.

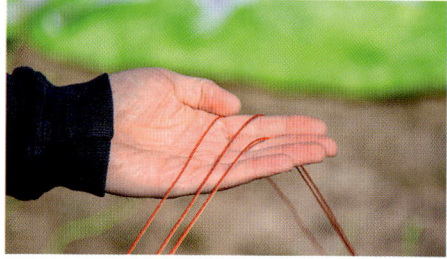

Check the lines are attached to the glider and the maillons. Run each set of lines and brake lines through your hand, walking from riser to glider, feeling for any nicks, knots or damage. Discolouration can mean internal damage.

Check the brake popper or magnet works. Check brake-keepers and see that the brake line runs freely through them, all the way up to, and including, where the lines fan out and connect to the trailing edge.

Check brake handles are not worn. Check the knots between brake handle and brake line are secure. Gliders are supplied with the brakes at a certain length – it's not recommended to change them.

▶ LINE LENGTHS

Some lines are sheathed, others aren't. Occasionally lines can shrink or stretch, if they get damp for example, and a wrinkled sheath might be evidence of this. Get to know what your lines look like, so that you'll know when something's wrong with one of them.

Higher-performing gliders can tolerate only very small changes in line length, while other wings can tolerate more. Some manufacturers suggest pilots have their lines professionally checked after the first 15 hours, to make sure the glider stays in trim.

Risers

Check risers are not twisted, worn or damaged. Check they are connected to the paraglider properly. Check that the speed bar line is running cleanly and not wrapped around or through the riser.

Where there are trimmers, check these are not stuck shut and are in good order. Some gliders have fabric sleeves that cover the pulleys or other elements of the risers – lift these up and give what's underneath a visual check.

Speed system

Check the speed system pulleys, speed bar, and line. If lines are worn, they tend to snap in flight just when you need them most! Check the pulleys are connected properly, there are no twists and that any maillon rapides are closed.

Brummel hooks have an irritating habit of separating – check them every time you fly. There are many different solutions to prevent this, from using maillon rapides to rubber bands or 3D printed covers.

▶ HANG ON TO IT

If there is a danger of your helmet rolling down the hill, you can put it on your head and fasten the strap. Fastening the strap straight away means you won't take off with your helmet undone. If you take your helmet off again while walking around the launch, clip it to something. Yours wouldn't be the first one rolling off the hill with you chasing after it. Stow the glider bag and anything else you don't need in the back pocket of your harness. Don't leave anything on take-off as you most likely will not return there.

▶ HARNESS FITTING

Harnesses come in different sizes, and you should use one that fits you correctly. Most manufacturers size them by minimum and maximum pilot height, for example 160cm-185cm. Fly a harness that fits.

Before you fly a harness for the first time, fit it correctly by hanging it up and sitting in it, using a pair of ropes tied to a beam. While you're sitting in the harness, adjust its straps evenly until you're in a comfortable position.

Paragliders are tested with sit harnesses with the chest strap at a width of 42 to 45cm, indicated in the manual. If you fly a harness wildly out of this range, you can expect the glider to react differently.

Harness

Check your harness each time you fly. Check straps are in good order, back protection is fitted correctly, fabric is not ripped and that karabiners are not wearing away any material. Check that it's set up symmetrically.

Unless you're at the very beginning of your learning phase, your harness will be equipped with a reserve parachute and will incorporate a speed system too. It's vital to check both of these before you launch. See the corresponding boxes on these pages.

Many harnesses have zip pockets on the back and at the side. Use these to store your glider bag and other things. Before you fly, check the zips are closed properly and that what is inside is stowed securely and can't fall out or leak.

Reserve parachute

Check the curved steel pins or plastic rods are threaded correctly. A reserve pin should be centred, not pushed all the way through. The handle itself should stand proud, so it can be grabbed if needed.

Check that any Velcro elements are not squashed shut. It's not uncommon for Velcro surfaces to stick together firmly – if this is the case, run your finger between them and clean away any dirt. Put the Velcro back together gently.

Check that any zip fasteners are free of dirt and not obstructed. Zips have started to replace Velcro in many new harnesses – this is because the hooks on Velcro can damage lightweight fabric.

Flight deck

Before you take off, make sure any instruments are attached securely with a short lanyard and not simply stuck onto the Velcro – that's an easy way to lose an expensive flight instrument.

▶ CHECK IT, PACK IT

A reserve parachute should be taken out of the harness, aired, dried and repacked by a qualified packer according to the manufacturers' recommendations, usually at least every year. You can train to repack it yourself and many schools and clubs organise repack days. When the canopy is out and airing, check the lines and fabric just like you check the glider. Clean out all the dirt and check for damp or mold. Also check the manufacturing date of the reserve: most manufacturers don't recommend using a reserve that is more than 10 years old.

▲ GETTING INTO THE AIR
After completing your pre-flight checks the next phase is launching. You need to find a clear spot, assess the wind, check for other air traffic, and then execute a safe and controlled take-off. Easy!
Photo: Jérôme Maupoint

▶ THE LAUNCH PHASE

Be systematic

Depending on how you've been taught, your harness and glider will either already be attached, or will be separate. Some people prefer to clip in to their harness and then attach the glider. Others prefer to attach the harness to the glider and then clip in.

Whichever system you adopt, if you make it a systematic process you're less likely to forget any steps. And once you start the process of clipping in to your harness and glider don't stop: don't get distracted by friends or your phone.

Modern harnesses have safety-locking systems that make it 'impossible' to take off and then fall out. However, once you're in your harness, it's a bad habit to sit there with one or two buckles undone for comfort. It's too easy to think: "It's launchable!" and take off with a buckle undone. Struggling to close a buckle in flight can be an alarming experience, even if you're not in any real danger.

Pay close attention to your connections and harness buckles – you are clipping in to a safety harness that is designed to keep you secure. Once you're clipped in, don't be afraid to do a buddy check with a friend on launch.

Choose your spot

Securely buckled in, it's time to launch. Choose the place you want to launch from. Your runway must be long enough and free from obstacles. Note how much distance you have to abort the launch if something is wrong. If there's enough wind you'll need less room to run than if there's no wind.

Spread out your canopy. Sort the lines, starting with the brake lines and then from As to Cs (or Ds if you have them), making sure there are no knots, loops or sticks caught in them. If you've not already done so, connect the risers to the karabiners of the harness, ensuring that they're not twisted and the fronts of the risers point forwards. If you have a speed system, connect it. Check the settings of the trimmers if you have those.

Ideally the wind will be blowing directly onto the slope. Lay out your canopy in an arc, perpendicular to the wind, with the centre higher up the hill than the wingtips. This ensures during launch the cells in the centre will fill with air first, followed by the rest of the canopy.

Crosswind

If the wind is blowing on to the hill at an angle, this is a **crosswind**. A crosswind of up to 45° either side usually poses no problem when launching a paraglider (although some sites can be more sensitive to crosswinds than others) so typically we have a launch wind-window of 90°.

For example, let's say you're on a north-facing launch (zero/360°). Your wind-window for this site is NW through to NE, or 315° through to 45°. If you're on launch and the wind is coming from 330°, you have a 30° crosswind. As you face out from the hill the wind will come from the left, so lay out your glider facing left and start your launch facing left.

If the wind is more than 45° off the air will start to become turbulent and potentially dangerous – you'll need to wait for it to come around again, or change launches. Be wary of trying to launch with a **backwind**, when the wind is from behind; the air can be turbulent and potentially dangerous.

▼ **CROSSWIND LAUNCH**
A slope that faces due north (0°) can typically be flown in a 45° crosswind, ie from NW (315°) to NE (45°). If the wind is more than 45° cross then the air will become turbulent, uncomfortable and potentially dangerous to fly in

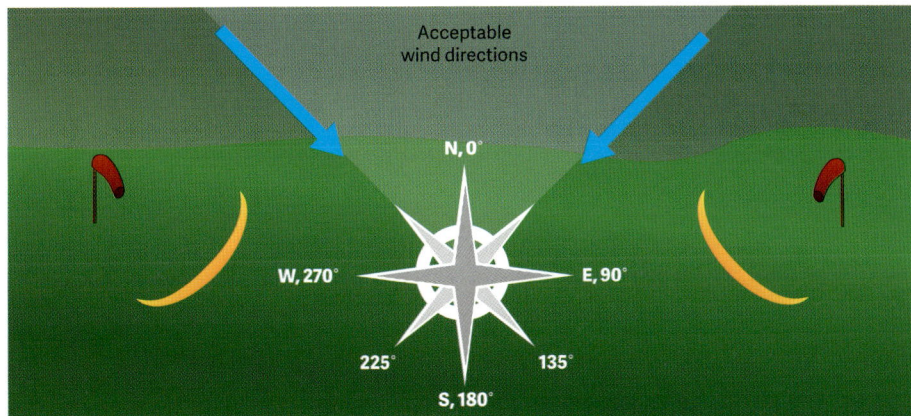

Acceptable wind directions

N, 0°

W, 270°

E, 90°

225°

135°

S, 180°

Pilot
Check your harness is done up properly, and that you are clipped in

Lines
Check they are free of tangles. Check brake lines for twists, and that they run clear

Canopy
Make sure there are no lines over the glider, and that it is laid out nicely

Airspace
Keep an eye on other pilots and give them space

Wind
Keep checking this for strength and direction. If it changes, adjust your plan

Ready for take-off?

There are many variations of this list of **pre-launch checks**, but they're always aimed at making sure you and your equipment are ready and safe to launch. The sequence presented here starts with the pilot and works outwards. Get into the habit of doing the same checks every flight.

1 Pilot and harness The main thing is the leg straps. Are they securely fastened? Are the chest strap and other straps also connected? Are the karabiners closed and locked? Are the reserve pins secure and is the handle in place? Helmet on and strap fastened? Is your clothing safe and laces tightened? Finally, check your radio volume and frequency with your instructor.

2 Lines Are all lines free of knots, branches or loops? No **line-overs**? Are your risers straight and not backwards or twisted? Karabiners closed and locked? Speed system connected and not twisted?

3 Canopy Is the canopy laid out in an arc, free of large folds or tucks? Is it straight into wind? If it is inflating more on one side than another, then it is not centred. Adust your stance by taking a step to the left or right until the glider sits evenly.

4 Wind Is the wind still from the right direction? How strong is it? Do you see any changes in the weather? Can you take off safely in these conditions?

5 Airspace Check the area and the air. Who else is around you, ready to launch or in the air? Is anyone flying close to the take-off area? Are others about to take off at the same time? Is your runway clear? If everything is fine, you're ready to launch.

Forward launch

The **forward launch**, also called the **Alpine launch**, is probably the first launch technique you will learn. It's called the Alpine launch because it is commonly used in the nil-wind or light-wind conditions found in the Alps.

First lay the glider out in a nice arc, making sure the lines are clear and there are no twists or tangles. Check the canopy visually. Then, clipped in and facing forwards in the direction you want to launch, take the brake handles and the A-risers in your hands. The right brake and riser should be in the right hand, and the left brake and riser should be in the left hand. Brake lines, lines and risers should be free of tangles and not twisted. Stand in front of the centre of your canopy, facing forward. Hold your hands loosely closed at shoulder height. Check the wind and other air traffic for a final time. At some busy launches it's customary to call out "Launching!" just before you start your run. This lets others know you're about to take off.

The forward launch can be divided into four phases:

1. Inflation phase: By taking a few steps forward you put tension on the A-lines, causing the cells to open and fill with air. The canopy will start to rise. Guide the As upwards while you continue to walk. Lean forward and look ahead at where you're going. The speed of your walk is highly dependent on the wind. Without wind, you'll need more speed, perhaps a run. With wind, you merely need to put tension on the As and lean forward.

2. Control phase: As soon as the canopy is straight overhead, you need to control it. Check the canopy by looking straight up: is it completely filled with air? Are the lines and risers free of knots, loops, twists or sticks? Let go of the A-risers and put some tension on the brake lines. This prevents the canopy from shooting over your head. Abort your launch if you feel or see that something is not right, by pulling both controls down towards your knees and holding them there.

3 Acceleration phase: When the canopy is under control, move your hands with the controls back with the palms facing out and the thumbs up (think about opening a newspaper). Make sure your centre of gravity is in front of your toes by pushing your chest forward. In this position, you have a little bit of tension on the brake lines and your bodyweight accelerates the canopy. Walk forward with large steps and increasing speed, while looking where you're going. If you take off with a crosswind, this is the time to steer the canopy straight down the hill. Keep moving and leaning forward until you're several metres up in the air. If you stop moving too early or lean back, you'll hit the ground. Don't try to 'jump' into the air early – it doesn't work.

4 Fly away: Fly away from the hill and bring your hands slowly back to shoulder or ear height. Watch for other pilots and airspace users, and fly towards open space. Sit back in your harness by pulling your knees up towards your nose. If necessary, help yourself into the harness by putting both controls in one hand and holding them in the centre above your head, then push yourself into the harness with the other hand. (Don't pull down both brakes as you push yourself into your harness.) Now it's time to enjoy your flight!

Reverse launch

The forward launch has some disadvantages, especially in strong winds. During the inflation phase, the canopy is behind you and you can't see it. In this position, the canopy has the most power and is most likely to pull you backwards or lift you up. To counter this you need to walk towards the canopy, but walking backwards is not as easy as forwards. So in a strong wind, it's safer to execute a reverse launch.

For a **reverse launch**, you turn around and face the canopy for the inflation (1) and control (2) phases. This has several advantages. You can see the canopy during inflation and immediately check for knots, sticks or **line-overs**. Second, you can easily walk towards the canopy if it rises too quickly. This slows down the canopy so you don't need to apply a big brake input to stop it from **overshooting**. Brake input generates lift, causing you to be pulled off your feet, so the less you need, the smaller this risk. Finally, facing the canopy allows easier use of your bodyweight to control it.

There are several different reverse launch techniques, all valid. The easiest way to start is to connect the risers to the harness in the usual way and grab the controls as you're used to. Then turn around so that the risers are crossed in front of you. The brake lines are also crossed: the left control (which now crosses to your right) is in your left hand and the right control is in your right hand. After inflation, you don't need to switch controls.

Now pick up one A-riser in each hand, but don't cross your hands; grab the right A-riser with your left hand and vice versa. Alternatively, you can pick up both A-risers with one hand. Pull the As upwards lightly and the canopy will start to rise. Take a few steps toward the canopy to de-power it if necessary.

Bring it straight over your head by taking a few steps towards the lower tip of the canopy if necessary. Then let go of the As and control the canopy with the brakes and by making sure you're standing right under the centre of the leading edge.

With the canopy under control, you can turn around (3), while making sure to keep pressure on the risers by leaning forward. Be careful at this point to turn in the right direction – so that your risers untwist cleanly; otherwise you'll put a twist into the risers and will have to abort your take-off. Moving forwards, and with commitment, you can then accelerate and take off.

▲ OTHER LAUNCH METHODS
The pilot on the left is using the rear risers to control the glider. Using As and Cs (or Ds) to launch can be useful in strong wind. The pilot on the right is using the cobra launch – useful in strong wind and confined spaces
Photos: Bastienne Wentzel / Ant Green

Rear-riser method

Another reverse launch technique involves holding both As in one hand and both rear risers (usually the Cs or Ds) with the other. This is sometimes called the **Australian technique** or **Mitsos launch** and is particularly useful for managing the glider in strong wind.

The controls are held as above. Inflate the canopy by moving the As upward with one hand. With the other, you can control the speed with which the canopy rises by pulling lightly on the rear risers to slow it down. Correct the direction of the canopy by moving your hand on the rear risers towards the lower tip of the canopy.

With the canopy straight overhead, you can control the glider with the rear risers only, or turn around and take off as normal.

In strong winds the advantage of this method is that you can very effectively control the speed with which the canopy rises, and also pull it back to the ground if necessary. As we saw before, brake input generates lift, but braking the canopy using the rear risers does not generate lift. This method therefore creates less risk of being pulled off your feet.

Cobra launch

Finally, you can inflate the canopy asymmetrically. This means that you don't pull both A-risers simultaneously, but inflate one side of the canopy first. In strong wind this ensures that the canopy rises at the edge of the **wind window** instead of in the centre of it, where the strongest forces are. The forces are much smaller, and you're much less likely to be dragged or lifted by the wing before it's overhead. A well-known asymmetric launch technique is the **cobra launch**.

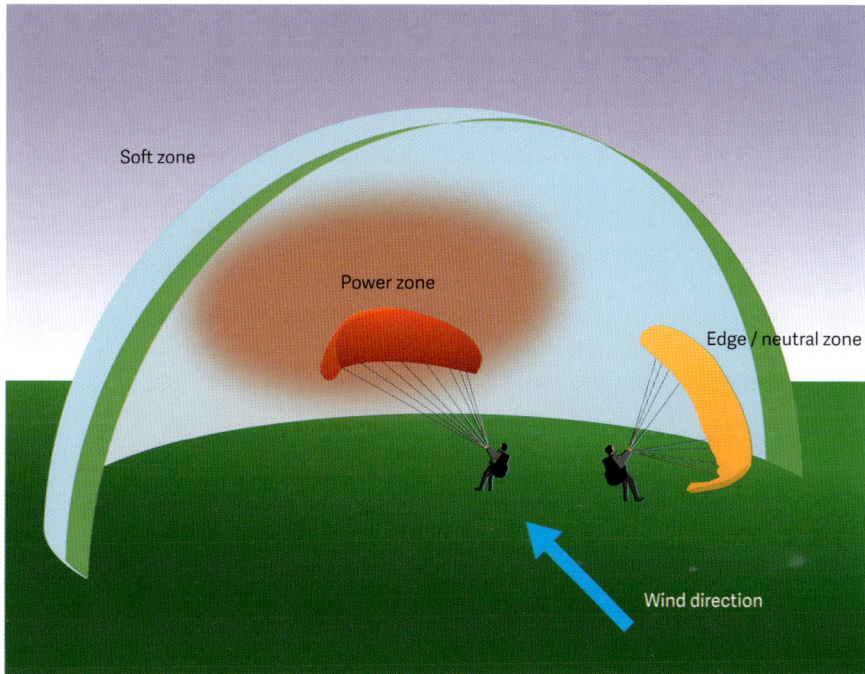

▶ THE WIND WINDOW

Soft zone

Power zone

Edge / neutral zone

Wind direction

The **wind window** is the space downwind of you where you can kite your glider while groundhandling. It extends left and right of you, above you, and ahead of you when facing the wing. It has the shape of a quarter-sphere. The concept of the wind window is a fundamental theory of kite-boarding, and we use it in the same way.

We can divide the space covered by this quarter-sphere into three zones. The first is the edge of the wind window, the green stripe in this illustration. We call this the **edge**, or the **neutral zone**. The glider has least power on the edge of the wind window. In a steady wind it is easy to hold the glider in this position and manage the wing without pulling. For example, when it is above your head or fully to one side of you on its tip like the yellow glider.

The **intermediate area**, or the **soft zone**, is the blue area. The glider will move dynamically and produce power. The power is less at the edge and stronger towards the power zone.

The **power zone** is the centre of the wind window. It's the red area in the illustration. This is the most powerful area within the wind window. The glider needs to be kept under constant control in the power zone. When groundhandling the glider will pull hard in the power zone as it accelerates towards the soft zone and the edge. Facing the wing, with the wind at your back, the power zone is directly downwind of you from ground level to about 45-degrees.

You can use this information when groundhandling or landing in strong winds by making sure that the glider doesn't enter the power zone but instead remains as close to the edge of the wind window as possible. This is why in strong wind you need to use a control method that manages the wing well in the power zone (As and Cs) or launches from outside the power zone (the cobra method).

Tow launch

For a **tow launch** a **launch marshal** is usually present. The marshal assists the pilot and communicates with the **tow operator**. During launch preparations, a tow release is connected to the karabiners or attachment loops of the harness. The tow line is connected to this release.

After the pre-launch checks, the launch marshal will ensure that everyone is ready and then ask the operator to take up the slack from the tow line. Resist the pull until you're ready to inflate the glider.

The first two phases of a tow launch are similar to a forward launch. Inflate your glider and control it overhead. When it's under control, tell the launch marshal to start the acceleration phase; they will relay this to the operator.

The operator will start pulling the line. Hold your hands up high and keep walking until you're in the air. You don't need to lean forward -- the tow line provides the necessary acceleration.

With a crosswind, inflate your glider straight into wind and correct its direction after the control phase. It's important to keep your course straight toward the tow once you're in the air, with the tow line exactly straight ahead. Be prepared to correct your course, especially with crosswinds. If your course is too far off, you risk a **lock-out**, where the wing becomes unmanageable.

When making directional corrections, it's best not to pull too much brake. The wing is already far behind you as a result of the tow line tension. Braking too much may induce a stall, causing the wing to stop flying.

When you're flying almost over the tow installation, the operator will slow down the winch, release the tension on the tow line, and then tell you over the radio that you can release. Make sure the tow line is no longer connected after you've released, and fly away normally from the tow area to avoid interference with the towing operation.

Don't release if there's still tension on the tow line. This will cause the line to snap back and jam the drum. If there's an emergency and you have to release, try to notify the operator by spreading your legs forward and holding them there. In an absolute emergency, choose safety first and release.

If the tow line breaks, don't release the rest of it, but try to bring it in if that's safely possible. If you release the line, it may fall over roads or people, causing a dangerous situation. Alternatively, unlock the release but bring the line in so that you can drop it if it becomes tangled in a tree or other object. Release and don't hold on if the line is tangled, as it may pull your glider down.

Step towing

A special form of towing is **step towing**. The purpose is to get higher in the air by flying towards the tow and back to launch a number of times. During these 'steps', if the operator or the pilot notices a thermal, you can be released right in the middle of it. It's a great starting point for a flatland cross-country flight.

You need a special step-tow release and a **certified winch** and operator. When you reach the winch after the first tow, the operator tells you to turn 180 degrees, usually specifying left or right. This direction depends on the wind, so follow the instructions carefully as there's a good reason for them.

Make sure that the tow line doesn't accidentally pull the handle of your reserve parachute, if they're on the same side. However, don't take the line between your feet or in your hand to avoid this, because then you effectively eliminate the safety mechanism of the step-tow release (see the chapter on Equipment).

When you're approximately over the launch area, or when you want, or if you're low, or when the operator tells you, turn towards the winch again, in the opposite direction of your turn away from the winch. The operator will take up the tension on the line again and pull you up higher than the first round. This process can be repeated until you run out of towline. After multiple steps, the operator will tell you when to release in the normal way.

▼ STEP TOWING
Popular in the flatlands, step towing lets you get in the air by winch without needing to use a huge field

▶ HANDS UP!

Whether you get in the air from a hill launch or a tow launch, you must keep your hands high, near the brake-keepers. This is so you don't slow the glider down too much, or, in the worst case, stall it by mistake. This can happen if a pilot's hands are down by their waist. In your training you will get used to hearing your instructor command "Hands up! Keep your hands high!" as you go through the launch phase.

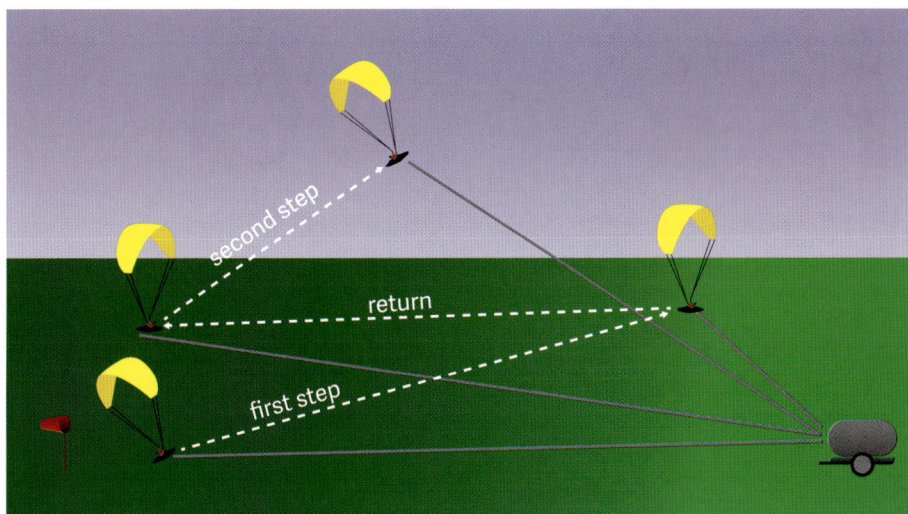

▶ HOLDING THE BRAKES

The way you hold your brake handles is largely personal and may depend on the shape and size of the handles and also on your flying style and discipline. Most important is that you have a good grip and a quick release. In a manoeuvre the forces can get relatively high, so make sure the handles can not suddenly be pulled out of your hand. On the other hand, but just as important, in an emergency you should be able to release the handle immediately, pull your hand out and grab your reserve handle. These are the most used grips:

The standard grip

This is the way many pilots are taught when learning to fly. There is nothing wrong with this grip, but it can be uncomfortable or tiring for a long flight, and some pilots find that the grip lacks sensitivity, because of the muscles it uses. It's very easy to release in an emergency, which is a plus point.

The half-wrap

Your fingers are through the handle with the thumb outside, and you lightly hold the middle of the handle or the stiffener. By rolling your wrist out and around you grab the line just above the handle. This grip does not slip and should not be tiring, while still being easy to let go if needed.

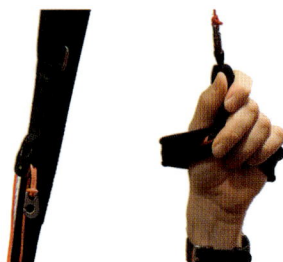

The acro grip or dragon grip

This grip, used a lot by acro pilots, usually requires a large brake handle. You slip your full hand through the loop so it is on your wrist, then grab the line above the handle. It is a tight grip for delivering lots of force without being tiring. Test releasing your hand without effort, including with gloves on. Reject it if that doesn't work for you.

Other possibilities

Loose grip: Some pilots just hold the handle right above the loop. Be aware that the loop can be pulled out of your hand, which can be a problem. Works well with acro handles.
Full wrap: If you temporarily need to shorten your brakes for a manoeuvre or good flare, you can wrap the line around your hand. Wear gloves because this can hurt your hand.

▲ **READY TO FLY**
Committing aviation in the south of France
Photo: Marcus King

▶**FLYING**

Once you're in the air, relax, take a look around and enjoy the view. Now it's time for the real thing: piloting the paraglider in the air.

Controlling the glider
The pilot controls the paraglider using the brakes or controls. The brakes are attached to the brake lines, which are in turn attached to the trailing edge of the paraglider canopy. Applying brake changes the speed of the paraglider. How much brake you should apply depends on the situation that you're in and what you want to do. Learning how much brake to apply and when to apply it is a key technical skill in flying a paraglider.

A paraglider flies at a certain speed with respect to the surrounding air. This is called **airspeed**. If you don't touch the brakes, the airspeed of a typical paraglider is equal to its **trim speed**: around 38km/h for most paragliders.

The paraglider also has a speed with respect to the ground: the **groundspeed**. Without wind, the groundspeed is equal to the airspeed, but with wind it is not. Finally, the **wind speed** is the speed of the air with respect to the ground. There are some examples in the box on this page to help you get to grips with these important concepts.

How much brake?
Hands up: With your hands fully up, the brakes will touch the brake pulleys. The paraglider is now flying at trim speed.

Contact position: By bringing your hands down approximately 10cm you'll feel a bit of tension on the brake lines. You're now 'in contact' with the wing. The paraglider is still flying close to its trim speed.

Minimum sink postition: Different gliders have different minimum sink points. For a modern performance glider minimum-sink position is close to trim speed, that is, the hands-up position. For older gliders, minimum sink is flying with about one-third brake.

▶UNDERSTANDING SPEED

A paraglider flies with a certain speed with respect to the surrounding air, the **airspeed**. A paraglider also has a certain speed with respect to the ground, **groundspeed**. In nil-wind airspeed is equal to groundspeed (**a**). With a headwind the airspeed of a paraglider is still the same, but the groundspeed decreases (**b**). Flying downwind airspeed is still the same but groundspeed is higher (wind speed + airspeed) (**c**).

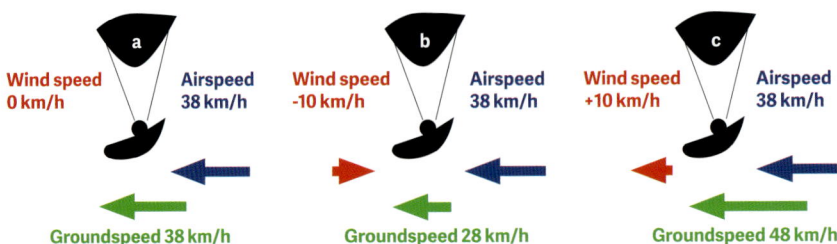

a	**b**	**c**
Wind speed 0 km/h — Airspeed 38 km/h	Wind speed -10 km/h — Airspeed 38 km/h	Wind speed +10 km/h — Airspeed 38 km/h
Groundspeed 38 km/h	Groundspeed 28 km/h	Groundspeed 48 km/h

▶ PITCH, ROLL AND YAW

A paraglider moves in three different directions. **Pitch** is the rotation around the horizontal axis. **Roll** is the movement around the longitudinal axis. **Yaw** is movement around the yaw axis.

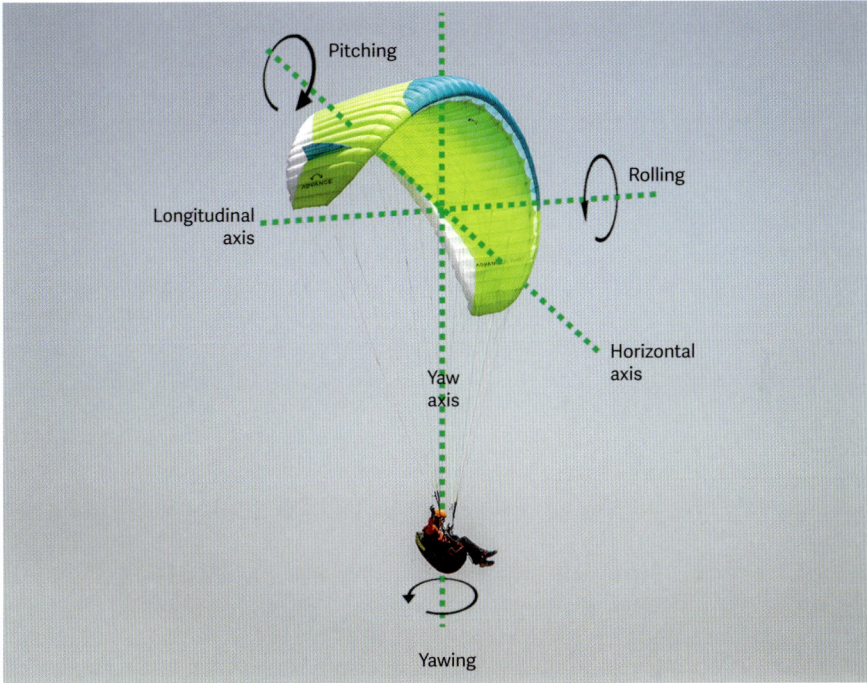

Pitching

Rolling

Longitudinal axis

Horizontal axis

Yaw axis

Yawing

Full stall position: Most paragliders have a brake range of 55cm-65cm. If you hold your hands with the controls at hip height, you are braking the paraglider at its maximum 100% brake. The wing will stop flying and you'll fall out of the air. This is a **full stall**, or **stalling**. In normal flight you should not pull 100% brake while flying. For steady flight keep your hands at ear height, the contact position.

Pitch, roll and yaw

When flying a paraglider the canopy will move around, and you will swing under it like a pendulum. The glider moves around three different axes. Understanding these movements is at the core of paraglider control.

Pitch means rotation around the **horizontal axis** that runs from left to right through the canopy. Pitch is like going back and forth like a swing.

Roll is rotation around the **longitudinal axis**; the axis that runs from front to back. It is the movement of the canopy from left to right: like bending left and right at the waist.

Yaw is rotation around the **vertical axis**. Yaw is like twisting left and right at the waist, or imagine you're twirling.

Pitch, roll and yaw are controlled throughout the flight by using brakes and applying weightshift.

97

Turning a paraglider

Turning a paraglider is not hard. The mechanics of it are simple: if you add drag to one side of the glider you slow that side down; the other side is now flying relatively faster, so the glider starts to turn.

If you lean to the left, the paraglider goes left. If you pull the left brake, the paraglider goes left. With some practice, a subtle combination of weightshift and brake input will get the paraglider to turn exactly as you want it to.

The most important rule when turning is to look before you turn, and continue to look as you complete the turn. In this way you'll maintain your **heading**, you'll be able to watch for other air traffic, and you'll naturally feel your way around the turn. As in driving a car or riding a bicycle, pilots who don't look before turning can be a danger to themselves and others.

Your first low training flights will probably not involve turning the glider much. The instructor will focus on learning to launch and land and becoming familiar with the new equipment and environment. Any turns will be limited to one or two. However, once you go higher, you must learn to turn.

Types of turn

As you progress, you'll be introduced to turns in a systematic way. We talk about turns in degrees, left or right. So there is a **90-degree turn** (left or right), a **180-degree turn** (you end up facing the other way), and a **360-degree turn** (full circle). We also talk about **S-turns**, which are gentle turns to the left then right, like a meandering river. S-turns are typically used to lose excess height while you're on final approach to a landing field.

At every stage the aim is to execute a smooth, controlled turn, where you maintain **situational awareness** throughout. You're not turning a bicycle on the flat – you're flying an aircraft in three dimensions, and always going up or down as well as forwards. To some people this situational awareness comes very naturally; others have to learn it.

The ultimate aim of learning to turn well is not simply to be able to land where

▶TURNING

A **90-degree**, **180-degree** and **360-degree** turn. The aim is to execute a smooth, controlled turn, while maintaining situational awareness with respect to the ground and others.

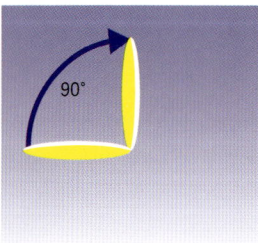

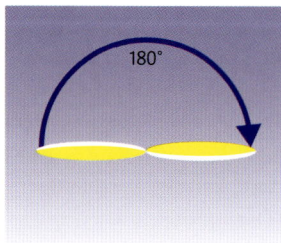

you want in the landing field. It is to let you turn in rising air – lift – and stay up. In narrow lift bands close to hillsides or on the coast, pilots need to be able to fly **beats**, turning 180 degrees at either end. In thermal flying, pilots must fly 360-degree circles to stay in the rising columns of air. Add other pilots into the mix in either situation, and you can see how this can at times become demanding.

First turns

Your first turns will be flown in clear air, away from the hillside and other pilots. Your instructor will brief you, but the process will be something like this. Before you start to turn, decide how far you want to turn. Find a point on the horizon that's on your new course. Look around over your shoulder and up and down in the direction of your turn. That way you can see if your intended flight path is clear, and it also brings your weight in that direction.

Lean gently into the turn. As soon as the paraglider starts to turn, you can gently pull the brake handle on that same side. A few centimetres of brake is all you need at first. If you want to stop the turn, simply bring your hand back up and then sit straight with your weight neutral.

By flying a **flat turn** you lose as little height as possible. To make a flat turn, start by flying straight with a little bit of brake pressure. Now bring one hand down a bit while bringing the other up.

Under instruction you'll be guided through different exercises to help you understand the potential and the limits of your paraglider. You'll notice that when you do a flat turn, you lose less height, but the turn takes a long time. When you

▶ **WEIGHTSHIFTING**

Weightshifting is used to help turn the glider efficiently.

Weightshifting should be a whole body movement. Don't simply swing a leg over your knee and pull the brake.

Rather, shift your whole body across. A good tip is to get your nose in line with your risers and lean into the turn.

▲ DREAM LOCATION
Rainbow beach, Queensland, Australia. Paragliders can stay up for hours in the lift band created by the wind hitting a hillside or coastal cliff. Stronger wind creates a bigger lift band, while weaker wind means less lift. Mastering soaring is a crucial step in becoming a pilot. Photo: Tex Beck

use weightshift and apply more brake on the turning side (the inside brake) you lose more height but you complete your turn more quickly.

Depending on how you progress, your instructor may encourage you to practice 90-degree and 180-degree turns for quite some time. Depending on where you're learning, the aim here is to bring you on to the next stage, which is **soaring** flight. This involves making consistent smooth 180-degree turns close to the hill, perhaps while other pilots are also flying.

Flying beats

Having perfected your launch and landing skills on a series of straightforward top-to-bottom training flights and learnt the basics about turns, most students are eager to progress to the next stage. In order to stay up in a lift band pilots must perfect the art of flying back and forth along the ridge. This is called **flying beats**.

To help you learn this art, the instructor will probably ask you to perform a series of 180-degree turns in a ridge-soaring pattern. Unless conditions are perfect, you'll probably complete these further out from the hill, away from the lift band. You should always turn away from the hillside, never towards it.

You might experience going up for part of the flight as you fly through lift, and then coming down again. The aim here is to introduce you to the idea and the techniques involved in soaring flight safely, well away from the hillside.

The key thing that you're learning about is your relative position to the hillside and the landing field. Although you're under instruction, you'll be required to demonstrate an awareness of where you are in the sky. There's no point flying perfect beats all the way down the slope if you're then too low to turn and fly out to make the landing field. There's a lot to think about in flying beats!

Ridge soaring

Once you've shown the instructor that you're competent at flying beats, they'll bring you closer in towards the hillside. The aim of **ridge soaring** is to get you flying in the lift band, so that you stay up.

At this point you're not actually being taught anything you don't already know. You're simply tightening up what you do know, and flying in the lift band.

This is a remarkable feeling, and the first time you fly in lift without going down is memorable. In the best case you'll be out front and up high in lots of lift, and it will be easy. It gets harder to fly when the lift is lighter and you need to **scratch** in close to the hillside or coastline to stay up. Either way, keep a close eye on other traffic, the hillside, your take-off spot, and where the landing is.

Later, when flying like this but without an instructor, you'll need to watch the weather too. Soaring in strong conditions can be a lot of fun, but you do need to keep one eye on the weather and the wind – if it gets too strong while you're in the air you can be blown backwards behind take-off.

With time and experience you can learn to slope-land in light conditions, and land back where you started – top-land – in good conditions.

360-degree turns

It's possible to learn to ridge-soar and top-land without ever learning to fly a

▼ **RIDGE SOARING**
A good soaring pattern allows a pilot to get established in the air by flying beats in the rising air close to the hill. Always turn away from the hill at the end of each beat, never towards the hill: otherwise you might be blown back behind the hill into turbulent air or, if low, there is also the chance of hitting the ground while flying downwind.

360-degree turn. Pilots who fly on the coast or in hill country where ridge soaring is popular do this all the time. The reason is the 'never turn towards the hill' rule in ridge soaring. It means you're always turning into wind and away from the hill, never making more than 180-degree turns.

However, pilots who learn to fly in the mountains where there's lots of height, on tow, or at easy thermic sites will come to flying 360-degree turns early on.

In still air a 360-degree turn is simply a full circle, a smooth continuation of a

▶ FLAT OR EFFICIENT

Pilots sometimes confuse a **flat turn** with an **efficient turn**. In fact, an efficient turn is the best turn to use in the current conditions. There's no point making a wide flat turn in a narrow lift band – you'll simply drop out of it, which is not efficient flying. Making a tighter, quicker turn that means you stay in the lift band is more efficient in this instance.

90-degree or 180-degree turn. You shift your weight, apply a little brake, regulate the turn with your outside brake, and around you go. Flying down from the mountains in smooth air in the morning and flying lazy 360s over the landing area 500m below you is a simple and nice way to enjoy the flight and the view.

The issue comes when there's wind – because then the 360-degree turn has a downwind component. If you fly perfect 360s over your landing field and there's wind, you'll drift away from the field.

When you're flying 360-degree turns, therefore, you always need to take account of what the wind is doing. This is especially true if you're close to the hillside. Your slow into-wind leg will become a fast, accelerated sweep as soon as you turn downwind. It's easy to be caught out when flying a 360 close to the hill and end up either hitting the ground or sweeping low and fast over the top of the hill and finding yourself behind it. Neither is a good option.

This becomes especially pertinent later in your career when you're using ridge lift to stay up while waiting for a thermal to come through. You might be flying ridge-soaring beats close in, and then suddenly need to turn a tight 360 when a thermal releases. It takes skill and experience to execute this well.

Figure-of-eights

Figure-of-eight describes the pattern you make through the sky as you fly coordinated and linked turns, for example when ridge soaring. Flying figure-of-eights gets more demanding the tighter the figure-of-eight becomes. Flying two 360-degree turns in sequence in opposite

▶ TURNING IN CIRCLES

When making a turn in nil-wind the pilot finishes where they started. As the wind increases the downwind component also increases. In strong wind move out, or you might hit the hill

directions sounds easy enough, but requires quite a lot of piloting skill.

The direction of the turn must be managed carefully. When executed carelessly, this can result in an uncontrolled roll of the wing. If you exit a turn too quickly the wing will pitch back and forth. With a perfectly executed tight figure-of-eight, neither of these will be observable.

Practising figure-of-eights is a good exercise. It teaches you a lot about how to manage roll and pitch in turns. That in

turn is good practice for when you start to thermal. In thermalling you will often need to turn quickly, to get back into lift you have flown through for example. You may also fly figure-of-eights on a landing approach. These get increasingly tighter as you approach the ground. In both situations good pitch and roll management is important.

Tight 360s and spiral dives

A **tight 360** is one where, from trim speed, you weightshift to one side, and then, as the glider starts to turn, you pull

▼ FIGURE-OF-EIGHTS
Figure-of-eights can be elongated and involve slow, smooth applications of brake. Or they can be tighter and demand more application of brake with weightshift. Flying figure-of-eights is good training in learning to manage the pitch and roll of your glider.

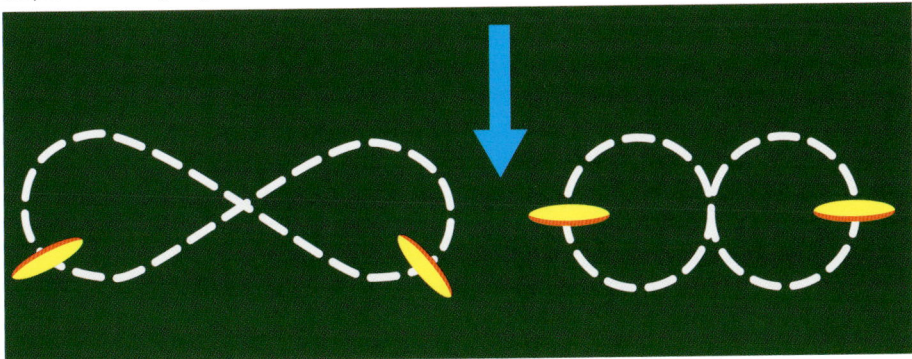

▲ HIGH FLIGHTS
Flying from high take-offs is exciting and exhilarating, but can also be intimidating. Approach launch and landing exactly as you have been taught. The difference is the feeling of exposure and the amount of time in the air. You can also go further, which means it's easy to end up missing your landing field. Photo: Marcus King

more inner brake and accelerate into the turn quickly. You pick up airspeed fast and lose a lot of height. You control your descent rate by managing both inside and outside brakes.

This type of turn is useful if you need to avoid something in the air, or to get down quickly. It's not advisable to make steep turns close to the hillside or low. You don't want to 'bury the brake', but rather apply the inner brake evenly and firmly. The speed and forces in this manoeuvre can increase very quickly until you reach a **spiral dive**. In a spiral dive pilots descend at 10m/s or more, and can feel forces of up to about 4G, which is easily enough to make a pilot black out.

It's only recommended for experienced pilots who have had the proper training.

It's actually very easy to do, and in fact it's not uncommon for new pilots to experiment with spiral dives and get into trouble. If you want to learn how to execute a good spiral dive, the best way is to go on a **manoeuvres course** or **SIV course** and learn over water, with a safety boat to hand. Pulling too much brake too quickly may cause that side of the wing to stop flying. This results in a dangerous situation called a 'spin' (see the chapter on Advanced Flying)

Learn tight 360s and spiral dives progressively and responsibly with plenty of height, as a rule of thumb, never below 200m.

High flights

If you learn to fly in the Alps or other mountains, you'll be flying from high launches very early on. But it's not unusual for newly qualified pilots who have learned to fly at the coast, for example, to find themselves feeling exposed on their first **high flight** – say 300m or more – in the mountains or hills.

It may be intimidating at first, but height means safety. A high flight means plenty of time to practise skills like steep 360-degree turns or figures of eight. Approach it like any other flight containing take-off, flight and landing phases.

You'll need to give yourself time to adjust to the exposure, if that is new to you, so don't plan to do too much on your first day. Get used to the slower feeling of simply hanging there, silently progressing, without the constant reference of the ground nearby.

Having a **flight plan** is essential for a high flight, as is reaching the landing with enough altitude. It's better to get there early and have to wind off the height with a series of 360s than to arrive too low and land in the lake instead of the landing zone.

When flying from a new, high launch site, allow yourself extra margins of time and space until you get used to the new environment. Then simply sit back and enjoy it!

▶ FLYING WITH OTHERS

After your training you will often fly with other paragliders and air traffic – from model aircraft to sailplanes. The most important thing while flying with others is to be aware of your surroundings. Look around and take notice of where the other air traffic is and where it is going. Pilots have a responsibility to avoid collisions, and you can only avoid what you see coming. That means being aware of what's going on around you, flying in a predictable way, anticipating what others are doing, and obeying the rules of the air. We'll learn more about the rules of the air later. Photo: Andy Busslinger

▲ HAPPY LANDINGS
A large but busy landing field. Watching gliders and the windsock will show you which way the wind is blowing. Hazards include the buildings, trees, a river, the road and of course other pilots in the air and people on the ground
Photo: Marcus King

▶ LANDING

Landing is arguably the most important part of flying. On take-off you always have the choice not to fly. But once in the air you're going to have to land, no matter what. No paraglider pilot has ever stayed up forever – they always eventually come down. The important thing is to land safely and at a place and in a way that you choose. Thinking ahead and making a plan for landing is essential.

The wind and landing

As already discussed, thinking about your landing starts before you've even taken off, in the flight planning stage. This includes visiting the landing field, looking at the options, spotting the windsock, and planning how you will make your approach in different winds.

You should keep your landing options in mind throughout your flight, and start to focus on the landing field when you're in the final phase of your flight.

It's wise not to fly too far away from it, particularly on the **downwind** side. There's always the chance that the headwind that you face on the way back will be too strong and you won't make it. This is especially true on a ridge run or coastal run where there's a slight crosswind. You can fly off at speed downwind, but turning and making progress back **upwind** will be harder.

106

The prime consideration for any landing is that you need to land into wind. Look at the **windsock** for information about the wind direction and strength. Watch other paragliders and their landing circuits for the same reason.

If you can't see those, there are lots of other **wind indicators**: chimney smoke; washing on a line; the breeze in crops or trees; ripples on water; the way birds land (always into wind); the way pilots are groundhandling; by flying 360s above the side of the landing field and assessing your drift; by checking the speed on your flight instrument. Be aware that the wind in the landing zone might be different to the wind at the take-off.

Sometimes, especially if it's light, it can be difficult to determine the wind in the landing field. In that case, do your best to judge it and then commit to your final approach. Avoid making last-minute tight turns low, as this can be more damaging than simply having to run-out a fast downwind landing while flaring hard.

Landing approach

The perfect place to land in a landing field is in the first third. If you plan to land in the last third, what will you do if you overshoot? Aim to land in the first 30% of the landing field; that way if you misjudge your approach, you simply fly on and land further down the field.

While you're losing height for landing, stay above the boundaries of the landing field; this keeps you close and within reach if you should suddenly lose some height. Try to avoid flying low over the landing field except for the last leg – this can be confusing for other pilots who are also landing.

▶ SIGNALLING THE WIND

On some landings there is a **landing T**. This is a marker indicating the main wind direction and the preferred landing direction. The tail points downwind. The landing direction is over the tail onto the top of the T. To help fellow pilots when there is no windsock or T, make one yourself from a jacket, or stand with your arms spread and your back into wind. When others have seen you, they can acknowledge it by opening and closing their legs. They land 'in your arms'.

The final leg of your landing approach is simply called **final approach, final** or finals. For a perfect landing, you'll fly on a straight line into wind, at close to maximum speed but with a bit of pressure on the brakes. Flying fast like this means the glider will cut through any turbulence better and will suffer less from any **wind gradient** close to the ground. Wind gradient is where the wind lessens sharply close to the ground because of friction.

Fly straight, without making any sharp turns. Just before you touch down, **flare**

▲ LANDING SAFELY
The pilot keeps their speed high as they approach, before they execute a clean and decisive flare to stall the wing. Slowly applying brake or 'mushing' a glider into a landing field is bad practice and can result in a hard landing
Photos: Mac Para

the glider smoothly and confidently – unless there's a fairly strong wind. This slows you right down, stalls the wing so it stops flying, and should enable you to land gently on your feet. Keep your hands down and take a few steps forwards to ensure the canopy falls behind you.

Managing the flare
In nil or light winds, flaring the glider will involve fully applying both brakes. But in stronger wind you'll need to flare less, and in very strong wind hardly or not at all. If you apply 100% brake in strong wind, you're liable to be dragged as the wing will turn into a very large kite.

Instead, after landing in strong wind without using brakes, turn around with the glider still above your head, control it using the risers (As and Cs are good), and collapse it. If you find yourself in a situation where you can't control the wing and it's dragging you, run towards it and get behind it as you pull it down, and pull in on brakes or risers.

If you see someone being dragged in strong wind don't start trying to grab their lines or risers. Instead, run behind their paraglider and collapse it with your body – this takes all the energy out if it immediately.

In still air or very light wind, try to make sure that you don't let the glider overshoot you and hit the ground leading-edge first. This can damage the cells, or it might fall over something. To make sure the glider falls behind you in light winds, keep the brakes down and take a step or two forwards as you turn to face the canopy. It should float down softly.

In all cases, after landing bundle up the canopy and clear the landing field quickly while keeping an eye out for others who are just about to land. Give them ample space to land. Do this even if you're the only one in the landing field. An open glider laid out on the ground and not being visibly packed up is understood among pilots as a **distress call** – pilots still flying above you might think you need emergency help.

Landing circuits

Many official landing fields have a recommended or required approach, known as a **landing circuit**. This is a way to make sure that every pilot approaches the landing via the same route. The risk of a mid-air collision is a lot smaller when pilots are all flying in the same direction.

There are a number of different circuits, of which the **constant-aspect approach** or **U-circuit** is the most frequently used. This approach is also used in many other aviation disciplines.

The major advantage of a constant-aspect approach is that you fly upwind during your final approach. This means if the wind increases during your approach you should always be able to reach the landing field by cutting short the downwind and the crosswind part of the circuit.

▶ SPOT LANDING

A useful skill to master is **spot landing**. This requires you to touch down in a predetermined circle of about 15m in diameter. The closer you are to the bulls-eye the better. The landing needs to be safe and on your feet, and it must be preceded by a correct landing circuit.

If you can do this almost every time in various conditions, you know you have the skills to land in tight spots anywhere. This is very helpful when it comes to flying away from your home site and going cross country, as it opens up many more landing options than if you need to land in a giant field every time.

Remember that spot landing like this is meant to be fun – lots of pilots have broken an ankle by flaring in from too high in an attempt to be the closest among their friends. Don't let that be you! If you're going to overshoot, just fly past and land normally. There's always next time.

The circuit starts at the point where you lose excess height by doing 360-degree turns. You fly these turns **upwind** and to the side of the landing field. For a left-handed U-circuit, you turn left and vice versa.

The direction of the circuit for popular sites is usually set and depends on the prevailing wind direction and obstacles around the field. Internationally, the rule is to turn left, unless otherwise noted.

When you've lost enough height, turn onto the **downwind leg**. You fly above the edge of the field with the wind at your back. Next, turn 90 degrees left to the **base leg** and again a 90-degree turn left for your **final leg**, into wind and towards the target.

If you've misjudged your height, distance or speed, you can adjust the length of any of these legs by turning earlier or later. Do not make any large corrections during your final glide.

Strong or rough control movements may cause the paraglider to pitch or roll, and your touchdown may be hard.

Alternatively, you can approach the landing field via an **S-circuit**. Fly long S-turns or figure-of-eights along the **downwind** side of the landing field until you've lost enough height to fly the final leg. The advantage of this approach is that you always face the landing field. Watch that you don't fly closer to the target with every turn; turn back on to your original course at the edge of the field, or you may overshoot the landing field. The disadvantage of an S-circuit in strong wind is the risk of increasing winds. These may blow you back away from the field. Always make sure you can still reach the field in the current conditions. Another disadvantage is if there are several pilots it's easy to get in the way of each other.

As before, after landing bundle your glider and take it to the side of the field to pack.

▼ U-CIRCUIT / CONSTANT ASPECT APPROACH

This shows a left-handed U-circuit, or constant aspect approach. Altitude is wound off with 360-degree turns upwind of the landing zone, before a U-shape final approach is made. This allows the pilot to gauge how much height they have before making the final into-wind turn.

▼ S-CIRCUIT

During an S-circuit, altitude is wound off by flying 180-degree turns at the end of the landing field. The pilot always faces the landing field and flies beats along a base-leg. The disadvantages of this approach are that turns can get tight as you approach the ground, and pilots can get in the way of each other if it's busy.

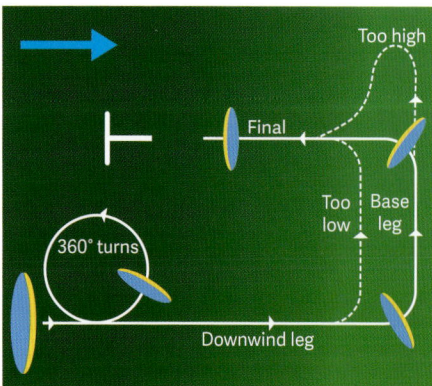

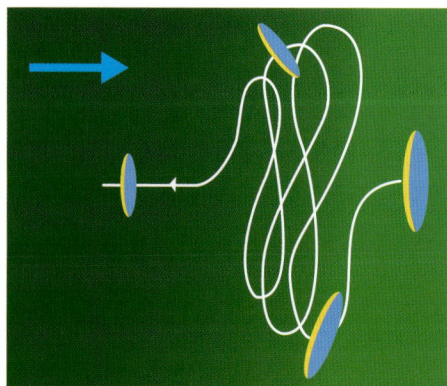

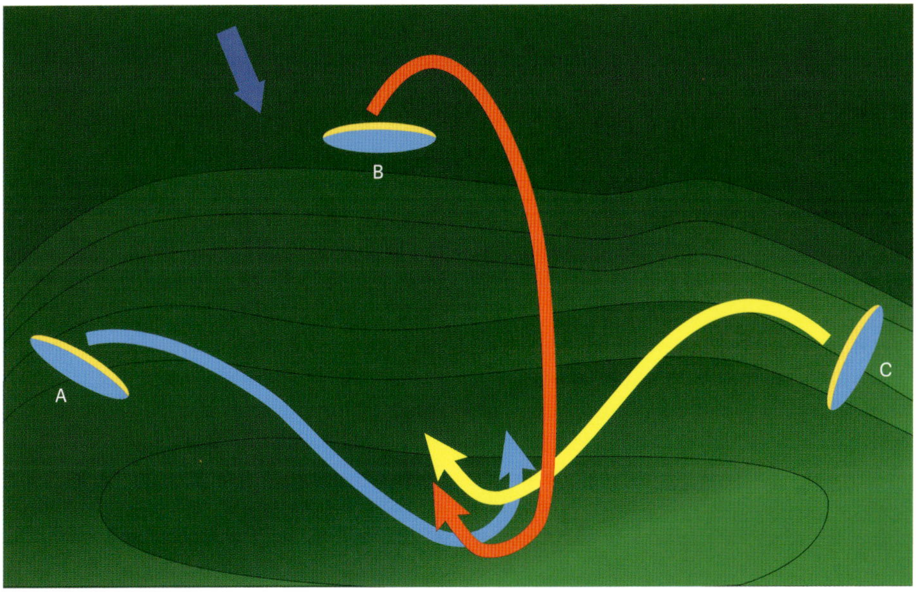

▲ **TOP-LANDING APPROACHES, WITH A CROSSWIND FROM THE LEFT**
A. Crabbing from the left is ok but requires a sharp turn just before touchdown, to turn into wind
B. Flying directly downwind is not a good option, with no room for error. You must make a quick 180-degree turn into wind on the windiest part of the hill. If you are low and get it wrong, you may even collide with the hill
C. Flying into wind is the easiest option in this situation, you can drift along for an easy touchdown

Top-landing and slope- landing

A top-landing is a good alternative to landing in the valley. If the terrain and the conditions are suitable, **top-landing** saves you a trip from the landing back up for the next flight or to pick up your vehicle.

Before trying to top-land, make sure you're allowed to do it at the site where you're flying. The top should be reasonably flat and free of obstacles to ensure that there's no turbulence (see the chapter on Advanced Flying Techniques for terrain assessment). Next, assess the wind direction.

In the example shown in the illustration above, approaching from the side (**C**) is the safest option. As the wind is slightly cross, this approach will be mostly into wind. It involves flying parallel to the hillside and turning into wind just before landing. If the wind is exactly at 90 degrees to the hillside choose the side with the fewest obstacles (**A** or **C** would both be options). If you're too high or too low, abort the landing and fly away from the hill.

The downwind approach (**B**) involves flying head-on over the ridge. This requires some skill in assessing the amount of turbulence over the top of the ridge. It's not a good approach if low as you will be flying downwind at trim speed plus wind speed (say 60km/h). Everything happens quickly at that speed and there is no room for error.

Top-landings when ridge soaring will be in reasonably strong winds, as otherwise the hill would not have produced enough lift to get you up above take-off. On touchdown, therefore, make sure you don't flare more than is necessary, but keep your hands high and turn around to groundhandle the glider. Then you can collapse it, or even kite it to the launch area (watch out for others!) and re-launch.

If the launch area is not near the top of a hill, or you find a suitable place on a hillside, a **slope-landing** is an option. The approach for a slope landing is always parallel with the slope similar to **C**, but never straight towards it or down the slope. Fly figures of eight (again always turning away from the slope) until you reach the proper height. Don't turn into wind just before touchdown, because this will usually mean you'll glide along the slope and never touch the ground. A slope-landing should be executed only when the wind is upslope. If the wind is downslope, you are flying in the lee of the wind – turn and fly away, because the air will be sinking, turbulent and potentially dangerous.

Magnetic boots
Finally, try not to hit anything in the landing field. This sounds obvious but there is a standing joke in paragliding that if there is a single tree in an otherwise empty landing field, at least one pilot will hit it. This phenomenon is known as **object fixation** or, more colloquially, **magnetic boots**.

It works when pilots are worried about an object in a landing area – it can be a tree, a house, a pylon or a bull – and fixate on it. The result is that they unconsciously steer towards it and end up perfectly lined up on it. As they get closer they start to worry more and more about hitting the object and keep looking at it, and therefore steering towards it. Quite quickly all their brain power is taken up with stress and worry – there's simply no mental bandwidth for clear-headed decision making. They literally get stuck on their glide path, effectively give up ("It's in the hands of the gods now"), take no avoiding action and end up hitting the object. This can be funny for both onlookers and pilot if it's a small bush, but much less so if it's a 15m tree.

The trick to avoiding this is to look at where you want to land. Take note of obstacles and store them away as something to avoid, but don't fixate on them. That's done most easily by having a good look at the landing site, having a clear flight plan, and understanding the different landing approaches possible – all before you launch.

▶**LEARN MORE**

- **USHPA New Pilot digital magazine**
  ushpa.org/page/magazine

- **Cross Country magazine**
  xcmag.com

- **DHV beginners (English subtitles)**
  tinyurl.com/dhvbasics

- **Basics explained (YouTube)**
  tinyurl.com/BandarraBasics

- **Paragliding tips (YouTube)**
  youtube.com/FlybubbleParagliding

▲ **GOING PLACES**
Spectacular flying in the Italian Dolomites
Photos: Gudrun Öchsl

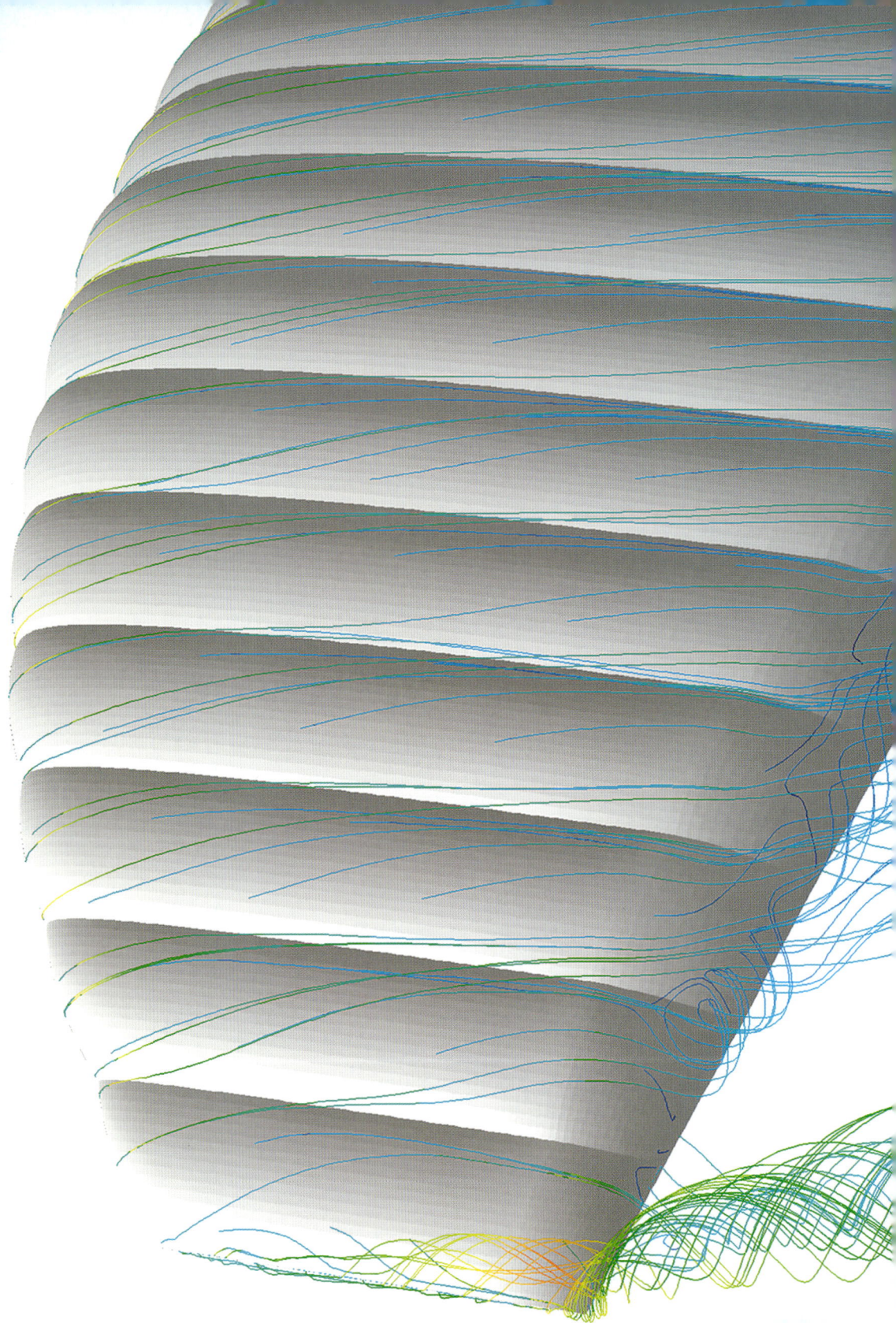

#4

AERO
DYNAMICS

▶ **THE FORCE OF AIR**

▶ **LIFT AND DRAG**

▶ **AERODYNAMICS OF FLYING**

▶ **AERODYNAMICS IN PRACTICE**

Understanding the air we are in

Why does a paraglider fly? It's simply a piece of fabric with some lines attached. Once in the air, the canopy takes on the shape of a wing and generates enough lift for it to fly. But why does a wing generate lift? Which forces hold the paraglider in the air?

Aerodynamics is the study of the forces that air exerts on objects such as paragliders. In this chapter, we'll show that some knowledge of these aerodynamic forces makes it easier to understand why a wing flies and what happens when it stops flying.

You'll start to understand why one paraglider flies differently from another, and perhaps even improve your flying style, based on a better understanding of aerodynamics.

▲ **AIRFLOW OVER A PARAGLIDER**
Computer modelling allows
designers to create more
efficient gliders
Photo: Tom Lolies / BGD

▶ THE FORCE OF AIR

To study aerodynamics – the forces that air exerts on objects like a paraglider – it's useful to know a bit more about air itself.

Air pressure

Air consists of particles. Imagine these particles as very tiny beads that move constantly. These beads have mass. If they're deflected or slowed down in their movement, they exert a force.

Try holding your hand out of the window of a moving car, or hold up an umbrella on a windy day. In the first case you feel the force of the air particles through which your hand moves. In the second case, the air itself moves, and the air particles collide with the umbrella that you're holding. Notice that it doesn't matter which is moving: the object, the air, or both.

It's not only moving air that exerts a force; so does the weight of the air particles. Air is relatively light, but when there's a lot of it, such as all the air in the atmosphere, this force can be fairly large. A column of air a metre square rising all the way up through the atmosphere weighs about 10,000kg. But since the air presses on us from all sides, we hardly notice it, and we're not crushed by its enormous weight.

The total air pressure is a combination of the weight of the air and movement of, or through, the air. The first one is called **static air pressure** (or simply **air pressure**), the second one is **dynamic air pressure**.

Flowing air

The following experiment shows the effect of moving air on an object. Take

▶ AIR PRESSURE

The red and blue arrows in this box indicate the force that the air exerts on an object. Blue represents a higher air pressure, hence a larger force. Red represents a lower air pressure and a lower force.

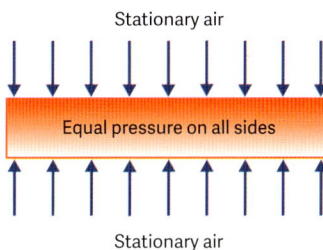

Stationary air

Equal pressure on all sides

Stationary air

Still air
In still air, the air presses on an object from all sides equally.

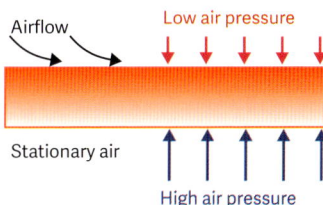

Airflow

Low air pressure

Stationary air

High air pressure

Moving air
Airflow brushing the surface of an object presses less efficiently and hence applies less force on the object. The air pressure is lower because the air moves.

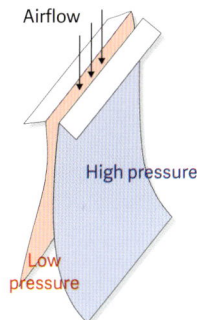

Airflow

High pressure

Low pressure

Try this
Fold two sheets of paper like so. Blow between them. What happens?

▶ DEFLECTION

More deflection
Low air pressure

Less deflection
High air pressure

Airflow

Deflection
Airflow deflects around a wing. The air presses less efficiently on the upper side of the wing than the lower side. Air pressure is lower above than below.

Lower pressure:
2/3 of lift

Higher pressure:
1/3 of lift

Differences in air pressure
Arrows indicate the direction of the force generated by the difference in air pressure. Two-thirds of the air-pressure difference is caused by lower pressure above the wing and one-third by higher pressure beneath

Pressure zones
Air pressure below and above a wing in an airflow computer illustration. Purple, red and yellow indicate lower air pressure. Higher air pressures are shades of blue. Image: Paul Nylander / bugman123.com

two sheets of A4 paper. Fold back a few centimetres of one short side of each sheet. Hold the folded sides, one in each hand, and keep them a few centimetres apart. Now blow gently in the middle between the two sheets as if trying to blow them apart. What happens?

You'll have seen the sheets of paper move towards each other. That's odd, because you were trying to blow them apart. What's going on here?

The air pressure diagrams on the previous page show what happened. When the air is not moving, it pushes equally hard on both sides of each sheet of paper. That's the static air pressure. But by blowing, you cause the air to flow between the sheets. Now we have air that's moving, mainly in one direction. The air particles brush the surfaces at an angle. Therefore, they push less efficiently against the sheets of paper, and the air exerts less pressure.

So the fact that the air is moving between the sheets causes lower air pressure. But on the outside of the sheets of paper, the air doesn't move, so the pressure has not changed and it remains a bit higher than that between the sheets. The result is that the pieces of paper are pushed towards each other.

When air flows over a wing, the same thing happens. Deflection of the airflow at the upper side of the wing causes the pressure to drop. On the lower side, the wing pushes down on the air leading to a higher pressure under the wing. How much the air pressure drops on the top surface of the wing, and how much it increases on the bottom surface, depends on the angle with which the wing moves through the air.

Another effect also plays a role: the air along the upper surface of the wing moves faster, and along the lower surface it moves slower. It follows from **Bernoulli's principle** that the air pressure on the upper side of the wing must be lower.

Lift and drag

As we've seen above, a well designed object such as a wing, set in an airflow, causes a difference in air pressure between the upper surface and the lower surface. The air pressure is a bit lower on the upper side and a bit higher on the lower side. The result is **lift**; the wing is pushed up.

Lift results from an object pushing against and deflecting flowing air. About two-thirds of the lift that a paraglider wing develops is caused by the lower air pressure over the wing, and one-third by the higher air pressure under the wing, as shown in the diagram opposite. Note that the largest pressure difference occurs on the front half of the top side of the wing. This is where most of the lift is generated.

The shape of the object in an airflow and its angle to the airflow determine the amount of lift that the object feels. These factors also determine the amount of **drag** that it encounters. Drag is the resistance that the object feels from the air. The shape and position of a wing in an airflow together determine the ratio of lift to drag.

For example: your flat hand sticking upright out of the window of a driving car will encounter only drag. If you tilt your hand with an angle toward the air flow, lift is generated. You'll feel your hand not only being pushed back but also up (or down, depending on the angle). A wing in an airflow at a small angle generates a lot of lift, but only a little drag.

▸ A COMMON MISCONCEPTION

Air flows faster over the top side of a wing moving through air, and the air pressure is lower than on the bottom side. This generates lift.

An incorrect explanation for the air moving faster over the wing than under assumes that parcels of air, which were separated at the stagnation point into a part that moves over the wing and a part that moves under the wing, need to come together at the trailing edge.

The argument is that the parcels must travel a longer distance over the curved upper side. To rejoin each other at the rear, these parcels must travel faster than their counterparts traveling under the wing.

However, there's no reason that the parcels of air should reunite at the trailing edge. Indeed, this does not happen.

As long as an object generates lift, there's drag as well. Even a perfectly designed wing always creates a little bit of drag.

Forces

In graphs, a force that's acting on an object is represented by an arrow. The length of the arrow represents the relative size of the force. The direction in which the arrow points is the direction in which the force acts.

To become familiar with forces, try the experiment over the page. Grab a hairdryer and a ping-pong ball. Turn on the hairdryer at its highest power and float the ball in the airstream. Now two forces act on the ball: **gravity** is pulling

▶ BERNOULLI AND NEWTON

DANIEL BERNOULLI

ISAAC NEWTON

Lift is an extremely complex theory within the discipline of aerodynamics. Several descriptive models have been developed. The two models that we present here are the most important for paragliders.

A physical description of the generation of lift is often given using the **Bernoulli principle**. This states that in a flow of gas such as air, an increase in the speed of the gas is accompanied by a decrease in the pressure of the gas. Both phenomena occur simultaneously; one is not a result of the other.

For an aerofoil to generate lift, air pressure must be lower on the upper side and higher on the bottom. According to the Bernoulli principle, the speed of the air must therefore be higher over the aerofoil. The above describes the generation of lift. Bernoulli's principle does not explain the generation of lift. That is a more complex issue.

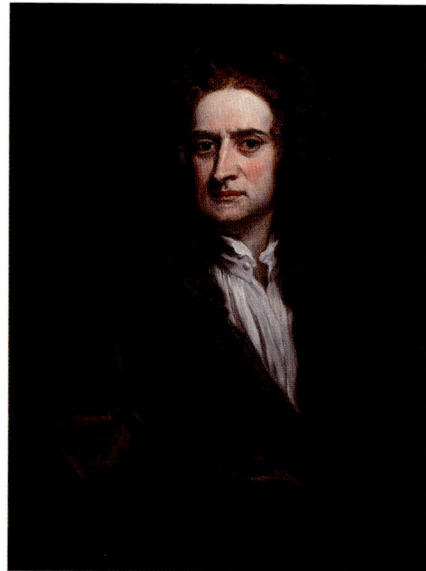

Lift can be explained and calculated using **Newton's laws**.

Air flows around an aerofoil at a slight angle. The aerofoil exerts a force on the airflow to deflect its path. This is a force directed downward. Newton's laws ('action equals reaction') tell us that the air must exert an equal but opposite force on the aerofoil as well. The air exerts a force upward on the aerofoil. This force is called lift.

It is possible to calculate the exact magnitude of the lift by calculating the force that each individual air particle exerts on the aerofoil. But air consists of countless particles which move chaotically. Therefore, these calculations are extremely complex.

Daniel Bernoulli (1700-1782). From an engraving by Johann Rudolf Huber / Dibner Library. **Isaac Newton** (1642-1727), painted in 1702 by Godfrey Kneller

it down and the air is pushing it up. The ball is floating in the airflow, so these two forces must be in equilibrium. That means the forces are equal in size and opposite in direction.

Now, with the ball still floating in the airflow, tilt the hairdryer slowly a bit to the side. You'll notice that the ball will still float, even though the air is not now flowing straight up. The main reason for this is lift. We've already seen in the previous paragraphs that an airflow which is pushed aside and deflected creates lift and drag. This is exactly what happens here. The airflow is deflected by the ball, creating lift and drag. Drag is parallel to the airflow. Lift is perpendicular to the airflow. The resulting force or **resultant** (that is, the sum of the two arrows taking their direction into

▶ FORCES IN AN AIRFLOW

a. A ping-pong ball in an airflow will float because the forces acting on it are in equilibrium. The force pulling it down (gravity) is equal but opposite to the one pushing it up (the reaction force).

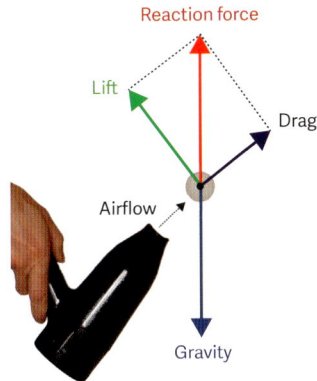

b. When the airflow hits the ball at an angle from the vertical, lift and drag are generated. A ball in a slanted airflow will float because lift and drag together add up to the reaction force, which again is equal but opposite to gravity.

account) is the aerodynamic reaction force, abbreviated as **R**. R is made up of **lift (L)** and **drag (D)**. Finally, as long as the ball floats in the airflow, R is always in equilibrium with **gravity (G)** (also called weight). This, of course, also holds for a paraglider, as you can see in the box below.

Forces in steady flight

When all forces acting on a paraglider are in equilibrium with each other, the paraglider will fly in a straight line and will not accelerate or decelerate. This is called **steady flight**. In steady flight, the reaction force (R) and gravity (G) are in equilibrium with each other.

Gravity (G) is equal to the weight of the pilot plus all their equipment, the all-up weight. The all-up weight does not change during flight, so G does not

change during flight. And considering R is equal (and opposite) to G, R does not change during flight either.

Forces in turns

When you fly a turn, you feel you're being pushed to the outside of the turn. You'll end up slightly offset under the canopy. The turn causes a third force to act on the paraglider, the **centrifugal force**.

The effect of centrifugal force is that the pilot appears to become heavier. During a quick turn, the force on the pilot may be two or three times higher (2G or 3G) because of the added centrifugal force.

When you experience this G-force you will feel your arms getting heavier, and you will be pushed more firmly into your harness by the extra force.

▶ FORCES ON A PARAGLIDER WING

The same forces acting on a ball in an airflow also act on a paraglider. On the left all the forces are acting on the ball. On the right the same forces are applied to a paraglider.

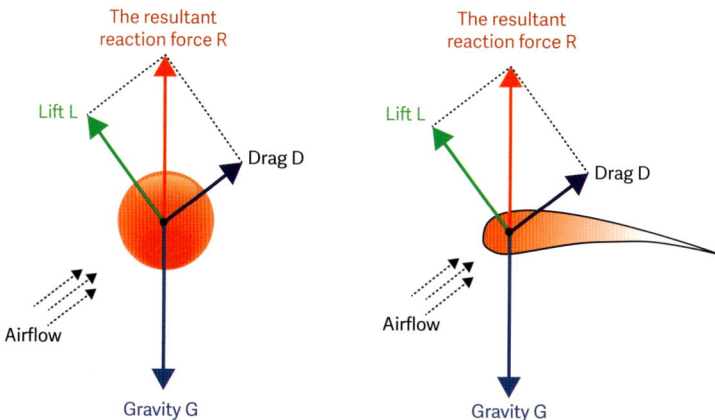

The resultant reaction force R

Lift L

Drag D

Airflow

Gravity G

The resultant reaction force R

Lift L

Drag D

Airflow

Gravity G

During stationary flight, **reaction force (R)** and **gravity (G)** are in equilibrium. In a turn, the pilot feels **centrifugal force (C)**, pushing out from the centre of rotation

Reaction force R

Gravity G

Centrifugal force C

G   2G

The reaction force R is the same size as the resultant of the forces that are acting in the opposite direction. Therefore, R is the sum of the gravity and the centrifugal force when flying a turn. And since R is made up of lift L and drag D as we saw before, these quantities are larger as well. You'll notice this when flying a turn because you fly faster and you descend faster.

▶ LIFT AND DRAG

The lift formula
At the beginning of this chapter we saw that a paraglider wing generates lift because it deflects an airflow. The shape of the wing, also called an **aerofoil**, causes the air to deflect. But lift is not only dependent on the shape of the paraglider. It also depends on the speed of the airflow, or in other words, the speed of the paraglider with respect to the air. Additionally, the size of the wing and the density of the air play a role. These quantities are put into a formula called the **lift formula**.

From this formula, we can derive a number of conclusions that are important for flying paragliders:

- At higher altitude there's less air. That means lower **air density**. Lower air density means less lift, according to the lift formula.

- The paraglider will fly faster at higher altitudes to compensate for the decrease in lift. The descent rate

▶ LIFT FORMULA

$$L = \tfrac{1}{2}\, \rho \, v^2 \, S \, C_L$$

where:

L = Lift
ρ = Air density
v = Speed of the paraglider relative to the airflow
S = Surface of the wing
C_L = Lift coefficient

will also increase, because there's less lift.

- You'll notice the decreased lift at higher altitudes because you have to run faster to take off.

- Running or flying twice as fast will give you four times as much lift, because the speed is squared in the lift formula.

- A larger wing has more surface area and therefore will give more lift, for example to carry a heavier pilot. A surface that's twice as large gives twice as much lift.

- If you make the surface of the wing smaller, for example by pulling big ears, the lift decreases proportionally.

- The shape of the wing, expressed as the lift coefficient C_L, also has an influence on the amount of lift. A 'better' aerofoil has a larger lift coefficient and therefore more lift.

▶ DRAG FORMULA

$$D = \frac{1}{2} \rho \, v^2 \, S \, C_D$$

where:
D = Drag
ρ = Air density
v = Speed of the paraglider relative to the airflow
S = Surface of the wing
C_D = Drag coefficient

The drag formula

We've noticed by sticking our hands out of the car window that drag of an object in an airflow depends on the shape and the angle of the object in the flow. In the Form Drag box opposite you'll see several shapes lined up in order of decreasing form drag. Note that a cube has a lot more drag than a cone or, even better, an aerofoil. But just as for lift, drag depends on more than just the shape. This is put into the **drag formula**.

As with lift, we can reach some interesting conclusions from this formula. Lift and drag are both related to the aerodynamic reaction force. It is no surprise that the formulae, and the conclusions we derive from them, are strikingly similar.

- At a higher altitude there is less air, which means lower air density. According to the drag formula, this leads to less drag. At a high take-off or while flying at high altitude, a paraglider will have less drag (provided you fly at the same speed).

- But because of the decreased drag, the paraglider will fly faster, which increases drag again to reach a new equilibrium. Increasing the flying speed by a factor of two increases the drag by a factor of four, because the speed is squared in the formula.

- Doubling the surface area of the wing will double the drag.

- The drag of a wing in an airflow depends on its shape, given by the drag coefficient C_D. An object with an aerofoil shape (a wing) has more than twenty times less drag than a cube under the same conditions.

Types of drag

There are several types of drag. For a paraglider, **parasitic drag** and **lift-induced drag** are important. Parasitic drag is caused by the form of the paraglider: its canopy, lines, the pilot and the harness. These together are also called **form drag**, because it is the drag caused by the form or shape of the object. Additionally, **skin friction drag** adds to the parasitic drag. That is how much the air 'sticks' to the surface of the paraglider.

Parasitic drag is, well, parasitic to the flying characteristics. About 20% of the total drag is caused by the lines, 20% by the pilot and 20% by the canopy. Parasitic drag is therefore approximately 60% of the total drag. These harmful factors can be reduced, for example by flying with an aerodynamic harness or using fewer lines in constructing the paraglider.

Lift-induced drag is caused by the pressure differences that are created when an aerofoil moves through the air. It's drag that occurs whenever a moving object deflects the airflow coming at it. A large part of lift-induced drag is caused by the **tip vortices**. These vortices arise when the air on the upper side of the wing collides with the air on the lower side, at the very tips of the wing.

Below the wing the air pressure is a bit higher, as we have seen. The air will flow from high to low pressure at the tips, causing the swirls that induce drag. This induced drag amounts to about 40% of the total drag of a paraglider. Wings with a high aspect ratio have relatively less induced drag, because the wingtips form a smaller proportion of the total surface area of these wings.

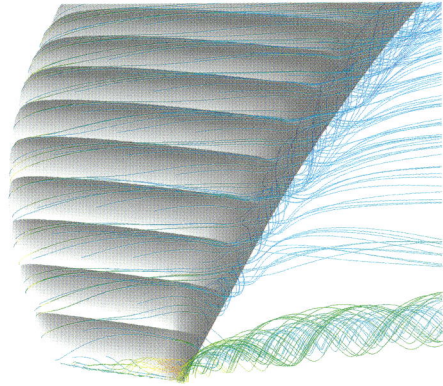

▲ LIFT-INDUCED DRAG
In this computer simulation of airflow over a paraglider the tip vortex is clearly visible
Image: Nova Paragliders

▶ FORM DRAG

Objects with different shapes have different drag. The **drag coefficient (C_D)** is a measure for this form drag. A wing-shaped object (an aerofoil) has a low drag coefficient, and therefore low form drag.

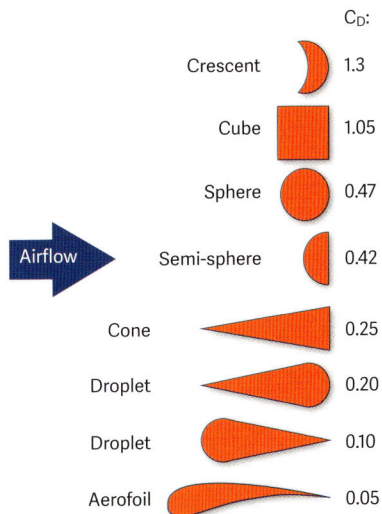

	C_D:
Crescent	1.3
Cube	1.05
Sphere	0.47
Semi-sphere	0.42
Cone	0.25
Droplet	0.20
Droplet	0.10
Aerofoil	0.05

Airflow

Angle of attack α

Flight path

α

Chord

Relative airflow

Angle of incidence i

i

Horizon

Chord

▲ **ANGLE OF ATTACK, AND ANGLE OF INCIDENCE**

The angle of attack (α) is the angle between the paraglider's chord and its flight path – its straight-line trajectory as it descends through the air. The angle of attack (AoA) doesn't reference the ground. Change the AoA by applying brakes, and you affect how much lift is produced

The angle of incidence (i) is between the chord and the horizon. It is a fixed number, built into the design and follows from the line length. It changes if you engage the speed bar or release trim tabs, as these affect line length.

▶ THE AERODYNAMICS OF FLYING

Airflow and flight path

A paraglider is always descending with respect to the air. Gravity is responsible for that; it pulls the paraglider down. A paraglider has no engine to provide thrust remember, and no elevator to direct it upwards – it is always gliding down. This downward trajectory of a paraglider is called its **flight path**. The direction of the air flowing over the wing is known as relative airflow. **Relative airflow** is always parallel with and directly opposite a paraglider's flight path.

So even if the surrounding air is going up – in a thermal for example – a paraglider is always going down through the air. For example, assume the air in a thermal is rising at a speed of 3m/s. A paraglider typically descends with respect to the air at 1m/s. The result is that the paraglider flying in this thermal will ascend at a speed of 2m/s.

Angle of attack

As we saw in the Equipment chapter, airflow hits the profile of a paraglider at its stagnation point. The angle at which the airflow hits the profile is known as the **angle of attack**.

The angle of attack is defined as the angle between the chord and the flight path. Therefore the angle of attack is also equal to the angle between the chord and the direction of the relative airflow. It is indicated with the symbol α (alpha). (Remember the chord is the imaginary line between the leading edge and the trailing edge.)

The angle of attack, together with the shape of the wing, determines the amount of lift generated. As we have seen, as soon as there's lift, there's drag. The ratio between lift and drag determines how far you can fly. If there is more lift and less drag, you can fly further.

The angle of attack is therefore also an important factor in the performance of

126

Flight Path

Angle of
incidence i

Glide
angle γ

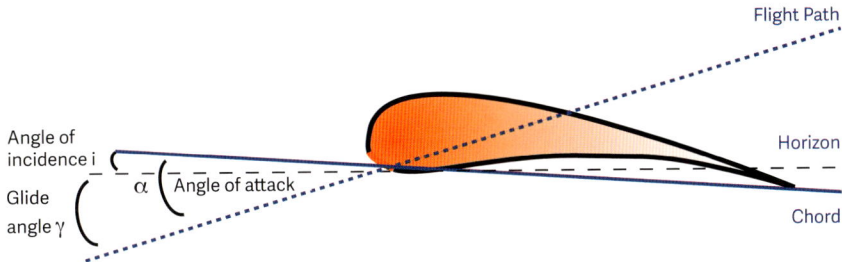

α   Angle of attack

Horizon

Chord

Angle of attack

- is the angle between the chord and relative airflow
- related to glide angle and angle of incidence
- is influenced by pulling the brakes

Angle of incidence

- is the angle between horizon and chord
- is a fixed property determined by line lengths

Glide angle

- is the angle between horizon and the flight path
- is the angle between forward speed and sink rate, with respect to relative airflow
- related to angle of attack and incidence

Flight path

- is the trajectory of the paraglider as it travels through the air
- relative airflow is parallel with and directly opposite the flight path

Flight path with wind

- when there is wind the flight path changes with respect to the ground
- is determined by the ratio between the groundspeed and the sink rate

Glide ratio

- is the ratio between the paraglider's forward speed and sink rate
- is also the ratio between lift and drag (L/D ratio).

a paraglider. For any shape and design of paraglider wing, there's an optimum angle of attack which is calculated by the designer. For paragliders, this angle is usually about five to eight degrees.

Angle of incidence

The **angle of incidence** indicates how the wing is tilted with respect to the horizon. It's defined as the angle between the chord and the horizon, and it is indicated with the symbol i. In the case

of a paraglider, the angle of incidence is above the horizon, ie we call it 'positive'.

The angle of incidence is a fixed property of the wing. The designer determines it by choosing the line lengths. The angle of incidence does not normally change during flight. There are two exceptions to this: engaging the speed system or opening the trim tabs changes the angle of incidence by pointing the nose of the wing down a bit more, thereby making

▶ FLIGHT PATH AND GLIDE ANGLE

At trim speed

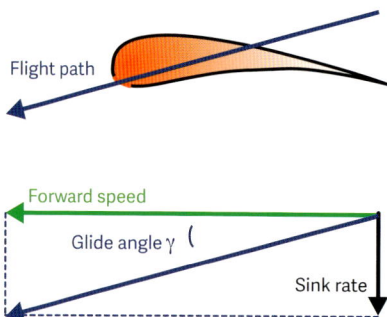

The blue arrow indicates the flight path. Forward speed and sink rate are deduced from the flight path. The angle between the forward speed and the sink rate is the glide angle.

Brake applied

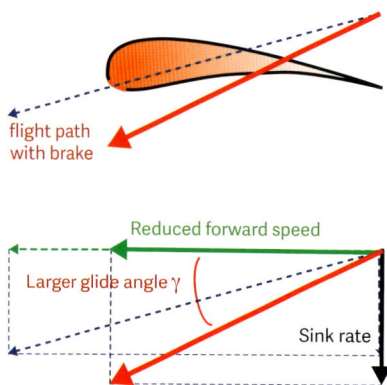

When you pull brakes, forward speed decreases and the sink rate may increase. The new flight path, in red, is steeper. The glide angle γ has increased. Therefore the angle of attack has increased as well.

the flight path steeper and causing the paraglider to fly faster.

Glide angle

The **glide angle** of a paraglider is defined as the angle between the flight path and the horizon. The glide angle therefore follows from the angle of attack and the angle of incidence, as shown in the illustration on p127. It's indicated with the symbol γ (gamma). In still air it's also the angle between the direction of the airflow coming at the paraglider and the horizon. However, the glide angle is greatly influenced by wind.

For example, let's say a paraglider is flying at its trim speed of 36km/h into-wind (assuming the air is not going up or down). The wind is blowing at 36km/h. The paraglider will have no forward speed with respect to the ground, and it will slowly descend straight down. The flight path is therefore pointing straight down and the glide angle is 90° in this case. Note that with respect to the relative air flow, the paraglider still flies at the same angle as it would without any wind. That means the angle of attack does not change when flying into wind.

Speed and descent rate

The flight path is determined by the **forward speed** and the **descent rate** (or **sink rate**) of the paraglider. The forward speed is the horizontal component of the flight path (the green arrow in the illustration on the left). The descent rate is the vertical component (the black arrow).

When a paraglider slows down, for example when the pilot pulls the brakes, the flight path changes. The forward speed decreases and, in most cases, the sink rate increases.

That means the angle of the flight path will get steeper (the red arrow). The angle between the flight path and the horizon (the glide angle) has increased. Therefore the angle of attack has increased as well.

Glide ratio

The ratio between the forward speed and the sink rate determines how far you can fly. Let's say you fly in nil-wind at a speed of 36km/h (10m/s) and the sink rate is 1m/s. For every one metre of height you lose, you can fly a distance of 10 metres. The **glide ratio** is 10:1.

The glide ratio is one of the factors a designer considers when choosing the angle of incidence of a paraglider. This angle is determined on the one hand by the optimum angle of attack for the aerofoil design that they have chosen. On the other hand, the designer has a certain glide ratio in mind for their newly developed glider. Therefore the glide angle is given.

If the glide angle and the angle of attack are given, the angle of incidence that the designer must achieve, by choosing line lengths, is also set. You can see this in the illustration on p127. To obtain it, take the angle of attack and subtract the glide angle.

For example, let's say the optimum angle of attack for a chosen aerofoil design is 7°. The designer wants the glider to have a glide ratio of 10:1. This corresponds to a glide angle of almost 6°.

Therefore, the angle of incidence i that the designer must build into this paraglider is 1° above the horizon ('positive').

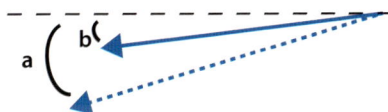

▶ A NOTE ON ANGLES

Correctly describing angles is a confusing business in paraglider aerodynamics. It is important to define what is meant by a 'larger' or a 'smaller' angle. Sometimes angles are called 'negative'.

Almost all angles we use to describe the position of a paraglider in the air are below the horizon, that is, they're pointing down.

In correct mathematical descriptions, these would be called 'negative' angles and be indicated with a minus-sign.

In this book, the minus-sign is omitted for the sake of clarity. In this book we define angles as follows: an angle is larger than another angle when its absolute value is larger.

When drawing angles, the large angle actually looks larger; the arms are further apart.

For example, an angle of ten degrees with respect to the horizon, pointing down (angle a in the illustration) is larger than an angle of five degrees with the horizon, also pointing down (angle b). Alternatively: angle a is more negative than angle b.

In some countries the paragliding exam has questions on understanding angles in relation to aerodynamics.

▲ AND NOW THE PRACTICAL
Classroom-based theory is all very well, but we are here to put it all into action. Here Xandi Meschuh and Benni Hörburger full stall a tandem – there's nothing boring about that when you're in the harness! Photo: Marcus King

▶ AERODYNAMICS IN PRACTICE

Lift over drag ratio

The ratio between speed and sink rate is the same as the ratio between lift L and drag D. A paraglider having a glide ratio of 10:1 has a forward speed that is ten times higher than the descent rate. It also has ten times more lift than drag.

Using the brakes, the pilot not only regulates forward speed and with that, the angle of attack of the wing; he or she also changes lift and drag and the ratio between these two, called the **L/D ratio**. We can therefore use the L/D ratio to derive some facts about the glide angle at different positions of the brakes. This determines how far you can fly and how long you can stay in the air. For example, when the L/D ratio is largest, you can fly the biggest distance. This maximum L/D ratio is equal to the maximum glide ratio and can thus be derived from the minimum glide angle of a paraglider.

The box opposite is a description of three situations representing various brake positions. They are for steady flight at a constant speed in a straight line. Note that the pictures on the right are similar to those in the 'Forces' box eight pages back. They are indeed the same figures, but here we've left out the paraglider, airflow and gravity, for clarity.

130

- **0% brake** – you fly with 'hands up'. The forward speed is at maximum. This is called **trim speed** because the paraglider is trimmed to this speed by the construction and line lengths. The angle of attack and the glide angle are at a minimum, which means the glide ratio is the best and the glider flies at a **minimum sink rate**. Keeping a small amount of pressure on the brakes (5-10%) to take the slack out of the lines lets you feel the movements of the glider better, but take care not to brake the glider, changing the angle of attack. Most modern paragliders achieve their **best glide** and minimum sink without any brake applied.

- **35-50% brake** – flying with a considerable amount of brake decreases the speed of the paraglider noticably. You feel less wind in your face. The angle of attack increases. Drag increases and the sink rate starts to increase as well. The ratio between forward speed and sink rate is much smaller. That means that the L/D ratio is also smaller. In other words: lift has decreased and drag has increased substantially. Braking even more causes the paraglider to fly at minimum speed.

- **100% brake** – when you lock your arms down holding the brakes, the paraglider will slow down below the minimum speed. The forward speed reduces to zero. The airflow can not follow the wing profile anymore. Lift is zero and drag is at a maximum. The paraglider stops flying. This is a **full stall** or a **landing flare**.

▶ INFLUENCE OF BRAKING ON THE L/D RATIO

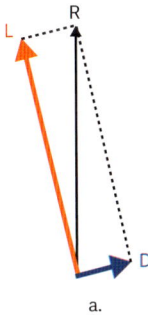

a.   b.   c.

L = Lift; D = Drag; R = Reaction force
Gravity has been left out in these diagrams. Note that the Reaction force is the same magnitude in all situations.

a. Hands up, no brake. Forward speed is large (trim speed), lift is at a maximum and drag is at a minimum. The glide ratio is best and the glider flies at a minimum sink rate.

b. About 50% brake causes the glider to slow down considerably. Lift decreases and drag increases.

c. Stall, 100% brake. The forward speed reduces to zero. The paraglider stops flying. There is no lift and maximum drag.

131

▶STALLS

Airflow

Airflow

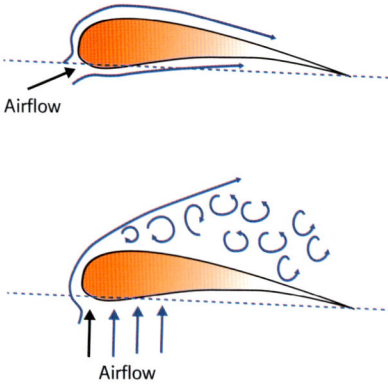

Paraglider stall

In the top illustration the paraglider flies above minimum speed. In the bottom the speed is below the minimum speed. The angle of attack has become too large for the airflow to follow the wing. There is no lift and the paraglider stops flying.

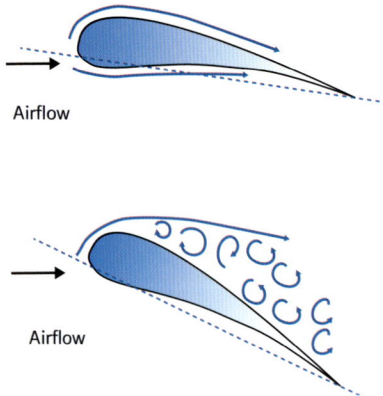

Airflow

Airflow

Stall of a powered plane

The aircraft flies at normal speed and angle of incidence. When this angle becomes too large (bottom illustration) because the plane pulls up its nose, the angle of attack will become too large as well. The airflow can not follow the wing anymore. There is no lift and the aircraft stops flying.

Heavy versus light pilot

From the previous paragraphs, you can deduce what the influence of a heavier versus a lighter pilot is on lift and drag. We assume that they're flying the same paraglider in identical circumstances and there's no wind. The larger weight of the heavier pilot means that G is larger. The reaction force R is therefore also larger. And since R is the resultant of L and D, both lift and drag will also be larger for a heavier pilot. That means the forward speed and sink rate are higher. The paraglider with the heavier pilot flies faster.

However, the glide ratio and glide angle are no different, since the ratio between L and D, and with that the ratio between speed and sink rate, does not change. Both the lighter and the heavier pilot fly the same distance, but the heavier pilot lands sooner because he flies and sinks faster.

Stalls

A **stall** of a paraglider means it stops flying. This happens when the paraglider is slowed down so much that its speed falls below its minimum flying speed. This **minimum speed** is reached when the angle of attack has increased so much that the airflow can't follow the wing's surface any more.

If there is no airflow around the wing, there's no lift. The air around the wing is now turbulent, as you can see in the computer simulation opposite.

The minimum speed is a property of the paraglider. For most paragliders it's just above 20km/h. However, the minimum speed increases if the lines of the paraglider have stretched or shrunk,

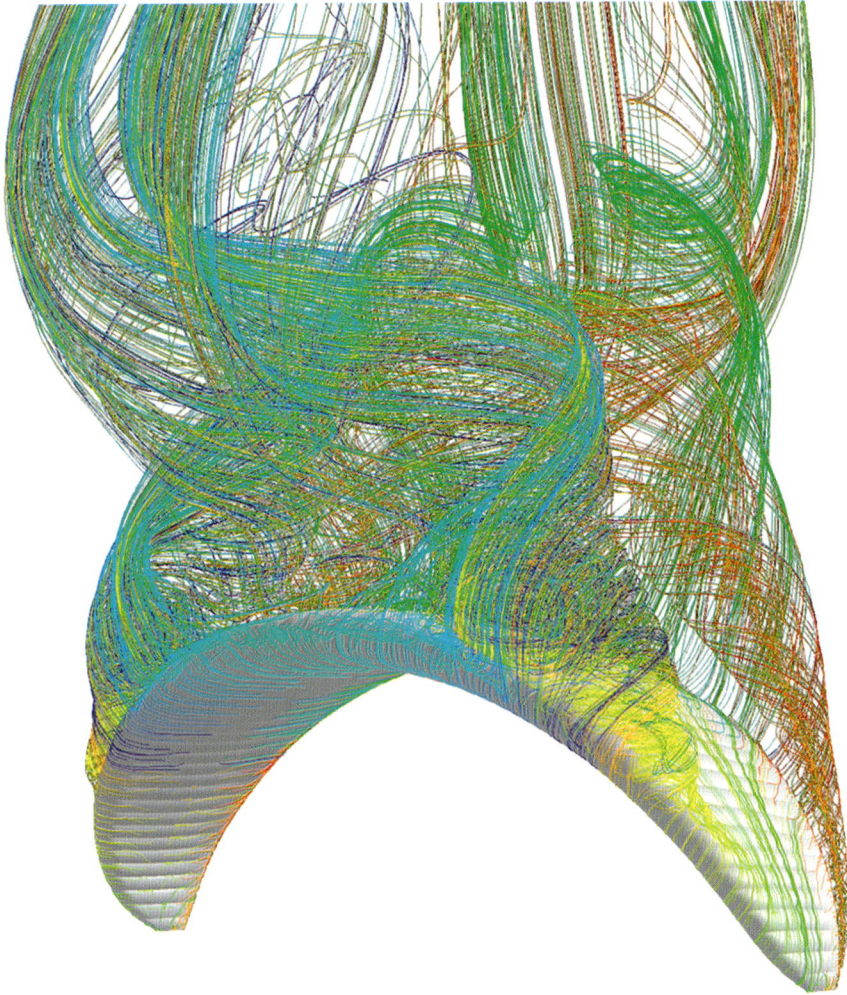

▲ **DEEP STALL**
A computer simulation of a paraglider in deep stall. The wing is still inflated but has no forward speed. It is clear that the airflow does not follow the profile of the wing any more over the top side. No lift is generated and the paraglider descends straight down. Illustration: Nova

if the fabric is old and porous, or if the surface is wet or has snow on it.

If a paraglider flies below the minimum speed, the wing stops flying. The forward speed is zero, the glide angle is 90° and the paraglider descends straight down. This is what happens during a **full stall**, when the pilot deliberately pulls the brakes all the way down.

A paraglider stall is slightly different from that of an aeroplane, although the cause is the same. In both cases the aircraft stops flying because the angle of attack is too large. However, a powered plane usually stalls when the nose is pulled up too far. The angle of incidence becomes very large, and the angle of attack increases so much that the airflow can't follow the wing anymore.

133

A paraglider can't pull up its nose, that is, increase the angle of incidence so much that it stalls. A paraglider stalls when its speed with respect to the airflow is too low. In some cases, a sudden change of the direction of the airflow, as in a strong thermal or turbulence, can cause the angle of attack to become locally too large, causing the wing or part of it to stall and collapse.

A **deep stall** is similar to a full stall in that the airflow has detached from the wing's surface, but in this case the cells of the paraglider are still filled with air. To the pilot, the wing looks as if it's still inflated and flying, but it's become very sensitive to small disruptions. A small brake input will make it turn violently. Deep stalls are rare, but they can happen if the glider is wet – one reason we don't fly in the rain.

Polar curves

A **polar curve** is a graphical representation of the performance of a gliding aircraft. In a polar curve, groundspeed is plotted against sink rate (below). A polar curve is constructed by measuring the sink rate of a paraglider at various speeds in steady flight (not changing speed or direction).

Measuring a neat polar curve is a fairly laborious job since, for example, there can be no wind variations at all. These graphs therefore give only a rough indication of reality.

From a polar curve you can see how flying slow or fast affects your sink rate. It's also possible to derive the glide ratio from a polar curve with a so-called **tangent**. For a tangent, draw a straight line from

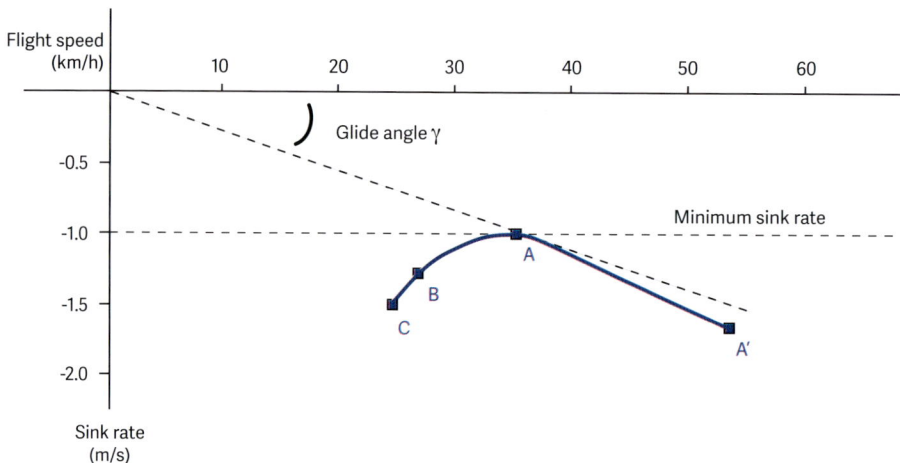

▲ **THE POLAR CURVE**
The polar curve of a typical EN-A paraglider
A' Speed system 100% engaged
A Trim speed (no brake)
B Slow flight (>50% brake)
C Stall speed (100% brake)

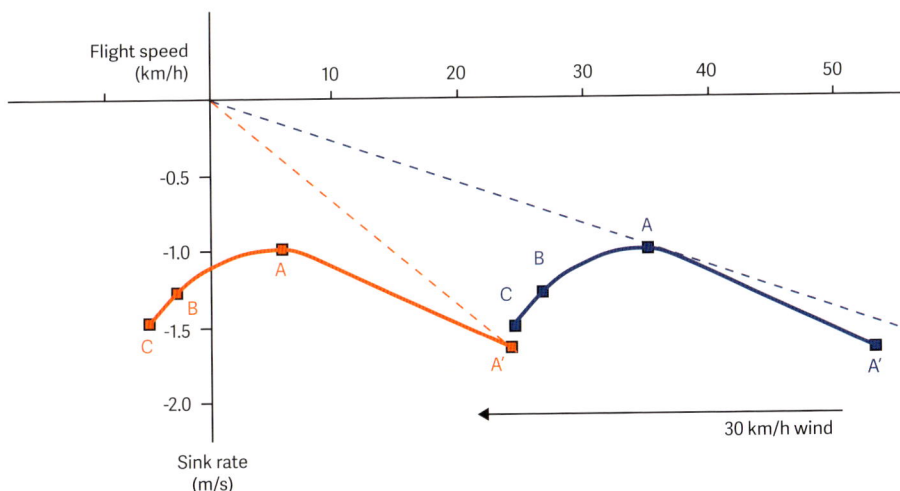

▲ **THE POLAR CURVE WITH WIND**
This polar curve shows the effect of a 30km/h headwind. The blue curve is a polar curve without wind. The letters correspond with the stages in the polar curve on the facing page. The orange curve represents a polar curve of the same paraglider flying in a 30km/h headwind. The curve is moved to the left by 30km/h. Note that the optimum glide angle corresponds to flying with full speed (orange dotted line).

the origin of the graph along the polar curve as you can see in the illustration opposite. The angle of this tangent with the horizontal axis is the glide angle. The glide ratio is given by its slope. The point at which the tangent touches the polar curve is the best glide speed (point **A**). As you can see, this is at trim speed. The top of the polar curve (the highest point) is the minimum sink. For modern gliders, this point coincides with the best glide speed (point **A**).

Therefore you can deduce from this polar curve that this glider flies best at trim speed, where it has its best glide and minimum sink.

Special conditions

When you fly into wind, the polar curve moves to the left of the graph, because the groundspeed decreases. The minimum and maximum speeds with respect to the ground will both be lower. The glide angle increases, and you will not fly as far.

At high wind speeds, the best glide speed will be so low that it approaches zero. In the polar curve on this page the orange curve represents a paraglider flying with a 30km/h headwind. In that case, best glide speed is almost zero. That means you will hardly have forward speed with your hands up.

If you apply brake when flying into a 30km/h headwind, you'll fly slowly backwards (point **B** on the orange curve).

The best glide angle is reached at maximum speed by fully engaging the speed system, ie flying at maximum speed. This can be deduced from the tangent (the orange dotted line) which touches the polar curve at point **A'** which corresponds to maximum speed.

Flight speed (km/h)

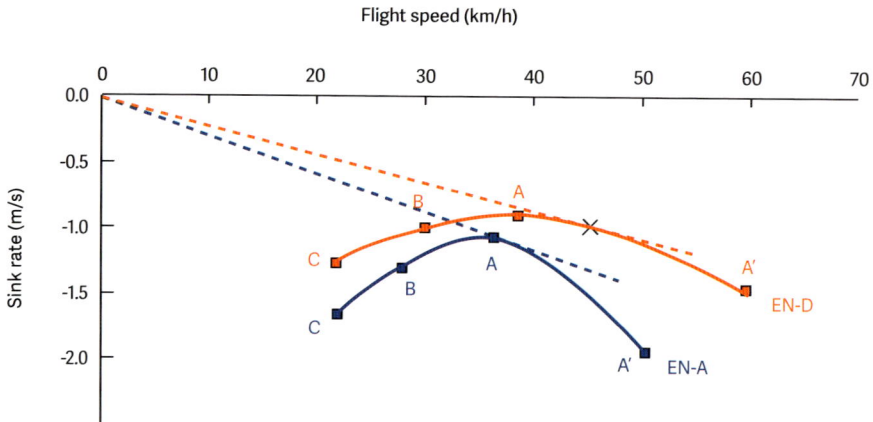

▲ **COMPARING PERFORMANCE**
You can compare different paragliders using their polar curves. This is a beginner's glider (EN A) and advanced glider (EN D). The dotted lines are the tangents from which you can work out the glide angle. Here, the EN-D glider has a smaller glide angle and therefore a larger glide ratio. Best glide is achieved at higher than trim speed (X). It has a similar stall speed C, a higher trim speed A and a higher maximum speed A' than the EN-A glider.

When flying downwind, the polar curve shifts to the right. Your groundspeed is higher than with nil wind. When flying in rising air, such as a thermal, the polar curve moves up since your sink rate with respect to the ground decreases, or it actually becomes an ascent rate.

In the same way you can deduce that the polar curve for a heavier pilot flying the same paraglider moves to the right and down with respect to the curve for a lighter pilot. By drawing a tangent to these curves, you will see that the glide angle and glide ratio are the same for the heavy and light pilot, as we already concluded before.

Finally, polar curves are useful for comparing the performance of different paragliders. The polar curve of a high-performance glider has a low sink rate over a large range of forward speeds, as you can see in the illustration above. This results in a flat polar curve.

▶ **LEARN MORE**

- **How Things Fly, Smithsonian Museum**
  howthingsfly.si.edu

- **NASA's easy guide to aerodynamics**
  tinyurl.com/NASAEasyAerodynamics

- **Understanding polar curves**
  tinyurl.com/PolarCurves

- **Airflow across a wing**
  tinyurl.com/AirflowOverWing

▲ **STALL**
Markus Gründhammer puts theory into practice
Photo: Markus Gründhammer

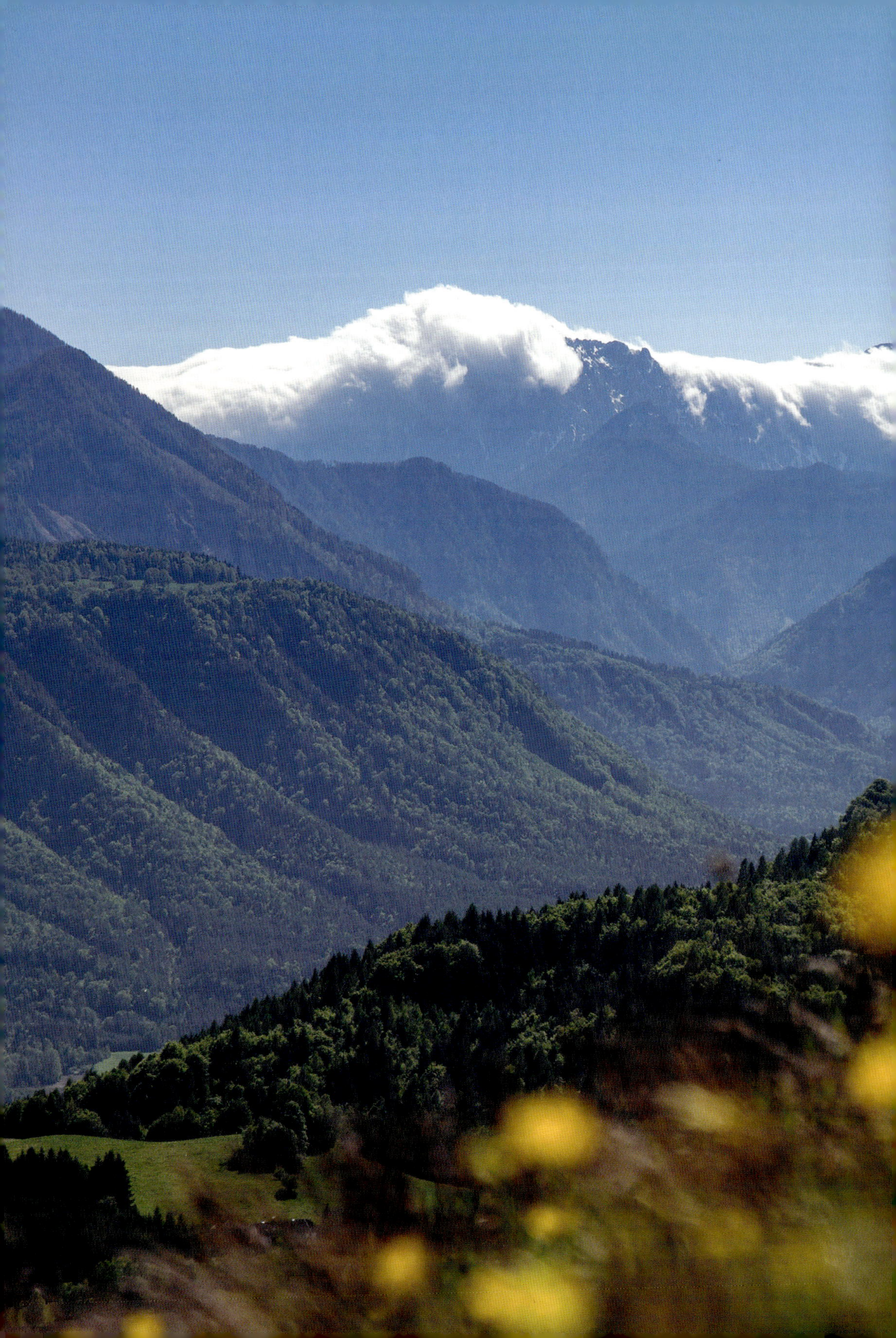

#5
WEATHER FOR PILOTS

How to predict the weather

The Earth is surrounded by a layer of gas only 100km thick: the atmosphere. This layer protects our planet, and everything that lives on it. The conditions in the atmosphere play an important role in our daily lives; we call this the weather. The study of the weather is meteorology, and with some knowledge of it we can, to a certain extent, predict the weather.

For paraglider pilots, the weather is crucial. It determines whether or not we can take off. If you want to fly a long way or for a long time, you need to know how the weather may develop during the day. It helps especially to know where to find rising air. Just as importantly, meteorology may help you to recognise turbulence, strong winds or bad weather before they get you into trouble.

You didn't know it at the time, but when you signed up for your paragliding course you also signed up for a life-long lesson in meteorology! Let's start learning.

▲ THE ATMOSPHERE
Our atmosphere is just a thin, blue layer around the Earth, as seen in this photo taken from the International Space Station. This thin layer protects us against radiation from space
Photo: NASA

140

▶ WATER

The atmosphere

The protective layer around the Earth that we call the **atmosphere** can be observed by astronauts on the International Space Station. From orbit, it's obvious how thin the atmosphere really is. It's this layer that protects us against harmful radiation from space and keeps the Earth at a comfortable temperature.

The gases that make up the atmosphere are responsible for this protection. Ninety-five percent of this gas is located in the 22km closest to the surface of the Earth. Only the lower 11km, called the **troposphere**, are of any importance to us humans, since we live in them and fly in them. Even airliners seldom fly higher than that.

The dry atmosphere consists mainly of two gases: nitrogen (78%) and **oxygen** (21%). The remaining 1% is argon and very small amounts of carbon dioxide (CO_2) and other gases.

But the atmosphere is seldom dry. It contains a percentage of **water vapour** ranging from 0% to 7%. This small amount of water in the air is responsible for almost all the phenomena that we call the **weather**.

Without water, there'd be virtually no weather. The properties of the atmosphere are determined by pressure, temperature, density and humidity. In this chapter, we'll cover all these aspects and how they influence the weather.

▶ PROPERTIES OF THE ATMOSPHERE

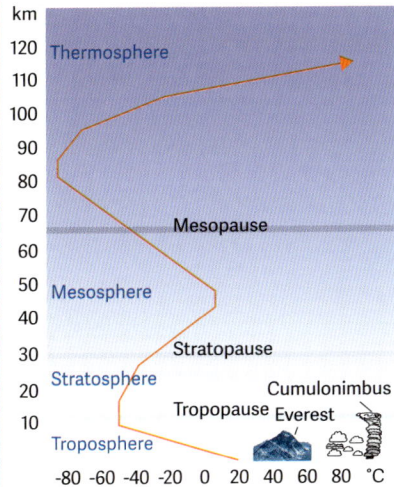

Our atmosphere is divided into layers. The troposphere, from the Earth's surface to about 11km altitude, is the most important layer for life on Earth. The orange line in the graph indicates the average course of the temperature at different altitudes. The composition of the dry atmosphere is:

Nitrogen 78%
Oxygen 21%
Argon 0.93%
Carbon dioxide 0.04%

▶ UNITS

Essential units with regard to weather:

Pressure
- hPa = hectopascal
- mbar = millibar
- atm = atmosphere (obsolete)
- 1 hPa = 1 mbar
- 1 atm = 1013 hPa
- Standard air pressure at sea level: 1013 hPa

Temperature
- °C = degrees Celsius
- °F = degrees Fahrenheit (32°F = 0°C)

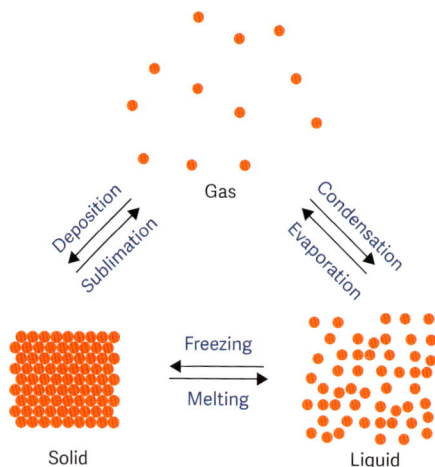

▲ THE THREE PHASES
All substances exist in three phases or states: solid, liquid and gas. All possible transitions between these states are shown here.

Water vapour

Some basic knowledge about this special substance, **water**, is useful in understanding its great influence on the weather. Water can exist in three **phases**, or states: **solid**, **liquid** or **gas**. The state of a substance depends on pressure and temperature. The standard pressure at sea level is 1013 hectopascals, abbreviated as hPa. We measure temperature in degrees Celsius (°C), or degrees Fahrenheit (°F) in the USA.

The first state is solid. Solid water is ice. At the standard pressure, ice forms at and below 0°C/32°F. You can imagine the molecules of water as beads, which in a solid are neatly stacked and hardly moving.

The next state is liquid. Liquid water is present at standard pressure between 0°C/32°F and 100°C/212°F. In liquid water, the molecules are not stacked but move around a bit.

The third state is gas. Gaseous water, which we call water vapour, can exist at all temperatures, not only above the

boiling point of water. If that sounds counterintuitive, imagine a cup sitting on the table containing a bit of water. After some time, all the water will have evaporated and therefore changed into the gas state. The water molecules in water vapour are floating freely around in the air.

All three states can change into each other. Two important **phase transitions** are **evaporation**, when a liquid changes into a gas, and the reverse process of **condensation**. **Freezing** and **melting** are the two other main phase transitions for water. Finally, the transition from water vapour to ice is called **deposition** and the reverse process is **sublimation**, also called **freeze-drying**.

Vapour pressure

The amount of water vapour is measured as a quantity called **vapour pressure**. This indicates the maximum amount of water vapour present at a given temperature and pressure. Note that vapour pressure is not the same as air pressure (simply referred to as pressure), but both are measured in hectopascals.

The vapour pressure of water increases when the temperature increases, because at higher temperatures, more water will be in the gas phase. We can plot this on a graph (Graph A on the page opposite). The blue line indicates the maximum amount of water vapour that can be present in the air at a given temperature.

For example, you can see in the left graph that the vapour pressure at 100°C is 1013hPa. Note that this is equal to the standard air pressure at sea level. That's no coincidence. Water has its boiling point at 100°C at sea level. From this, we

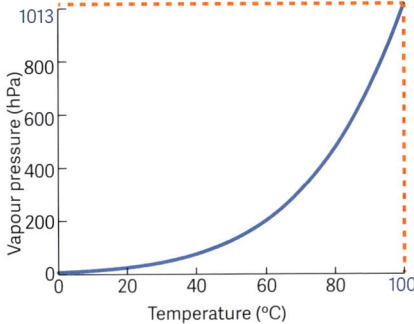

A From this graph you can read the vapour pressure of water at a given temperature. For example, note that the vapour pressure at 100°C/212°F is equal to the standard air pressure at sea level. This is the boiling point of water.

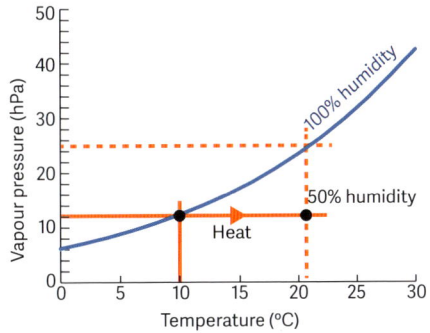

B The vapour pressure of water is 12hPa at 10°C/50°F. That means the relative humidity is 100% at 10°C/50°F if there is an amount of water present equal to 12hPa. When this air warms to 21°C/70°F during the day, the absolute amount of water corresponding to 12hPa is still there. But the relative humidity has decreased to 50%, because air of 21°C/50°F can contain up to 25hPa water vapour.

can derive the rule that a liquid boils when its vapour pressure is equal to the air pressure.

Graph B is a magnification of graph A to facilitate the readings at lower temperatures. At low temperatures, only a small amount of water is in the gas phase. As you can see in graph B the vapour pressure at 0°C/32°F is only 6hPa. At 10°C/50°F it's 12hPa.

Humidity and dew point

The **absolute humidity** is defined as the amount of water vapour (the weight of the water measured in grams) that is actually present in the air. But because grams of water vapour are not easy to measure, we usually represent the humidity in vapour pressure, measured in hPa, or as a percentage of the total amount of gases in the air. (The calculation from grams of water

vapour to hPa is not straightforward. You can find the calculations and values online.)

Let's assume that there is 9g of water in a volume of air of one cubic metre. This is equal to an absolute humidity of 12hPa. A vapour pressure of 12hPa amounts to 1.2% of 1013hPa (which is the standard air pressure). The absolute humidity in this example is therefore 1.2%.

Much more important for the weather is the **relative humidity**. This is expressed as a percentage of the maximum amount of water vapour that the air can contain.

This maximum is represented by the blue line in the graphs above. The blue line represents a relative humidity of 100%. At any point on this line you can read the maximum vapour pressure at a certain temperature.

143

▶ WHAT IS VAPOUR PRESSURE?

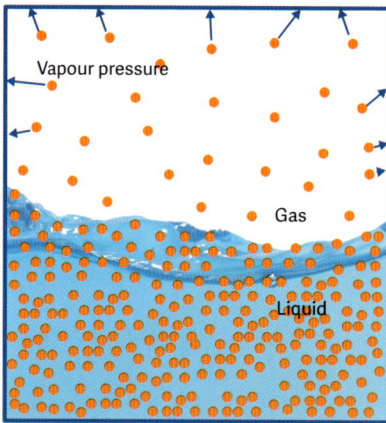

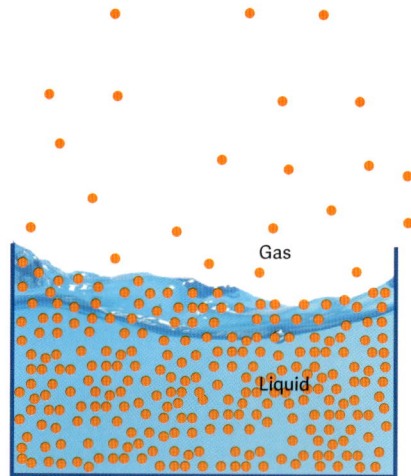

What is boiling? Most people will answer something like: "The transition from a liquid such as water, to a gas". But water is also present as a gas below its boiling point of 100°C. If it wasn't, the laundry on the line would never dry. The water evaporates, even though the temperature is not 100°C. So how can a liquid evaporate below boiling point? It's to do with vapour pressure.

Imagine a closed tank half filled with water. The water molecules in the liquid are in constant movement. Some of the molecules move so fast that they escape from the liquid and become a gas. They have evaporated. These gas molecules move around freely in the tank and collide with the walls from time to time. These collisions cause pressure: **vapour pressure**.

The quantity of water molecules in the gas phase determines how high the vapour pressure is. Vapour pressure therefore rises with temperature, because molecules move faster and collide more forcefully at higher temperatures. If you were to heat the closed tank, the vapour pressure inside would increase. If the tank were not closed, all the liquid water would evaporate over time.

The higher the temperature, the faster the evaporation. But that doesn't mean the liquid is boiling. After all, the laundry on the line isn't boiling, is it?

Boiling is a special form of **evaporation**. When the temperature of a liquid is raised to the level where the vapour pressure is the same as the air pressure around it, bubbles of gas will form in the liquid and we say that it's boiling. The vapour pressure of water, for example, is exactly 1013hPa at 100°C. That is equal to the air pressure at sea level. Water therefore boils at 100°C at sea level. Another example: the vapour pressure of pure alcohol is 1013hPa at 78°C, which is the boiling point of alcohol.

When you move up from sea level, the boiling points of liquids change as well. In the mountains, water boils at lower temperatures because the air pressure is lower.

Imagine you're in base camp on Mount Everest at almost 5,400m. Air pressure there is only 500hPa. The vapour pressure of water is equal to 500hPa at around 81°C. That means water boils at 81°C at Everest Basecamp. On the summit, the air pressure is only 300hPa and water boils at 68°C.

144

▲ IN THE CLOUDS
Flying to cloudbase and beyond. Cumulus clouds are formed by air rising and cooling with altitude – when the air mass reaches its dew point the water vapour in the air condenses, forming cloud. Photo: Adi Geisegger

If you know the absolute humidity, representing the amount of water vapour present in the air, you can read on the graph at what temperature a relative humidity of 100% is reached.

To do this, draw a horizontal line on the graph at the level of the absolute humidity. In our example, this was 12hPa. This line intersects with the blue line at 10°C. Therefore, at 10°C and 12hPa vapour pressure, the relative humidity is 100%.

This is called the **dew point**. The dew point is the temperature at which condensation first takes place.

Suppose the temperature rises during the day to 21°C. The relative humidity then decreases to 50%, as you can see in the graph (one page back).

If the temperature falls below the dew point in the evening (in this example, below 10°C), then clouds or mist will form through condensation. Daily temperature variations influence the relative humidity without affecting the absolute humidity, resulting in the formation of cloud or mist.

When the amount of water vapour in the air increases, for example by evaporation from a lake or from a moist surface, the relative humidity can also reach 100%. In this case, too, the excess water vapour in the air will condense.

▲ THE SUN
The sun influences all our flying. When it is high in the sky thermals will typically be stronger, and when it is lower in the sky – in the morning or evening – thermals will typically be weaker. This is why we sometimes wait until late afternoon or evening to fly, to take advantage of light but smooth conditions. Photo: Jérôme Maupoint

▶ AIR AND HEAT

So far, we have studied the properties of dry and humid air at **sea level**. That means we have assumed that the **air pressure** is 1013hPa. If we move to higher altitudes, the air pressure decreases.

At 5,500m the air pressure is only half that at sea level. A rule of thumb that holds at low altitudes is that the air pressure decreases by 1hPa with every nine metres that you climb.

But the air pressure does not decrease in a linear fashion with height, and so this rule does not apply over about 3,000m above sea level.

The **temperature** also varies with height. Normally, it decreases from sea level to about 11km. On average, this decrease is 0.65°C per 100m. But in practice this is often very different, as we shall see shortly.

To allow the calculation of some of the properties of the atmosphere, a **standard atmosphere** was defined, the properties of which are shown in the box on the right (The Standard Atmosphere).

The most important values are those at sea level: in the standard atmosphere, at sea level the air pressure is 1013.2hPa and the temperature is 15°C. The **air density** is also standardised. That's a measure of the weight of the air per cubic metre.

146

For general calculations and discussions, a standard atmosphere is very useful. But the air is seldom average. There are temperature differences because of sunshine and clouds, day and night, and the seasons. Some soils hold or radiate more heat than others. There are differences in humidity. There are several layers of air that do not mix. And finally, pressure and temperature differences cause currents of air such as wind or thermals. All these phenomena together determine the weather.

Heat

The Earth is heated by the sun. But **solar radiation** varies with time and place on Earth. A major factor is the angle at which the radiation reaches the surface. Radiation that reaches a surface at an angle is spread out over a larger area and is therefore less powerful than perpendicular radiation. It will heat the surface less. The angle of incidence is determined by its place on Earth, more specifically its distance from the equator. In Europe, the sun is never straight overhead. At the equator, it is. Solar radiation and heating by

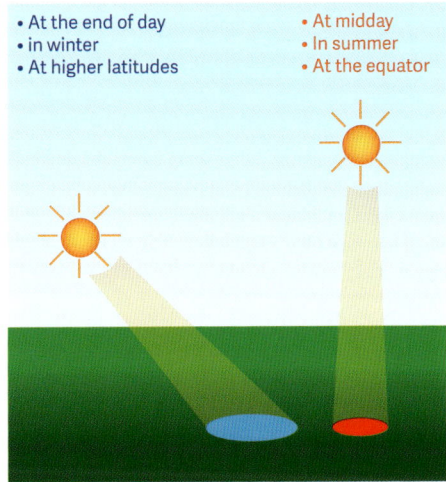

- At the end of day
- in winter
- At higher latitudes

- At midday
- In summer
- At the equator

▲ **SOLAR RADIATION**
Solar radiation that hits a surface at an angle is spread over a larger area and is therefore much less powerful than perpendicular radiation.

the sun are therefore stronger at the equator.

Time of day is another factor. In the mornings and evenings the sun is lower above the horizon than at midday. The position of the sun in the sky also varies with the seasons, and therefore so does the angle of incidence of the solar radiation. And in the northern

▶ THE STANDARD ATMOSPHERE

From ground level up to about 1,000m in the standard atmosphere, temperature decreases by 0.65°C every 100m. Air pressure decreases by 1 hPa every nine metres.

Altitude (m)	Temperature (°C)	Pressure (hPa)	Density (kg/m³)
0	15	1013.2	1.225
500	11.7	955	1.167
1000	8.5	899	1.112
1500	5.3	846	1.058
3000	-4.5	701	0.909
5500	-20.8	505	0.697

hemisphere, a south-facing slope receives more sun than a north-facing slope. That is why the best ski pistes always face north. In the southern hemisphere, of course, they face south.

Finally, the angle of a slope determines the amount of radiation it receives. If the angle of the slope is perpendicular to the angle of the incident light, the surface is heated much more efficiently because in this case too, the radiation is concentrated on a small area, just as when the sun shines on a flat surface from straight overhead.

Heat transfer

Apart from the amount of radiation that a surface receives, the type of surface also has an influence on the temperature that it will reach. How much a surface heats up depends on:

The **reflection** of sunlight. Light colours such as white sand or snow reflect the solar radiation and therefore absorb the least heat. Black surfaces such as dark rocks or asphalt absorb a lot of radiation.

The **conduction** of heat in the material of the surface. This determines whether only the surface heats up or the entire body. Water conducts heat very well, for example. Not only does the surface of a lake warm up, but the heat is transferred to deeper layers. Sand is a bad heat conductor, so that the surface heats up quickly but if you dig a hole, you'll feel cooler layers very soon.

The **humidity** of a surface. This is important because the heat from the radiation is first spent on evaporating moisture rather than heating the surface. A humid surface such as grass or deciduous forest will warm up less than a dry surface receiving the same radiation.

Secondly, the temperature that an object reaches depends on the rate at which it absorbs heat and releases it to its surroundings. This process is called heat transfer. There are three different mechanisms of heat transfer:

Radiation, or more precisely infrared radiation, does not need a medium (such as air or water) to transmit heat. The best example of this is solar heat. Space is a vacuum, but solar radiation still reaches the Earth. Heated surfaces such as rocks transfer heat by radiation to the air around them.

Conduction means the spreading of heat through an object. Metals conduct heat very well. Air does not conduct heat very well, or is said to insulate, as it does in double or triple glazing.

Convection or heat flow is the process in which the warm substance spreads itself and thereby distributes its heat. Central heating works in this way, by pumping heated water. Examples of convection in nature are warm streams in the oceans (like the Gulf Stream) and thermals (rising warm air).

Airflow

The process of warm air rising is called convection. The opposite is **subsidence**, where cool air sinks because cold air is heavier than warm air. This causes an **airflow** in the atmosphere of the Earth. In the most elementary model of the Earth, the air at the equator heats up and rises through convection. The air moves towards the poles, cools and moves down through subsidence. At

Subsidence · Convection

High pressure · Low pressure

▲ **CONVECTION AND SUBSIDENCE**
Warm air around the equator rises through convection and flows in the direction of the poles where it cools and sinks again through subsidence. Therefore, at the equator, mostly low pressure is found and at the poles, mostly high pressure is found.

▲ **AIR FLOW ON EARTH**
The Earth rotates counterclockwise, as seen from the North Pole. The airflow that exists because of convection and subsidence is deflected to the right, as a result of the Coriolis effect. Seen from the South Pole, the airflow is deflected to the left. The main wind directions on Earth – called trade winds – are determined by this deflected airflow. For example the main trade winds in the northern Sahara are northeasterly.

the equator, rising air leaves a void, giving rise to a **low-pressure area**. At the poles, sinking air causes a **high-pressure area**.

This model of the Earth and its atmosphere would be largely correct if the planet did not rotate. However, the Earth revolves around its axis once every 24 hours. For an observer on Earth (us), the rotation makes it look like the air flow is strongly deflected. This deflection is a result of the **Coriolis effect**. The Earth revolves underneath the airflow. Looking from the North Pole, the Earth revolves anti-clockwise. This causes a deflection

of the airflow to the right in the northern hemisphere. For an observer on the southern hemisphere, the airflow is deflected to the left.

Wind

Differences in air pressure on Earth cause **wind**. Air always flows from a high-pressure area to one of low pressure. Somewhere on Earth, the air heats up and rises. The resulting area of low pressure on the ground will be replenished with air from an area of higher pressure. This causes wind. Paraglider pilots sometimes call this **meteo wind**.

▲ **PLAYING WITH THE WIND**
As a paraglider pilot you will spend a lot of time playing with your glider in the wind, getting used to how it feels to control your wing in different wind strengths. There are different types of wind – the meteorological wind caused by air flowing from high to low pressure, and local winds. Photo: Jérôme Maupoint

The Coriolis effect causes the air in the northern hemisphere to turn left around an area of low pressure and right around an area of high pressure. If you stand with your back to the wind in the northern hemisphere, therefore, low pressure will be to your left. This is **Buys Ballot's law**. In an ideal situation, the wind blows exactly parallel to the **isobars**, the imaginary lines of equal pressure. This is called **geostrophic wind**. In practice, the wind never blows exactly parallel to the isobars as a result of friction and centrifugal forces.

Apart from the Coriolis effect, local phenomena influence local airflows.

Oceans and continents have an effect because of their location and temperature. Day/night temperature differences, which do not occur simultaneously all over the Earth, cause the air to flow.

The warm Caribbean is a source of humid low-pressure areas that flow via North America to Europe. Cold continental Russia, meanwhile, is a source of dry, high-pressure areas. Areas of high and low pressure therefore determine the wind over a scale of hundreds of kilometres. Local differences in radiation and heat transfer cause local winds, for example when cold air in a valley bottom warms up and rises.

150

Wind direction is indicated with a **compass rose**. North wind is wind that blows from the north, from the direction 0°. If the wind changes and turns clockwise it is said to be a **veering** wind. If it turns anti-clockwise it is a **backing** wind. A backing wind is changing for example from south (180°) to east (90°). It turns toward a lower number of degrees. A veering wind turns, for example from south (180°) to west (270°); that is, to a higher number of degrees.

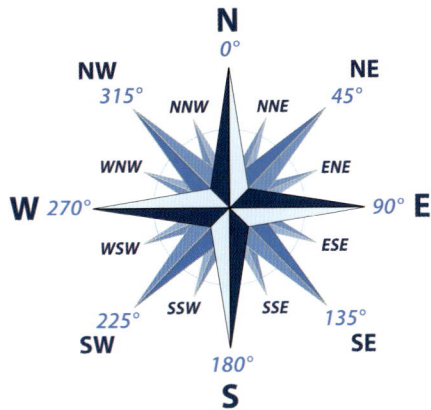

▶ CORIOLIS EFFECT

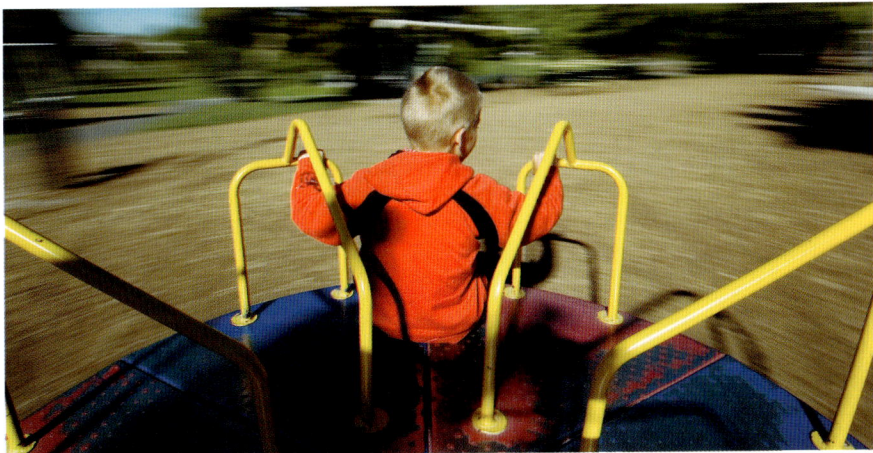

The Coriolis effect is a mathematical concept that describes how things floating or rolling over a spinning object appear to deflect from their straight course. Imagine you are standing on the North Pole of the Earth (which is rotating around its axis) and you throw a ball towards the Equator. As you throw, the Earth spins underneath the ball. Therefore, the ball ends up somewhere to the west of where you were aiming. The same happens to the air flowing around the rotating Earth. For an observer standing on Earth it looks like the airflow is strongly deflected, but this is just a result of the Earth rotating underneath the air.

The Coriolis effect does not apply only to the Earth and the air but to anything that spins. You can observe the Coriolis effect in action with a ball on a children's roundabout. As long as the roundabout is stationary, you can roll the ball to a friend opposite in a straight line. If you start to spin the roundabout, the ball ends up going to one side of your friend, even though you aimed straight ahead. In reality, the ball rolls straight ahead and the carousel rotates underneath it.

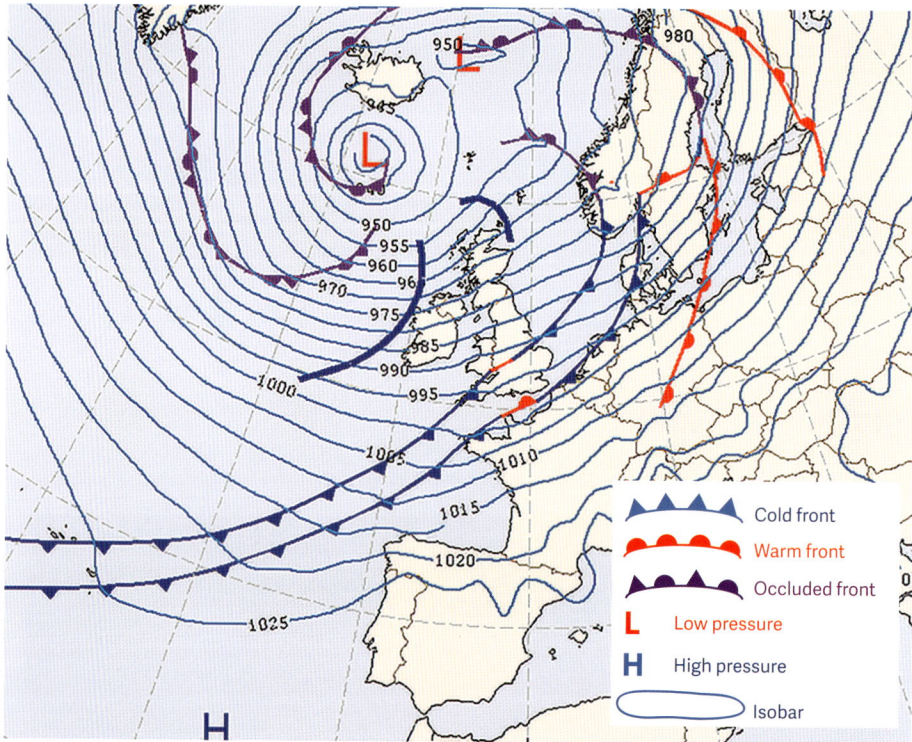

▲ PRESSURE CHART
The type of chart you will see in a daily forecast. It gives good general information about weather across a large area. Here, a low pressure is centred south of Iceland and two cold fronts are sweeping across the Atlantic towards Europe. Tightly packed isobars indicate high wind. Map: Royal Netherlands Meteorological Institute

▶ THE WEATHER

As we have seen, moving air can have a variety of causes. These moving masses of air may have a temperature different from their surroundings. Like oil and water, cold and warm air do not mix very well. Sooner or later, two masses of air with different temperatures will meet. The boundary between these is called a **front**.

A warm front

When a mass of warm air moves against a mass of cold air, a **warm front** is formed. As a warm front passes, an observer on Earth feels the cold air being replaced by warmer air. Because warm air is lighter than cold, the mass of warm air slides over the colder air. The latter does not move much, causing the front to stretch out over lengths of more than 1,500km. The front moves at a speed of about 30km/h, which means a warm front will take several days to pass. A warm front therefore usually causes a long period of bad weather with an overcast sky.

A cold front

If a mass of cold air encounters warmer air, it's a **cold front**. If a cold front passes, an observer on Earth feels the warm air being replaced by colder air. The colder, denser air replaces the warm air at ground level. Because the colder air pushes the warmer air away instead of sliding over it, a cold front moves faster than a warm front, sometimes reaching 50km/h. A cold front has a length of several hundred kilometres and usually passes within hours or a day. The weather is bad for a short period, often including thunderstorms. After the passing of the cold front, the weather clears and often leaves good flying conditions for paragliders.

An occluded front

When a cold front overtakes a warm front because it is moving faster, it creates an **occluded front**. Warm air is trapped on top of two layers of cooler air on the ground.

There are three different air masses present in an occlusion: the cold air that was pushed in front of the warm front; the warm air of the warm front; and the cold air that's overtaking the warm front.

Depending on the relative temperatures of these three masses of air, we can distinguish three different occlusions:

In a **warm occlusion**, the cold air in front of the warm front is even colder than the cool air that's overtaking the warm front. The cool air of the latter will move over the cold air of the first cold front. An occluded front is formed which has mostly warm front character.

A **cold occlusion** forms when the cold front that is overtaking the warm front is colder than the cool air in front of the warm front. The cold front pushes the warm front ahead, just like a normal cold front. A cold occlusion has mostly cold front character.

When the temperatures of the two cooler air masses are the same, a **neutral occlusion** is formed. The warm front is

▶ **FRONTS**

Warm front

Warm air is lighter than cold air, so warm air will move over cold air. A warm front moves at 10-30km/h. It causes long periods of bad weather with full cloud cover.

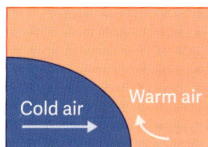

Cold front

Cold air slides under the warm air and pushes it up. A cold front moves with a speed of about 50km/h and causes a short period of heavy rain or thunderstorms. A day later, the weather may clear again.

▶OCCLUDED FRONTS

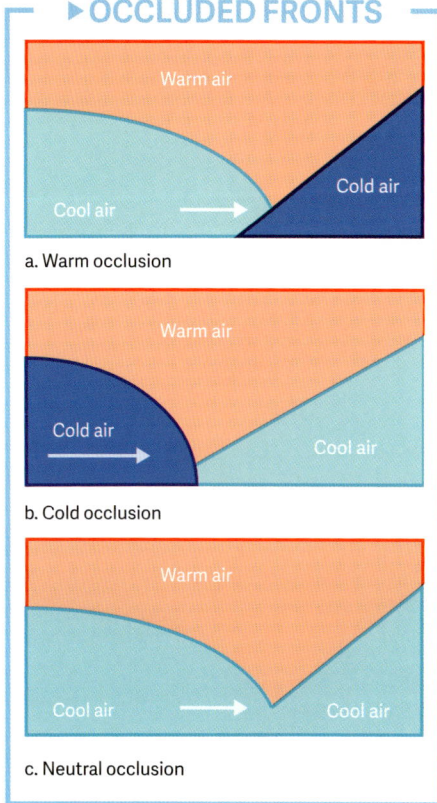

a. Warm occlusion

b. Cold occlusion

c. Neutral occlusion

Warm and cold fronts show the boundaries of masses of warm and cold air, respectively. A warm front is indicated by a red line with semicircles pointing in the direction of travel. A cold front is indicated by blue triangles (you can remember this because they look like icicles) also pointing in the direction of travel.

An occluded front is indicated by a line with semicircles and triangles, sometimes coloured purple.

Using this chart you can make a basic but good general **weather forecast**. First, you can determine the wind direction from the location of the areas of high and low pressure. In the northern hemisphere air flows anti-clockwise around a low pressure area and clockwise around a high pressure. (An easy way to remember this is to wave "Hi!" for high pressure – most people naturally wave their hand in a clockwise direction). If you put your right hand on your location on the weather chart with the thumb pointing towards the nearest low pressure area, your fingers are now pointing in the direction that the wind is blowing.

lifted, the cool air masses mix and the front dissolves.

Finally, a front can stay in one place for a long time. It's a boundary between two air masses, neither of which is strong enough to move the other. This is called a **stationary front** and it causes a long period of bad weather.

The weather chart

A **weather chart** or **surface pressure chart** is used to give an overview of the main weather phenomena. These include the areas of high and low pressure, indicated with an H and an L. In between these areas are the **isobars**, the lines that connect places with equal pressure.

The **wind speed** can be estimated from the distance between the isobars. When these are wide apart, there's hardly any wind. With the isobars close together, you can be sure of a strong wind.

It's also possible to make a general assessment of the weather. For example, an area of low pressure over Scandinavia gives rise to a north-westerly to south-westerly wind in the UK and western mainland of Europe. Cool and moist air is transported into these countries, resulting in bad weather. High pressure over Scandinavia meanwhile will give easterly or south-easterly winds in the western mainland of Europe. This sends dry, continental air in that direction, giving hot and clear weather in the summer and cold, clear weather in winter.

In the southern hemisphere air flows anti-clockwise around a high pressure and clockwise around a low pressure system. In Australia, for example, low pressure systems south of Tasmania spin clockwise, pulling in cold air from the south. These cold fronts can create big storms across mainland south Australia.

Weather forecast

Many specialised forecasts are available online from the **national weather services**. There are also specialist **soaring forecast** websites. For example, in the UK, the Met Office has a special General Aviation service.

Most **general aviation forecasts** use some specific language and abbreviations, for example for the type and degree of cloud cover. Part of the forecast may be coded, for example like this:

```
15UTC: 0500FT 060/15 -00
21UTC: 0500FT 060/20 -02
```

This says that at 15:00 hr UTC (standard time, equal to Greenwich Mean Time) at 500 feet altitude the wind will blow from the direction of 60° with a speed of 15 knots. The temperature at that altitude is 0°C. Six hours later, at 21:00 hr UTC, the wind direction has not changed but the wind has increased to 20 knots. The temperature is now -2°C.

More detailed aviation weather is given by the observations at airports all over the world. These observations are collected and published in a coded message called **METAR** (METeorological Aerodrome Report). Most national meteorological offices publish these messages, often including an explanation of the abbreviations used.

A **TAF** (Terminal Aerodrome Forecast) meanwhile is a weather forecast for a particular airfield. The codes and abbreviations are similar to those in the METAR, and the information in both messages is complementary.

Finally, the **GAFOR** (General Aviation Forecast) is a type of weather forecast used for worldwide aviation and airliners.

▶ WINDY AND APPS

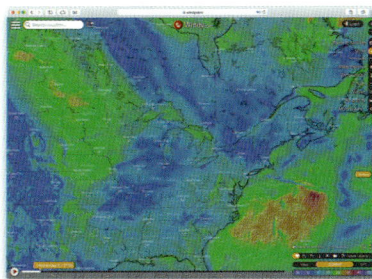

There is an enormous amount of weather data online, which can be very useful but also overwhelming to the new pilot. One good place to start is with the Windy.com website or app. It models winds around the globe, and also features thousands of paragliding sites. It uses the same weather data that informs the more traditional weather chart, but adds a real-time element with usuable forecasting up to five days in advance.

▲ COLD CLIMATE FLYING
Veso Ovcharov uses home-made down hand-warmers as he flies at extreme altitudes above 6,000m in the Hushe Valley in the Masherbrum area of the Karakoram, Pakistan. Keeping hands warm as you climb higher is critical
Photos: Veso Ovcharov

▶ TEMPERATURE

Lapse rate

At the start of this chapter, we defined the average temperature development with altitude in the standard atmosphere. On average, the temperature decreases 0.65°C with every 100m gain in altitude. But since the atmosphere is seldom average, this is not what happens in reality. For example, when a warm front passes, the air at ground level may be colder than several hundred metres up in the air, because the warm air behind the front moves over the colder air on the ground.

To analyse the temperature at the altitudes where we fly, we can draw a graph indicating the temperature on the horizontal axis and the altitude on the vertical axis. This temperature graph depicts the **lapse rate**, the rate at which the atmospheric temperature changes with an increase in altitude.

In the graph opposite, top right, you can see the lapse rate of a real situation. From the ground upwards, the temperature decreases as expected. But at a certain altitude, the temperature does not change any more, even if we rise. This is called an **isotherm**. 'Iso' means 'the same', and 'therm' means temperature. If we go even higher, a different situation arises, where the temperature increases with the altitude, contrary to what you might expect. This is called an **inversion**, a reverse of the usual development of the temperature in the atmosphere.

Thermals

When a surface, for example bare rock, is heated by the sun, a layer of warm air forms above the exposed rock. Warm air does not mix easily with colder air, meaning the warm air stays where it is. It will stay close to the surface until it's triggered and released, for example by wind blowing across the surface.

After the warm air has released from the surface it starts to rise. This is because warm air is lighter than cold air. This bubble of rising warm air is what we call a **thermal**. Thermals develop when a mass of air is heated to approximately 2°C warmer than its surroundings. Because air masses of different temperatures don't mix well, there's no exchange of heat between the thermal and its surroundings. The thermal is therefore called an **adiabatic system**; a mass of air that does not exchange heat with its surroundings.

The lack of **heat exchange** doesn't mean that the thermal does not change temperature during rising. It expands because the air pressure around it decreases with altitude. This expansion causes cooling – called **adiabatic cooling**. You can feel this effect when you open the valve on a gas bottle and the gas flows out. The gas expands and cools significantly, sometimes to the point where the valve freezes. The reverse process happens when you pump up the tyres on your bicycle. Compressing the air heats it up through **adiabatic heating**, as you can feel at the valve.

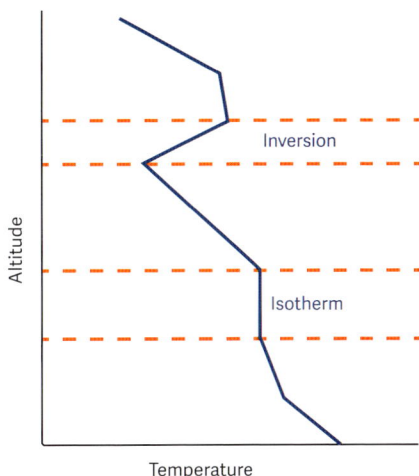

▲ **LAPSE RATE**
The rate at which the temperature changes with altitude is called the lapse rate. From a graph of the lapse rate, you can read the temperature at various altitudes.

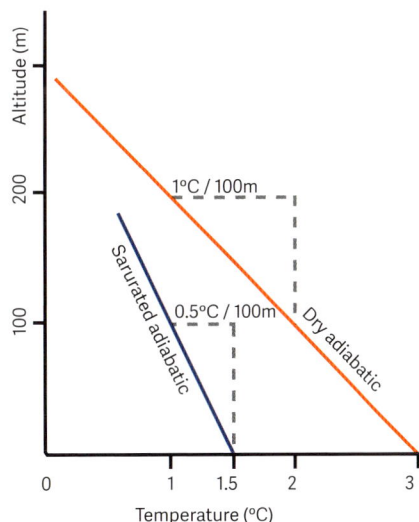

▲ **ADIABATS**
Dry (unsaturated) air cools with a rate of 1°C per 100m following the dry adiabat. Saturated or moist air cools with a rate of 0.5°C per 100m following the saturated adiabat. The saturated adiabat is therefore a steeper line on the graph than the dry adiabat.

157

a. unstable

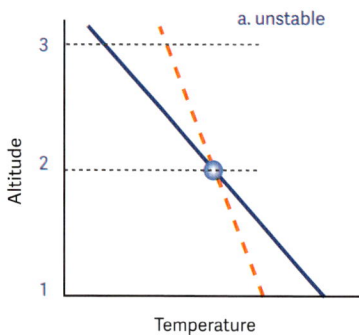

Altitude

Temperature

b. indifferent

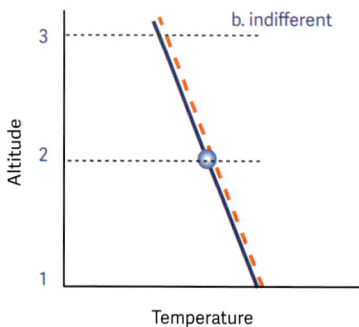

Altitude

Temperature

c. stable

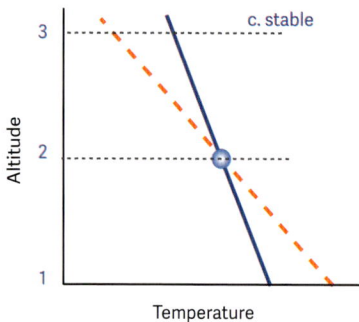

Altitude

Temperature

- - - - adiabatic
———— atmospheric lapse rate

▲ STABILITY
A thermal (blue dots) at Altitude 2 has the same temperature as the surrounding air (blue line). In these three graphs you can see what happens when this thermal rises (to Altitude 3) or sinks (to Altitude 1), in three different situations.

The rate at which the thermal cools depends on the humidity of the air inside the thermal. If the thermal is **saturated** with water vapour, this will cool and condense during its ascent. The process of condensation produces heat, which in turn causes the thermal to cool slower than it would if no condensation takes place.

Therefore, adiabatic cooling of air that is saturated with water vapour is slower than adiabatic cooling of air that is not saturated with moisture. Saturated air is sometimes referred to as **wet air** or **moist air**. **Unsaturated air** is usually referred to as **dry air** (although it's seldom completely free of water vapour).

As a rule of thumb, we can indicate the following adiabatic lapse rates for saturated and unsaturated air:

- **Dry adiabatic lapse rate**: 1°C every 100m

- **Saturated adiabatic lapse rate**: 0.5°C every 100m (varying with temperature).

- **Average lapse rate**: 0.65°C every 100m

Adiabatic cooling plotted on a graph is called the **adiabat** for short. Hence we have a **dry adiabat** and a **saturated adiabat**. The cooling rate (or lapse rate) of a rising thermal is given by one of these, depending on the amount of water vapour present in the thermal. A thermal consisting of air that's saturated with water vapour cools via the wet adiabat, which is slower than the cooling rate of a thermal consisting of dry air, which cools via the dry adiabat.

The opposite also happens: a mass of air that descends warms up via adiabatic heating. A saturated (wet) mass of air warms up via the saturated adiabat with 0.5°C per 100m descent. A dry mass of air warms up via the dry adiabat with 1.0°C per 100m descent.

Stable and unstable air

We've seen that a thermal, which is a mass of air that's warmer than its surroundings, will rise and cool during its ascent. As long as the thermal is warmer than its surroundings, it will keep rising. But at some point, its temperature will be the same as its surroundings. There's no more driving force for the thermal to rise any further, and it will stay where it is.

The cooling rate of the thermal follows the applicable adiabatic lapse rate. The lapse rate of its surroundings can be found in the temperature graph that we've seen at the beginning of this chapter. If you draw both lapse rates in one graph, at some point the lines will cross. At that point, corresponding to a particular altitude, the temperature of the thermal is equal to its surroundings.

During the ascent of the thermal, three different situations may arise. In the illustrations on the left the adiabat is represented by the orange dotted line. The temperature of the thermal follows this line. The lapse rate of the surrounding air is given by the blue line. Our starting point is a thermal that has released from the surface and is floating at Altitude 2. At that point, it has the same temperature as its surroundings. Let's assume this thermal gets disturbed and is moved upwards to Altitude 3. What will happen?

The thermal will cool while rising, at the lapse rate given by the orange line.

If the air is **unstable** that means the thermal cools, but not as strongly as its surroundings, which cool according to the blue line. The thermal will always be warmer than its surroundings and will keep rising. Unstable air leads to usable thermal activity for pilots. On the other hand, when the thermal is caused to descend from 2 to 1, it will warm up, but not as strongly as its surroundings. The thermal (which is now just a mass of air) will keep descending. Compare unstable air with a marble on a hilltop. Give the marble a small push and it will roll down ever faster without stopping.

If the air is **indifferent**, the thermal cools at exactly the same rate as its surroundings when it's moved upwards a little bit. Therefore, it will not continue to rise or sink but will instead dissipate; it's not a thermal anymore. Compare indifferent air with a marble on a flat surface. Given a small push, it will roll a little way, but then come to a stop.

If the air is **stable**, the thermal that rises a little bit from Altitude 2 to 3 will cool faster than its surroundings. It will immediately descend again, back to 2. The same happens if the thermal sinks a bit. It warms up faster than its surroundings and will rise back to Altitude 2. Compare stable air with a marble in a bowl. If given a push, the marble always returns to the lowest point.

Inversions

We can now understand that an **inversion** is a stable situation by definition. A thermal that runs into an inversion during its ascent will always encounter warmer air when it continues to rise. The cooler air of the thermal will always descend back to the level of the inversion.

159

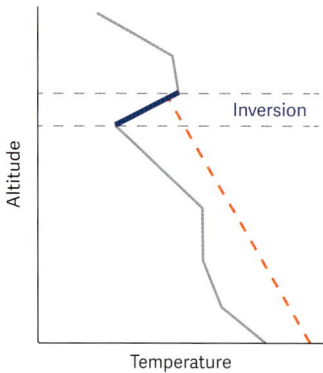

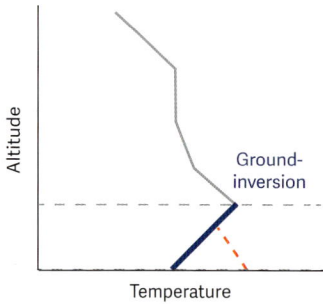

▲ **INVERSIONS**
An inversion is stable by definition. A thermal that would otherwise keep rising meets a warmer layer of air that stops it in its tracks. It can rise no further.

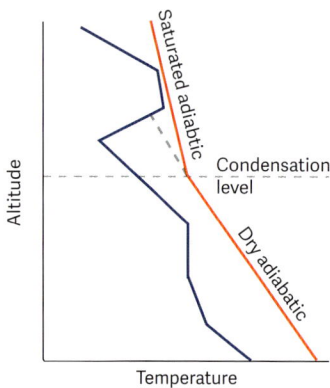

▲ **CONDENSATION**
When a mass of unsaturated air cools down to the dew point the water vapour will condense and the mass of air will continue to rise, following the saturated adiabat.

An inversion can also occur from ground level, usually in early morning. This is called a **ground inversion**. During the night, the ground cools faster than the air above it, causing a cool layer of air to be trapped beneath a warmer layer of air. This type of inversion only lifts after the sun heats up the ground enough for the air masses to mix.

Finally, subsidence can cause an inversion as well. Subsidence is a large mass of cool air that sinks and causes an area of high pressure. The temperature of this air mass rises through dry adiabatic heating, causing it to heat up more than the layer of air close to ground level. This results in a **subsidence inversion**. A tell-tale sign of a subsidence inversion is smog over a city.

Condensation

Almost all thermals contain some water vapour. As a thermal cools during its ascent, the air is able to contain ever less water vapour, until the dew point is reached. At the dew point, the air is saturated with water vapour. If the thermal cools even more, the excess of water vapour will condense and form **clouds**.

However, the condensation of water vapour has an effect on the temperature of the rising thermal. Since the air is now saturated with water vapour, its cooling rate slows down. The adiabatic lapse rate changes from the dry rate of 1.0°C per 100m to a slower 0.5°C per 100m.

In some cases, this change in lapse rate can enable the thermal to get through the inversion. Stability, such as an inversion, that holds only for the dry adiabatic lapse rate is called **conditional stability**.

Cloud formation actually ensures that the air in the thermal continues to rise. The condensation of water vapour releases energy which heats up the air. Warmer air rises faster than cooler air, so the thermal will start to rise faster, causing more condensation. This is what causes **cloud suck**. Cloud suck is the phenomenon that air beneath and inside a cloud rises faster than the air surrounding it.

A different effect caused by adiabatic cooling and heating is **föhn**. You'll find föhn in the Alps, but similar phenomena exist worldwide under different names.

On the southern side of the Alps, cool, moist but not saturated air is pushed against the mountains by a pressure difference. In general, when the pressure difference between the south and the north side of the mountain range reaches 4hPa, it is large enough for a föhn to

▶ **FÖHN**

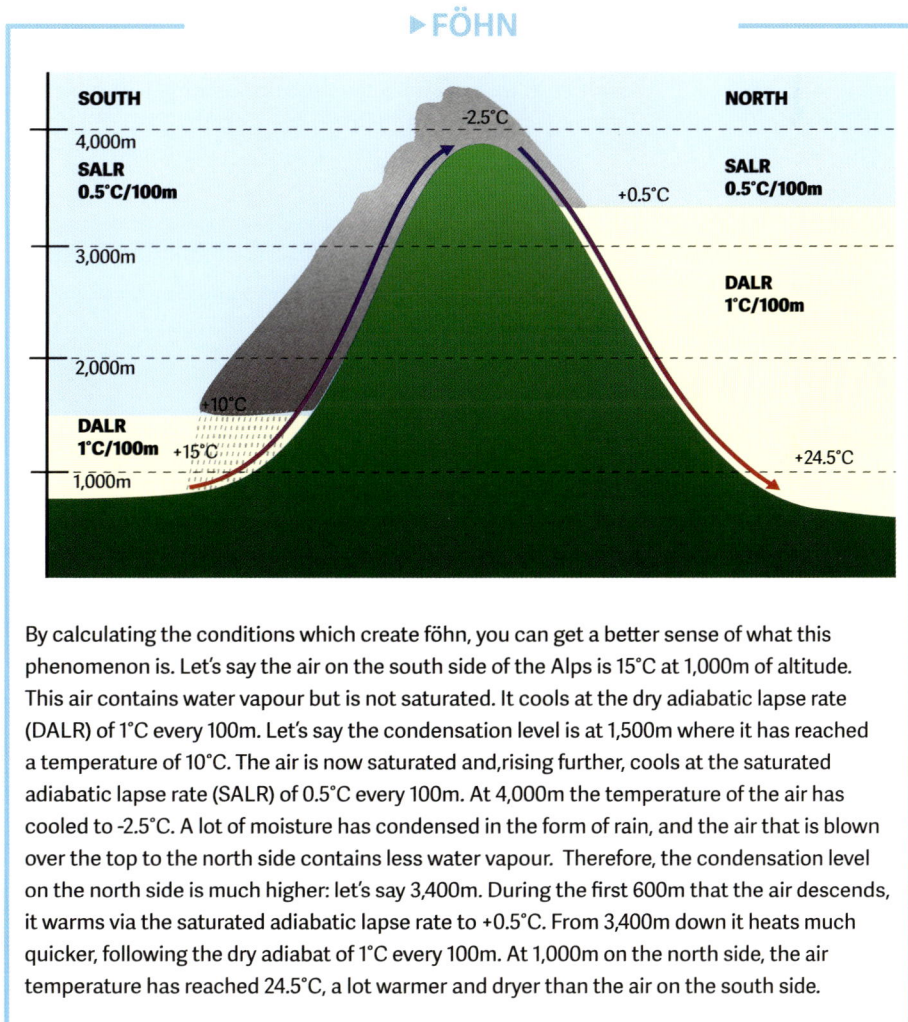

By calculating the conditions which create föhn, you can get a better sense of what this phenomenon is. Let's say the air on the south side of the Alps is 15°C at 1,000m of altitude. This air contains water vapour but is not saturated. It cools at the dry adiabatic lapse rate (DALR) of 1°C every 100m. Let's say the condensation level is at 1,500m where it has reached a temperature of 10°C. The air is now saturated and, rising further, cools at the saturated adiabatic lapse rate (SALR) of 0.5°C every 100m. At 4,000m the temperature of the air has cooled to -2.5°C. A lot of moisture has condensed in the form of rain, and the air that is blown over the top to the north side contains less water vapour. Therefore, the condensation level on the north side is much higher: let's say 3,400m. During the first 600m that the air descends, it warms via the saturated adiabatic lapse rate to +0.5°C. From 3,400m down it heats much quicker, following the dry adiabat of 1°C every 100m. At 1,000m on the north side, the air temperature has reached 24.5°C, a lot warmer and dryer than the air on the south side.

develop. But this number depends greatly on other circumstances such as temperature and humidity.

In any case, for the air the only way is up. It cools during its ascent, first at the dry adiabatic lapse rate of 1°C every 100m. When the air mass has reached its dew point, water vapour condenses and it rains. The air continues to rise and cool at the saturated adiabatic lapse rate of 0.5°C every 100m. It's blown over the top of the Alps, where you can see the typical föhn clouds over the peaks.

On the northern side, the air is much drier because the clouds have dropped their rain on the south side of the mountains. The condensation level at which the air mass reaches its dew point, is higher on this side. Below the condensation level, the air warms up via the dry adiabatic lapse rate, much quicker than it cooled on its way up on the other side. Therefore, the air is much warmer and drier when it reaches ground level, sometimes having a relative humidity of only 20%.

The warm, dry – and strong – wind that blows down from the mountain is called föhn wind. Pilots don't usually fly in föhn – because the air is sinking it can be very turbulent.

▼ FÖHN CLOUD IN AUSTRIA
Typical föhn cloud in Austria. Föhn describes a situation in the mountains where there is a big difference in air pressure on either side of a range. It rains on one side, and the dry air flows over and down the other side. Flying in föhn is not recommended as it can be extremely turbulent. Photo: Marcus King

▶ CLOUDS

Clouds consist of small drops of water or ice crystals, depending on the temperature. They appear when air that's saturated with water vapour cools (for example when it rises) and its **dew point** is reached. That's the temperature at which condensation takes place, forming clouds or mist.

The dew point depends on the humidity of the air and corresponds to a particular altitude, the **condensation level**. The condensation level can be calculated by multiplying the difference between the dew point and the surface temperature by 400. This is the altitude in feet above the surface at which clouds will form. We call this **cloudbase**.

Cloud types

There are numerous types of cloud. Meteorologists classify them according to their physical appearance, shape, method of formation and other properties. The types are ordered in an international system of cloud classification. The most important types of clouds, including their abbreviations used in weather forecasts, are shown at the end of this chapter.

Although the classification system is rather complex, we can break it down into a simplified form as follows. The system starts with three **cloud families** classified by their relative altitudes.

Higher than 6km above sea level we find **cirrus** clouds. Clouds at these altitudes always have the prefix **cirro-**. Between 2km and 6km altitude, clouds are named **alto-**.

Below 2km, the clouds do not have a prefix. If a cloud name does not start with cirro- or alto-, it's typically lower than 2km.

Secondly, the cloud is given a name according to its form or property, usually after the prefix. There are three groups of these, which combine with the families into the 10 main **genera**.

The best known **genus** is **cumulus**, meaning stacked. **Cirrocumulus** is therefore a stacked cloud at high altitude. Cumulus without a prefix are found below 2km altitude (or higher over mountains). Thermal clouds are cumulus.

The genus of **stratus** (meaning 'layer') is reserved for a solid layer of cloud. When the air looks grey, for example, you're

▶ CLOUD COVER

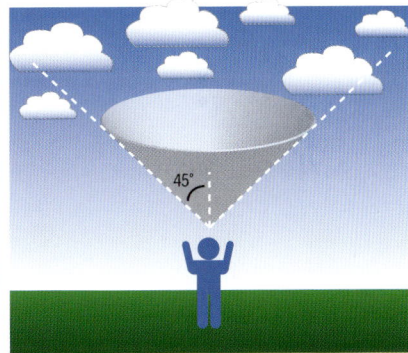

Determine the cloud cover by looking at the sky at an angle of 45° and estimate the amount of clouds. Below is a list of meteorological terms of cloud cover:

- FEW (few) 1/8 – 2/8
- SCT (scattered) 3/8 – 4/8
- BKN (broken) 5/8 – 7/8
- OVC (overcast) 8/8

— 10500m

BIRD FLIGHT
The Ruppell's griffon vulture has been confirmed flying at 11,000m

THE JET STREAM
Narrow bands of high wind of up to 450km/h that flow around the Earth

CRUISING ALTITUDE, 10,000M
Commercial aviation criss-crosses the planet while staying mainly above the weather

— 9000m

CIRRUS
Wispy clouds up high, like paint-brush strokes. They can indicate a change in the weather as a warm front approaches

— 7500m

CIRROCUMULUS
High level convection clouds, typically made of ice, that indicate upper-level instability. Sometimes called a "mackerel sky"

CIRROSTRATUS
Transparent high clouds, covering large areas of the sky. They sometimes produce a halo around the Sun. Suggest an approaching warm front and preceded by cirrus

— 6000m

ALTOCUMULUS
Mid-level heaped clouds that are usually made up of a mix of ice and water, giving them a more ethereal appearance than fluffy cumulus. Rain can fall from them, as virga – where rain re-evaporates before it reaches the surface

— 4500m

ALTOSTRATUS
Large mid-level sheets of thin cloud, often ahead of a warm front. As the front passes altostratus layer deepens to become nimbostratus – rain or snow clouds

CUMULONIMBUS
Thunderclouds. The base of a cu-nim is flat and dark and often relatively low. However, the top of the cloud can extend to 10,000m forming classic towers and the anvil shape. Lightning, heavy rain, thunder, hail and tornadoes are all associated with cu-nims. Stay away.

— 3000m

CUMULUS
Heaped clouds with a flat base, and what we look for in flying. A pilot's favourite cloud!

NIMBOSTRATUS
Grey layers of cloud, thick enough to block out the sun. Associated with continuous rain or snow they cover most of the sky

— 1500m

STRATUS
Low-level layers of grey cloud. Some rain might fall, but typically not very active. Often touching the hill tops

World's tallest building, Burj Khalifa, 828m

looking at altostratus clouds at 2km to 6km altitude.

Next, **nimbus** is an important genus for pilots. **Nimbo-** means rain. **Nimbostratus** is therefore a solid layer of cloud below 2km altitude which produces rain.

Finally, there is a separate genus that stretches from ground level to over 10km altitude, the vertically towering **cumulonimbus**. Besides these 10 main cloud genera, there are hundreds of types and subtypes classified according to their shape or properties.

Finally, for pilots, **cloud cover** is an important parameter. This is generally indicated in eighths or oktas, where 0/8 means a clear sky and 8/8 is overcast.

To estimate the cloud cover, look up at the sky at an angle of 45° all around you. If you looked at the entire sky down to the horizon, you would overestimate the amount of cloud. Instead of fractions, abbreviations are used to indicate cloud cover in weather forecasts.

Clouds accompanying fronts

By observing the type of clouds and their development, you can get an indication of the development of the weather. This is most clear in the passage of fronts.

A warm front announces itself with wisps of high cirrus cloud. Those mark the boundary of the warm layer of air at high altitude. The clouds gradually thicken

▼ CLOUDS AND FRONTS
Cold front (left) Cirrus and cirrocumulus appear before the passage of a cold front. When the front gets closer, altocumulus is seen. The clouds get lower until cumulus congestus and cumulonimbus form. Those can develop into thunderstorms. The air behind a cold front is clear, often with cumulus clouds – good flying conditions.
Warm front (right) Cirrus clouds followed by altostratus herald the arrival of a warm front. As the warm front draws closer the cloud lowers and thickens, to nimbostratus. Then, it starts to rain.

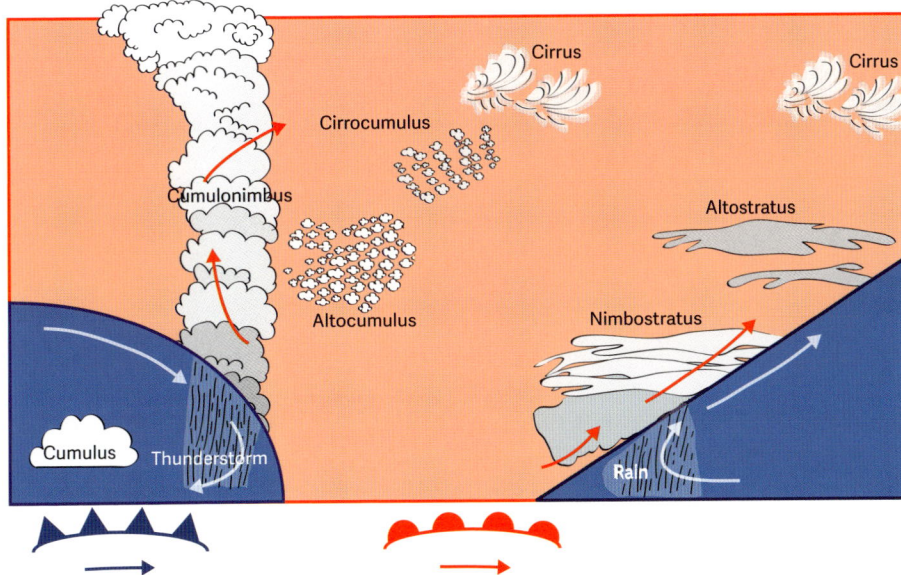

and lower into altostratus and finally a low nimbostratus, which produces prolonged rainfall. After the passing of the front, the wind will increase and veer again. A warm front usually announces a couple of days of non-flyable weather.

A cold front pushes the warm air ahead of it upwards, causing it to cool. The water vapour in the air condenses and forms cumulus clouds. Those may develop into cumulonimbus and thunderstorms.

After the front passes, the air pressure increases and the wind will increase and veer. Once it's passed, the weather is cooler with clear skies, allowing the sun to heat up the ground. Since the air is cool, large temperature differences may give rise to good thermals. After the passing of a cold front, the weather is usually good for paragliders.

Thermals and thunder

Thermals are associated with cumulus clouds: it's often said that cumulus clouds sit on top of thermals. Consider a cumulus cloud as a thermal marker.

Cumulus clouds form because a parcel of warm, moist air rises and cools. As soon as the dew point is reached, the water vapour starts to condense and an expanding cloud forms. If you see these cumulus clouds in the air and there's no other reason for them to form, you can be sure that they have been formed by convection – by thermals.

A thermal may also contain dry air, without any water vapour, or the air temperature may be below the dew point. The thermal is there, but you see no cloud. These are called **blue thermals**. The lack of cumulus cloud

therefore does not necessarily mean there are no thermals.

Cumulus congestus is the famous towering cumulus cloud. It indicates a strong upward current of air and will often lead to **overdevelopment**, in which it matures into **cumulonimbus**, giving **thunderstorms**. If you see overdevelopment after a warm day, usually in summer, this is called a **thermal thunderstorm**. When cumulus congestus and cumulonimbus are formed with the passing of a front, it's called a **frontal thunderstorm**.

If the cumulus congestus has sharp, flowering edges, it's still developing. You're sure to find a strong current of wind below and around the edges of the cloud, as well as below cloudbase and up to several kilometres distance. The strong winds are caused by the cloud drawing in air from its surroundings. Keep a close eye on the development of the cloud and land before the wind picks up or rain starts to fall from the cloud.

Special clouds

For paraglider pilots some types or subtypes of clouds are noteworthy because they indicate weather that influences our flying.

Cirrus consists of ice crystals and looks like thin wisps of cloud at high altitude. These high clouds announce the approach of a front.

Altocumulus lenticularis, or **lenticular** or lens-shaped clouds, are fairly high and seem to be stationary, even though their smooth, rounded shape indicates strong winds. The reality is that there are strong winds present, but the lenticulars appear stationary because they're formed in a wave of wind blowing over mountains. At the downwind side of the mountain, the air forms a wave, the lee wave. At the top of the wave, the air just reaches the dew point and condenses into a cloud. At the bottom, the cloud dissolves again. Something similar happens when a rock is placed in a fast stream of water. A wave is formed which seems to be stationary at some distance behind the rock. The stationary lenticular is in reality a continuous process of condensation and evaporation caused by the strong winds of the lee wave. Even though the wind may feel acceptable on launch, the presence of lenticulars in the air should be a warning that the winds are very strong at higher altitudes, with possible turbulence lower down.

Altocumulus castellanus are high banks of cloud that show a similarity to the battlements of a castle. These clouds accurately predict thunderstorms at the end of the day. The weather charts show no sign of fronts, but you still see cumulus clouds. They appear in the morning and dissolve as the sun heats up the air. They indicate the presence of a lot of energy in the atmosphere in the form of warm, moist air. When the air starts to cool again with the setting sun, all this water vapour condenses into fat cumulus clouds. Keep an eye out for cumulus congestus or cumulonimbus later in the day if you've seen castellanus in the morning.

Finally, in the mountains, thunderstorms may arise from an air mass being pushed up against a slope until the water vapour condenses. The clouds that develop this way may cause rain or thunderstorms, called **orographic thunder**. The width of the mountain range, the slope and the wind speed all influence the cloud formation and chances of precipitation.

▶ LEE WAVE

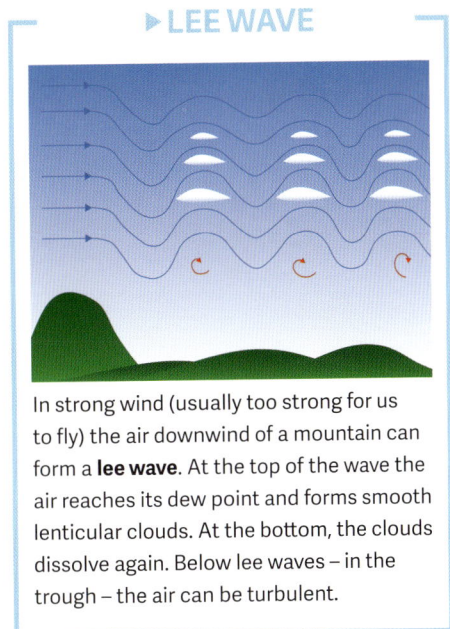

In strong wind (usually too strong for us to fly) the air downwind of a mountain can form a **lee wave**. At the top of the wave the air reaches its dew point and forms smooth lenticular clouds. At the bottom, the clouds dissolve again. Below lee waves – in the trough – the air can be turbulent.

Cloud Types

Cumulus (Cu)

Cumulus clouds are caused by convection – the sun heats the ground, warm air rises and condenses into a flat-based, fluffy looking cloud. These are what we look for in flying.

Cumulus castellanus (Cas)

So-called because they look like castles. These are fast-building cumulus clouds with a strong vertical profile. They indicate an unstable air mass, with probable thunderstorms later.

Cumulus congestus (Cu con)

These are large cumulus clouds, typically taller than they are wide. They build over a large area, have very strong updraughts and can reach 6,000m. Can often produce heavy showers.

Cumulonimbus (Cb)

A thunderstorm cloud, typically anvil-shaped. These are dense, towering clouds that can reach 10,000m. They can produce thunder, lightning, strong wind and rain.

Pileus

Latin for cap, pileus clouds are small cap clouds that form on the top of rapidly developing cumulus or Cb clouds. Indicate strong updraughts. Short-lived.

Mammatus

Heavy globs of cloud that develop below Cbs. Formed by cold air sinking down – the opposite of the Cu puffs created by convection. Associated with severe thunderstorms.

Cirrus (Cs)

Means "curling hair" in Latin and looks like wisps across the sky. High cloud (5,000m and above) that precedes a warm front, Also known as mares' tails.

Virga

Precipitation (rain or snow) that falls from a cloud but evaporates or sublimates before reaching the ground is called virga. Descending cool air can result in gusts on the ground.

Cloud Types

Mackerel Sky

A common term for rows of cirrocumulus or altocumulus clouds – the undulating pattern looks a bit like fish scales. Common ahead of a warm front, with rain 6-12 hours away.

Lenticular clouds

Spectacular lens-shaped stationary clouds formed by wave in the atmosphere. For example above the top of a mountain or mountain range. Indicate strong wind up high.

Orographic cloud

When wet air is forced to rise, by a mountain for example, it can condense into cloud and rain or snow can fall. Cloud that forms on the ground is called fog. Photo Tex Bex

Föhn

Föhn cloud is any cloud associated with a föhn wind (see p 161). It is usually an orographic cloud, a mountain wave cloud or a lenticular cloud. Photo: Thomas Hoflacher

Radiation fog

Low-level fog that forms when the ground cools overnight under a calm, clear sky – the air cools and condenses. Can be less than 1m thick. Most common in autumn and winter.

Glory

Circular rainbow caused by sunlight refracting on cloud. Rare to see as we are usually below cloud, but when pilots climb above clouds they can be rewarded if conditions are right.

▶ LEARN MORE

- **Check the flying weather anywhere,** windy.com, meteoparapente.com

- **Understanding the Sky by Dennis Pagen, classic weather textbook,** dennispagen.com

- **Honza's weather column, Cross Country Magazine,** xcmag.com

- **Backyard Meteorology, free online course via Harvard University**, edx.org

- **Met Office, UK, has a big online learning section**, metoffice.gov.uk/weather/learn-about/weather

- **US Aviation Weather Center,** aviationweather.gov

- **Australia Bureau of Met**, bom.gov.au

- **How to read a lapse rate diagram** youtube.com/user/xckelly/videos

- **The Cloud Appreciation Society** cloudappreciationsociety.org

- **Beautiful hurricane season simulation** tinyurl.com/hurricane-sim

- **Try this one-minute cloud quiz!** tinyurl.com/cloud-quiz

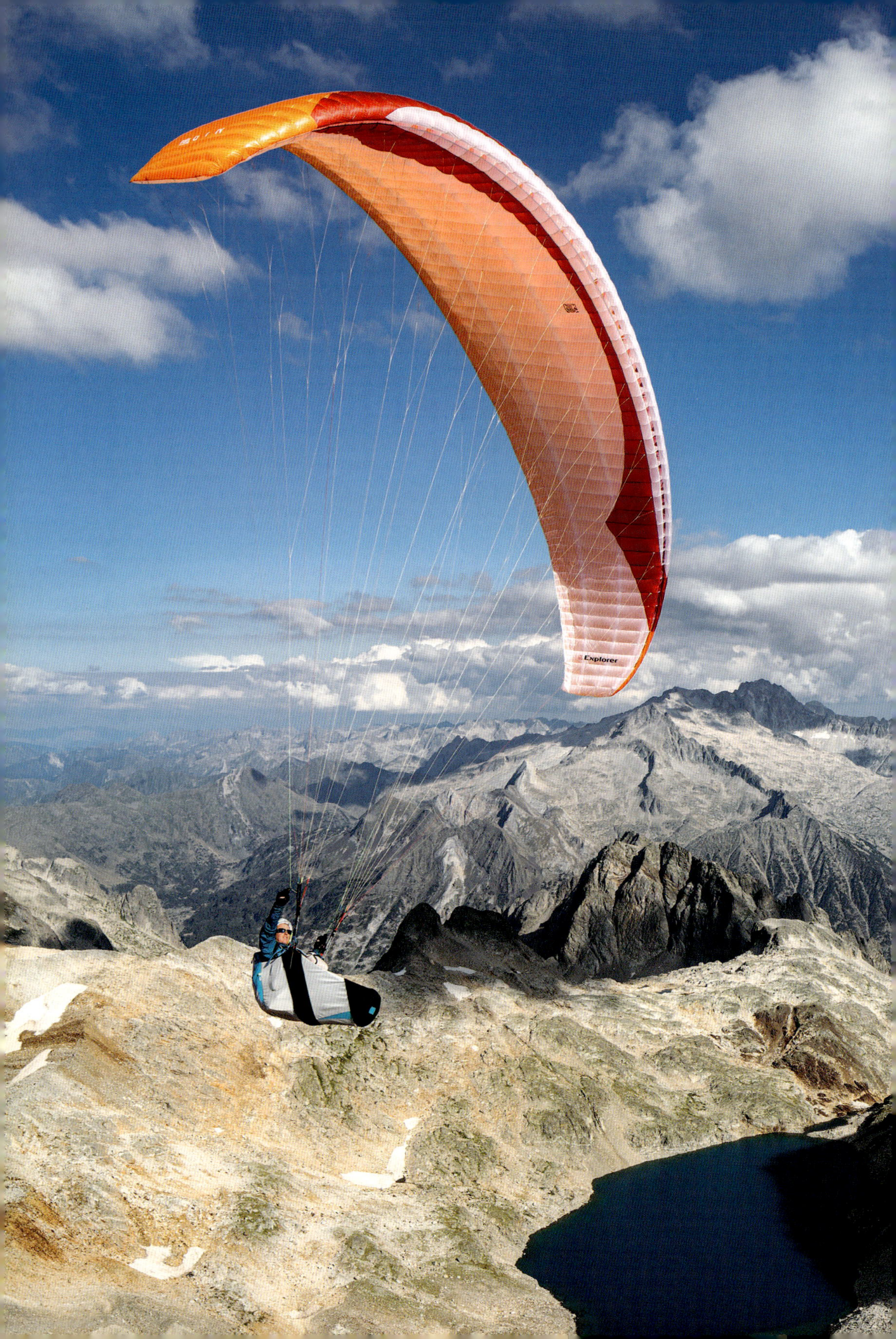
Explorer

#6
ADVANCED
FLYING

- ▶ SITE ASSESSMENT
- ▶ WIND, LIFT AND TURBULENCE
- ▶ THERMAL FLYING
- ▶ STRONG WIND TECHNIQUES
- ▶ DESCENT TECHNIQUES
- ▶ SIV AND MANOEUVRES CLINICS
- ▶ MANAGING EMERGENCIES

Becoming a better pilot

Your first flights were most likely in quiet circumstances. During these flights the air does not move much and your paraglider glides smoothly from top to bottom. You are flying in laminar conditions with little wind. Your instructor will have guided you during decision-making about site assessment and flying conditions.

But once you know the basics of how to operate a paraglider it is time to become an independent pilot. This not only includes learning advanced flying skills, it also means developing the knowledge to judge the air and surroundings that you are flying in – both before launch and while flying.

In this chapter we will discuss how air moves over the ground and in clear space, and how terrain and weather influences the airflow. We will talk about flying in rising or moving air, and where the movement of that air originates, where to expect it and how to anticipate it. We also look at how you can use it to your advantage to make long flights.

▲ **PERFECT SKY**
Cumulus clouds dot the sky in the flatlands of Dalby, Australia as a pilot is winch-launched into the air
Photo: Tex Beck

◄ **MOUNTAIN PILOT**
Flying high in the Pyrenees
Photo: Jérôme Maupoint

▶ SITE ASSESSMENT

In the Basic Techniques chapter we saw that it is vital to assess the site where you intend to fly before you take off. This includes looking at the topography, wind direction, wind strength, the aspect of any slopes, and any obstacles. It also includes knowing the site rules.

If you are flying at a popular site where other pilots are already in the air then making the decision to fly can be easy. But if you are at a new or remote site where no one has flown before, then making the decision to fly can be a lot harder – you have to examine the factors above carefully and work out how they will all interact with each other, and then make your assessment about whether the site is safe to fly or not.

Being able to make a good **site assessment** is critical to becoming a good pilot. No independent, autonomous pilot simply launches into the sky because someone else is already in the air – they always make their own assessment of the site and the conditions and relate it to themselves and their own flying ability. That is why learning how to make a competent site assessment early in your career is so important.

Flatlands, mountains or coast?

Before getting into the detail of the local **topography** of a particular site, it helps if we can identify the broad **geography** of the region we are flying in. In paragliding we talk about mountain, flatland or coastal flying. Knowing the basic geography of the area will give you a big clue as to what type of flying you will experience – because each type of landscape brings its own distinct weather and flying characteristics.

Mountains and hills are obvious high features, usually divided by valleys. The flatlands meanwhile are not necessarily completely flat. We might use a hill to launch from to fly into the flatlands, or there may be ripples, hillocks, rolling farmland or gullies and escarpments that, taken together, make up a region that is generally flat, or at least not uplands. The coast is generally taken to mean sites that face the sea and are largely influenced by coastal weather.

Hills and mountains

The most popular place to fly paragliders is in hills and mountains. This is because climbing a hill and flying off is an easy way to get into the air. In places like the Alps there are often cable cars that can carry us up 1,000m or more in minutes; in other places, pilots have to hike.

In the Alps and other high mountains, there are rocky summits, steep valleys, cliffs, gorges, waterfalls, forests, rivers and often snow, ice and glaciers. To fly in this environment we look for nice, calm days, with light winds. If there is too much wind, then the air becomes mixed up, broken and turbulent, and it becomes a dangerous place to fly.

To launch in the mountains, we look for sunny slopes to take off from in nil-wind or light-wind conditions. When flying, we usually fly with reference to the landscape, using the features of the landscape to direct our flights: following valleys, or hopping from spine to spine. Only rarely, on exceptional days, do we get to fly high above the high mountains with the snowy peaks below us, although it does happen!

▶ FLYING FROM EVEREST

When **Babu Sunuwar**, then 29, and **Lakpa Tsheri Sherpa**, 35, launched a tandem paraglider from the summit of Mount Everest (8,848m) on Saturday 21 May 2011 their site assessment skills came in handy.

After reaching the summit at 9am, they found zero wind – making launching a tandem in the thin air of the world's highest mountain almost impossible. So rather than take off from the obvious south side, Babu climbed to the northeast side, overlooking Tibet. There, as the sun rose higher, he suspected that thermals would start to roll up the east face, giving him an upslope breeze.

After being on top nearly an hour, a puff of wind did indeed come up the face. He used it to launch and then circled in the thermal as it took him up and over the summit. The pair then turned and flew south, into Nepal where they descended more than 5,000m over 42 minutes before landing safely near the Sherpa village of Namche Bazaar. They were only the third people to successfully paraglide from the top of Everest.

In lower hills we can fly in stronger wind than in the Alps. In fact we often seek out slopes and hills that face into wind – windward slopes – so we can soar and stay up. In this case we look for hills with a clean airflow, clear of obstacles out front, with good take-off and landing places. We can fly in a moderate to fresh wind, depending on other factors including how much sunshine there is and whether the air is thermic or not. Light wind mixed with strong thermals in hills makes for enjoyable flying conditions; strong wind and strong thermals makes for more turbulence and more demanding sport. When flying in hills, we will often climb out above them in thermals, but will often be looking at the landscape and topography to predict where the next thermal might come from.

Flatlands

We get into the air in the flatlands in two ways: launching from a hill or slope and then climbing out in a thermal; or by towing up. Either way, once in the air the topography has less impact on our flight than in the mountains. This is because we can go in any direction without hitting a mountain or glacier.

An important factor in flying in the flatlands is the wind: in flatland flying paraglider pilots tend to go downwind. When low we look at the terrain to give us clues on where thermals might be; when up high we look at the clouds and clues in the sky to show us where the lift is. If there is zero wind then we can and will fly in any direction, perhaps even completing a triangle circuit or an out-and-return. As a rule of thumb, we can generally fly in stronger wind in the flatlands than we can in the mountains or hills.

Coast

Pilots like to fly the coast because the air that comes across the sea is often smooth as butter and not turbulent. This makes for relaxed and easy flying. To take advantage of this we look for cliffs, bluffs or hills that face the wind coming from the sea. In a fresh breeze we can often soar and stay up for hours.

Coastal flying can also be predictable because of the predictable local weather. Sea breezes blow onshore during the day, and offshore at night. This means some coastal sites work 'like clockwork', 'switching on' when the local sea breeze sets up each afternoon. In some places by the coast it is flyable every day.

Not all sites near the coast offer this type of smooth, predictable and relaxed flying however. Mountains near the sea, for example, will experience mountain weather, including strong thermals and cumulus clouds, and require more complex site assessment. This can catch pilots out if they turn up to a site near the coast expecting benign conditions, but are instead faced with thermals and strong air. A good example of this is Babadağ in Turkey – this 1,969m mountain rises out of the Mediterranean Sea and is a very popular place to fly. It offers thermal flying during the day, with coastal sea breeze flying in the evening. Landing is on the beach in the resort of Ölüdeniz.

▼ **PERFECT COASTAL FLYING**
Torrey Pines in San Diego, California is a classic coastal site. Hundreds of pilots fly here every year, enjoying the regular sea breeze that sets up every day. It allows pilots to fly the coast for hours at a time. Photo: Annie Pearson

▶ Mountain flying

From grassy Alpine pastures to steep cliffs and frozen glaciers, flying in the mountains is always spectacular. Here's what to look for when finding a place to launch.

Into wind: Your take-off site should face into wind. Everything that flies takes off into the wind and we are no exception. Avoid setting up in dips or behind obstacles, which will make it difficult to read what the wind is actually doing.

Open face: Gently sloping with plenty of space to lay out and run for take-off is best.

Obstacle free: Obstacles cause turbulence and can hinder your take-off, eg buildings, boulders, power lines, trees or other hills.

Clean airflow: Air flows more cleanly over rounded hills and slopes, and tends to tumble around cliff edges or gullies. Cliff launches are always more demanding than hill launches because of this.

Space: There should be enough space to fly safely in clear air. You don't want to need to take immediate action to avoid a cable-car station, or to fly below or above a cable.

Landing: You should be able to reach a landing safely from launch. Be aware that valley winds can be strong during summer.

What's behind you? Are you on a smooth rounded hill or is it a knife-edge arête? Does the ground fall or rise? Are there flat fields, a pine forest or chalets and swimming pools? Take a good look around you – the full 360 degree view.

Photo: Vitek Ludvik / RBCP

Aspect
What is the sun doing? We want to fly the sunny slopes

Look out
Cable cars can be common – look for lines and infrastructure

Weather
Check the mountain forecast, ask about valley winds

Terrain
Follow the valleys, find thermals on peaks and spurs

Landings
Know where you can land safely and legally

Launch
Look for clear areas with plenty of room and clean airflow

▲ **OBSTACLE FREE?**
Always check for obstacles at launch, on the ground as well as in the air. The take-off here in Chamonix, opposite Mont Blanc in France is smooth and green but is also crowded and has a cable car right out front
Photo: Marcus King

Obstacles

As well as assessing the general topography of the site, at this point you should also be looking at potential **obstacles** and hazards. Some of these are obvious, others less so.

Water is a big one. Drowning is the main risk. Landing in a still lake in the Alps in summer is one thing; landing in the surf line on rocks is another. Moving water of any sort is something to be aware of and avoid at all costs – rivers, waterfalls and of course the sea. You should not fly a coastal site with no beach landing: it might be easy to stay up now, but what happens when the wind stops? Will you still be able to land safely?

Power lines and other cables are another big hazard, and are often not spotted by pilots new to an area. Single cables are very difficult to spot from the air: look for the tell-tale orange balls attached to the lines, these are there for that reason. Where those are not present, look for pylons and join the dots between them to track the path of cables and lines. Houses and buildings almost invariably have cables running into them, often running at angles of 45 degrees. They are a good place to start your visual search for cables. Telegraph poles and cables often follow the road too. Finally, look behind and above you on launch – can you safely pull up your glider and move back a few metres without hitting an overhead line? In the Alps the main cable cars are obvious, but smaller, service cable cars can often be impossible to spot – check the local air charts or hiking maps.

Trees are a third major hazard. There is a saying that there are two types of pilot: those who have landed in a tree; and those who will. Try to avoid landing in trees on take-off and landing. Don't fixate on them – note their presence and adjust your launch or landing approach accordingly. Large trees or forest can affect the wind and cause turbulence behind them, or they can provide shelter and mask the 'true' wind. In forested mountains some launches are narrow, just a cutting in the trees. In this case you must be confident in your launch technique, and aware of where your wingtips are, to avoid connecting with some of the lower branches. Trees can capture pilots in many ways – avoid them.

Other pilots can also be a hazard, especially if there are lots of them. Flying with others can be nerve-wracking, but it is something you learn to do as you progress. At the beginning of your flying career it can be easier to sit out the busiest part of the day, waiting until there are fewer pilots in the air. Or fly earlier, before the crowds arrive. When you do decide to launch with other pilots in the air, take note of where they are and what the conditions are like: 20 pilots on a site can be ok if conditions are good and they are high; but if conditions aren't great, then it can feel like you are dodging traffic as they crowd in close. Before launching look around for pilots who are taking off or landing; and when you have taken off, fly away from the launch area so others can then take off. Give way to pilots top-landing.

Airspace affects many sites, and it is the responsibility of each individual pilot to know about it. Just because another pilot is flying doesn't mean it's legal, so try not to follow others blindly. Airspace can include altitude limits, eg "500m above take-off", as well as prohibited areas, for example total exclusion from certain types of busy airspace or military zones. There is more on this in the next chapter. Your pilot teaching programme will cover airspace in some depth; learn to read the airspace maps, download any relevant apps, and make it a habit to keep up to date with local airspace changes.

Local rules affect all but the most open sites. Some are closed for lambing, others for shooting, some for the breeding season of a particular bird. Empty beaches you are allowed to land on in March are often out of bounds in crowded July. The reasons are numerous, but the effect is the same. Because of our high visibility it is hard for paraglider pilots to 'get away with it' and infringe local rules without being caught out, however many do. Unfortunately that is the way sites are lost, wherever you are in the world. Know the local rules and regulations, and observe them.

Landing fields should be large enough and free from obstacles. Look upwind for obstacles that can create turbulent air behind them, for example lines of trees or buildings. Check for power lines that might stretch across landing fields. Also check for livestock – animals can easily be spooked and can injure themselves in the race to get away from an approaching paraglider, or that lonely cow may in fact be a bull. In mountainous areas local valley winds can mean the wind is strong in the landing, even if it is light at launch.

181

South facing   North facing

Aspect

Aspect is a geographical term that describes which way a slope faces. For example, a slope on the eastern side of a mountain is described as having an easterly aspect.

An important part of site assessment in the mountains is understanding how the sun will affect it at different times of day. The simplest way of knowing this is to know the aspect of your site. In the northern hemisphere the sun rises in the east, moves through the south at midday, and sets in the west; in the southern hemisphere the sun rises in the east, moves through the north, and sets in the west. For pilots this is crucial information when flying in mountains. This means:

- In the morning, east-facing slopes will have sun on them first.

- By midday in the N hemisphere the south-facing slopes will be in full sun. In the S hemisphere the north-facing slopes will be in full sun.

- As sunset approaches, the west-facing slopes will be getting the sun.

The sun has a crucial influence on flying in the mountains. Basically, you want to take off on the sunny side and then continue to fly the sunny slopes of the mountains and valleys. This is because, in general, air rises in the sunlit areas, and sinks in the shade.

This means that in the hills and mountains in the northern hemisphere, you want to use east-facing take-offs and fly east-facing and southeast-facing slopes in the morning; south-facing take-offs and slopes in the middle of the day; and west-facing launches and slopes in the afternoon and evening.

This isn't just desirable, it's often essential. There is no point going to a west-facing launch at 9am expecting to find a sunny slope with a gentle breeze on it: that won't happen. However, an east-facing hillside will allow an early take-off.

This is why when you fly in the Alps you will often hear pilots refer to a site as a 'morning take-off' or 'an evening site'. Both are defined by aspect – the direction the slope faces – and say something about when the slope receives maximum sunshine.

182

Wind

The displacement of air is called **wind**, and it is caused by differences in atmospheric pressure. Air moves from areas of high pressure to low pressure, and it is this movement we know as wind. The strength of the wind is measured as **wind speed** in knots, m/s, mph or km/h or using the Beaufort scale (see next page).

Winds can be local or regional. While large-scale **regional wind** is a result of air moving from areas of high pressure to low pressure, **local winds** can be influenced by or associated with storms, sea breezes, ice and snow, the position of the sun, the strength of the sun, the time of year, mountains, ground cover and more. Having an understanding of what sort of wind you might expect at a site, including an up-to-date forecast, and a knowledge of weather, will help you make a good site assessment.

It's important to take note of and understand the wind because paraglider pilots are relatively vulnerable with regard to wind. To launch we prefer to have a light wind blowing into our face, but too much wind will make it hard to control the glider and can be dangerous. Too little wind is rarely dangerous, although it can make launching more difficult.

Direction of wind

As mentioned in the Weather for Pilots chapter, we talk about the wind with reference to the direction it is coming from. A wind blowing from south to north is called a south wind or a southerly. When we look west and feel the wind on our face, that wind is a westerly. If we look downslope and can feel a wind on our face, that is an **upslope**

▶ HIKE-AND-FLY ASPECT

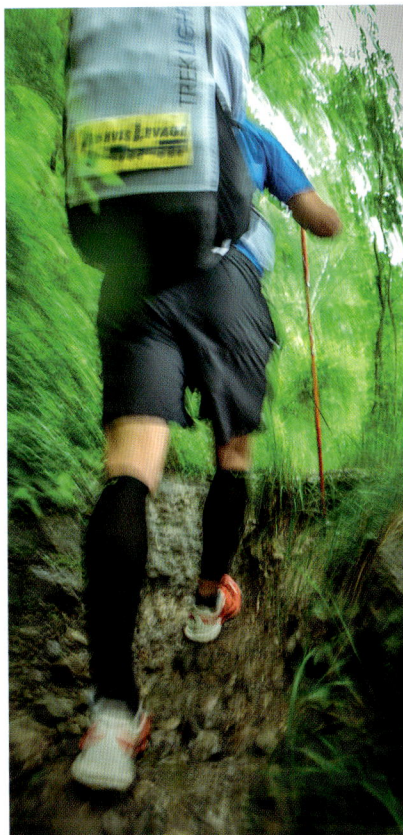

If you are hiking up a to a launch in the mountains, consider the aspect of your planned take-off spot and when you will get there. If you plan to take off from an east-facing slope but set off late, the sun may have moved around to the south (or north if you are in the southern hemisphere) by the time you get there. It might be impossible to launch. Choose a west-facing launch and hike up in the morning however, and you might have to wait several hours for the sun to come round and the wind to come 'on'. To avoid wasted trips, before you set off work out how long your hike will take and where the sun will be when you get there. Photo: Alain Doucé

▶ BACKING AND VEERING

When paraglider pilots talk about the wind **veering** it means the direction of the wind will rotate clockwise over time or height; **backing** means it will rotate anticlockwise. It is the same in the N and S hemisphere.

For example, "The wind on launch is forecast north in the morning but will back to NW by lunchtime as the front arrives." Or, "It's north on launch but expect the wind to veer northeast at about 1,000m."

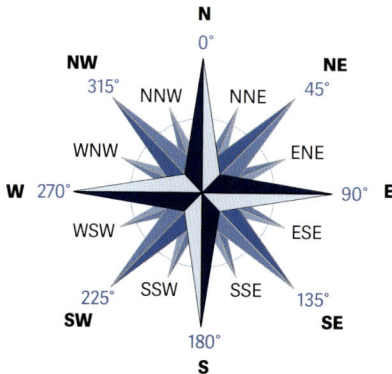

wind. If we stand on take-off looking at the direction we want to launch, but can feel a wind on the back of our neck, then that is a **backwind**.

In forecasts we might hear, "wind 270, veering 290". This means the wind is coming from the direction of 270 degrees, ie west, but it is forecast to swing round to almost WNW (west north west, 295 degrees).

Assessing the wind

Like many other activities that involve wind, in paragliding we use a **windsock** to give us a visual indication of the wind speed. Whereas we do not normally use an official windsock, there are windsocks that actually do indicate windspeed. Depending on the design, this may be three knots per stripe. Therefore, if two stripes are extended, the wind speed is around six knots or 11km/h.

However, most windsocks used at paragliding launches and landings are not meant to be used to give such

Beaufort	km/h	knots (kn)	m/s	Description	Windsock
0	<1	<1	0-0.5	Calm, smoke rises vertically	
1	1-5	1-3	0.5-1.5	Ripples on the water	
2	6-11	4-6	1.6-3.3	Wind felt on exposed skin, wind vanes begin to move	
3	12-19	7-10	3.4-5.4	Wave crests begin to break, scattered white caps, leaves and twigs move	
4	20-28	11-16	5.5-7.9	Branches move, fairly frequent white crests	
5	29-38	17-21	8.0-10.7	Small trees move, many white caps	
6	39-49	22-27	10.8-13.8	Hats and umbrellas blow away, long waves present	
7	50-61	28-33	13.9-17.1	Effort needed to walk against the wind, whole trees in motion	

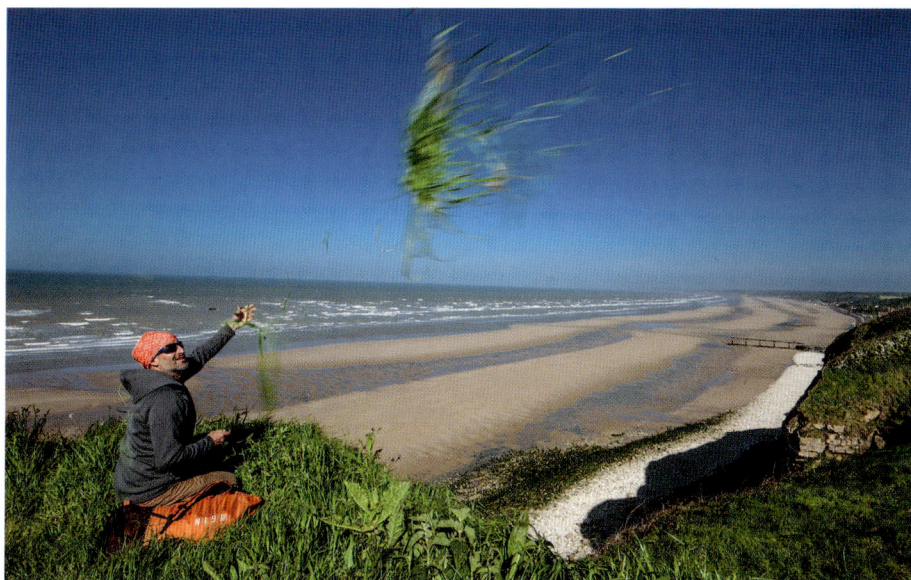

Omaha beach, France. Wind meters, windsocks, streamers, even grass can all help you determine the wind speed. Readings should be taken at the edge of launch, in clean airflow. Always consider the highest reading or strongest gust when making the decision about whether to fly or not. Photo: Jérôme Maupoint

accurate information. Rather they are used as wind indicators, to show the direction and the relative strength. Where there is no windsock you will often find wind **streamers** – these can be as simple as strips of ripstop fabric tied to a bush. Again, they are there to show the direction of the wind.

You will often see pilots assessing the wind in other ways too: picking grass and scattering it to the wind; kicking up dirt or dust on dry launches; holding a scarf or clothing aloft. It is a good idea to get into the habit of feeling the wind when you arrive at launch. This is best done on exposed skin: point into wind, close your eyes and feel the wind on your face.

In time you will develop your senses so that you know what a good flyable wind is compared with wind that is too strong to launch.

Wind speed and canopy size

For a weekend pilot with a standard paraglider, the maximum windspeed on launch that will allow a comfortable launch is 20-25km/h. Once in the air, we can handle a bit more wind because a paraglider's trim speed (hands up, no brakes) is around 38km/h. A headwind of less than 38km/h will therefore still leave us with some forward speed without having to apply the speed bar. For a safe landing however, this is again too much.

With more experience, or with a smaller wing with a faster trim speed, it is possible to expand your wind speed window. Soaring low dunes can be lots of fun with a mini wing of 14m² or smaller, for example, provided you have the skills. Flying a mini wing in strong wind in the high mountains is not a good idea – more wind means more turbulence, and even mini wings don't like that.

185

Types of wind

There are many types of wind that we can distinguish by origin, properties or location. We will discuss some of the main ones that are important for paraglider pilots here. For reference, the wind blows against the **windward** side and on that side we are **upwind**; the downwind side is the **lee**.

1 Meteo wind is what most people mean when they talk about 'wind'. It is the air flowing from areas of high pressure to low pressure. It can be determined by looking at a general weather forecast.

2 Dynamic wind, soaring wind or slope wind is wind that hits a slope and is directed up and over it. We often use this type of wind to fly – paraglider pilots are always looking for into-wind slopes that can be soared.

3 Thermic winds for our purposes are local or regional winds that are driven by the heating of the ground by the sun. The difference in temperature on the ground in turn warms the air, which drives the flow of air. This can happen on a small scale – one side of a canyon baking in the sun compared with the side that is in shade – or a much bigger scale. In general, standard, large-scale weather forecasting models do not predict thermic winds – we need to look at specific soaring forecasts, or understand how they work and predict and recognise them locally.

4 Anabatic winds blow uphill. Anabatic flow is when warm air rises upslope. Paraglider pilots use anabatic winds a lot when flying in the mountains. Anabatic flow is caused by the sun heating the ground, which in turn then releases heat. That warm air rises.

5 Katabatic winds blow downhill. Katabatic flow is the opposite of anabatic and arises when air cools and flows downslope. Pilots often experience katabatic winds when flying in the mountains in winter – snow cools the air and the air flows downhill. Large glaciers can have strong katabatic winds. Hills and mountains also 'turn katabatic' when the sun leaves them in shadow or sets. In this case conditions can go from launchable to a fairly strong backwind surprisingly quickly. Cool air descends.

6 Valley wind is the flow of air that arises when air in a mountainous region warms up and starts to rise. This leaves a void that has to be filled with air from somewhere else, so air starts to flow through the valley, being pulled in to the mountains. Valley winds are typically shallow, filling the lower depths of the valley to a few hundred metres, and will flow up-valley in the opposite direction to any rivers flowing down-valley. Where valley winds set up they tend to do so daily and with a degree of predictability.

7 Sea breeze is the wind that blows from the sea towards the land. During the day the land warms up more than the sea, causing the air to rise. This in turns pulls in more air from the direction of the sea, which creates an **onshore breeze**, the sea breeze. Where sea breezes set up they tend to do so daily and with a degree of predictability.

8 Land breeze is the opposite of a sea breeze. This happens at night when the sea cools less quickly than the land. The warmer air above the sea rises and the void is filled with air from the land. A land breeze or **offshore breeze** blows from land to sea.

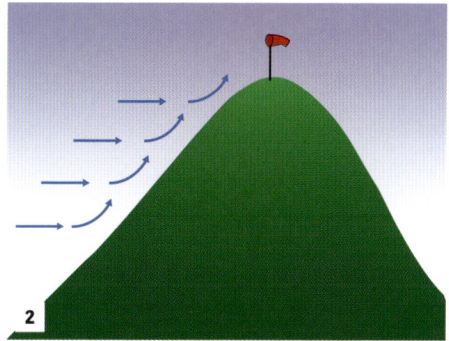

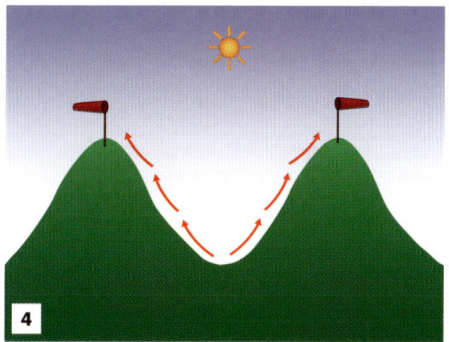

▲ TURBULENT FLOW
Air flows through the landscape like water flows along a river. Like water, where air meets an obstacle the flow will speed up, slow down, become broken and turbulent. Because air is invisible we must interpret the landscape and know the direction of the wind, and how it behaves to stay safe and avoid turbulence. Photo: iStock/Getty

Turbulence

Laminar airflow moves in one direction. When pilots talk of **laminar air** they mean smooth and easy air to fly in. The opposite to laminar air is **turbulent air**. Turbulence is caused when flowing air is deflected, slowed or accelerated by obstacles. A good way to imagine how air behaves as it flows over a landscape is to imagine how water would behave. Watching water flow down a river or stream will give you a good insight into how air behaves when it meets obstacles. Where the river is wide and slow and free of obstacles, the water flows calmly. But when it meets a boulder or a ledge, or where it narrows and is constricted, the flow changes: it becomes turbulent in the lee of the boulder; and it speeds up where it is constricted. Keep this idea in mind as we discuss some forms of turbulence that are important to pilots.

1 **Rotor** is a specific form of turbulence: a standing **vortex**. It is a swirl that rotates in one location, like an eddy in a stream that forms behind boulders. At the lee side of a mountain, you often find a rotor rotating around a horizontal axis. Imagine you are on a north-facing slope just below the top. If the meteo wind blows fairly strongly from the south, you can be sure that a rotor is present at the north side of the hill. You may feel wind in your face. But if you were to try to take off here, you would find it difficult,

turbulent and potentially dangerous. It is therefore essential to know the main wind direction, by reading the weather reports, by putting a windsock on the top of the hill or walking over to the other side of the slope. In this example, you would certainly notice the strong south meteo wind on the other side. You can also find a rotor around a vertical axis where a wind blows through a valley along protruding obstacles such as rocks or outcrops on the valley sides. Behind the obstacles you will find turbulence and possibly rotor.

2 Rotor on a cliff You will also find rotor at the edges of a **cliff** where the slope suddenly drops down vertically – both on top of the cliff and just below the edge. Cliff launches are only advisable for experienced pilots, and even then they should be approached with a lot of thought and care.

3 Turbulence behind objects may extend for quite some distance downwind. Quite how far downwind is an often-discussed point, and some pilots will confidently repeat some sort of formula: "Six (or 8, or 10) times the height of the obstacle," is typical. The reality though is how much turbulence is created downwind depends on the shape of the obstacle and the wind speed. Smoother objects create less turbulence than square-cornered objects: imagine the flow of water around a trout in a stream compared to a brick, for example.

All other things being equal, stronger wind will create more turbulence than lighter wind. Add a strong wind to a square-cornered holiday apartment building on the coast, for example, or a farm building in an empty field, and you can expect the turbulence to extend quite some distance downwind, with potentially dangerous rotors close to the building. As a result it is always wise to avoid landing in the lee of any big obstacles, especially in a strong wind.

4 Leeside thermals are thermals found in the **lee side** – downwind side – of a mountain or feature. The air on the lee side is turbulent. As pilots we can not soar it, but we can, if careful, use the thermals generated in the lee side to fly. These are known as leeside thermals. Typically they are strong – they have to be to rise through the sinking air – and rough, as they are disturbed by the wind. This makes them hard to use: recognising leeside thermals and using them safely requires a lot of experience. Only experienced pilots should fly leeside thermals. When in doubt, avoid flying them.

5 The Venturi effect describes the increase in wind speed that happens when wind has to flow through a constriction, or gap. This is important in paragliding because it means wind speed can double in areas where the landscape constricts or narrows, for example a narrow mountain valley or a pass. Flying into-wind with a wind speed of 20km/h is fine, but if the wind speed increases to 40km/h in the Venturi – gap – then that can be a problem as you will suddenly be going backwards. Because the wind speed is increased, there will be an increase in associated turbulence, both behind the gap and on the sides of the valley. Landing in a Venturi can be difficult because the wind is so much stronger and more turbulent. The Venturi effect is named after Giovanni Battista Venturi (1746-1822), an Italian physicist.

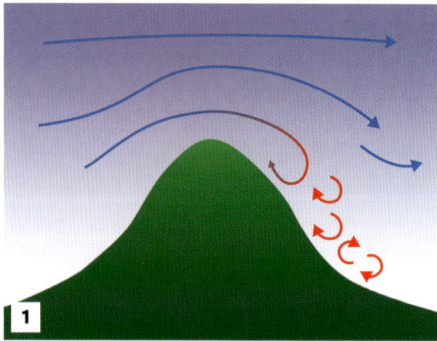

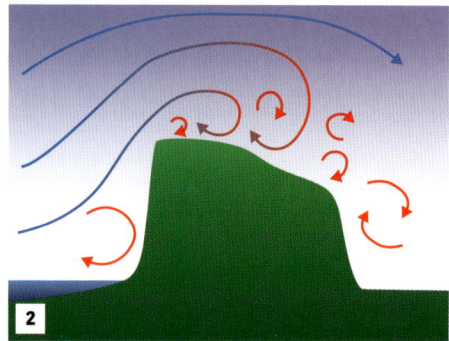

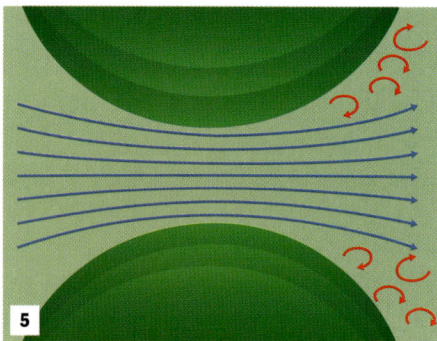

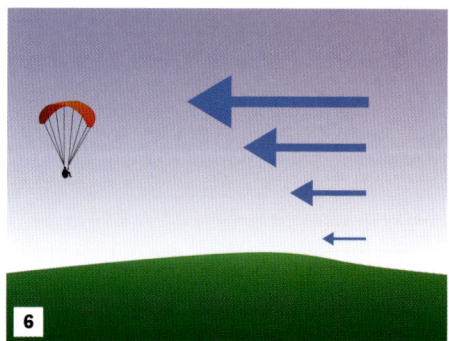

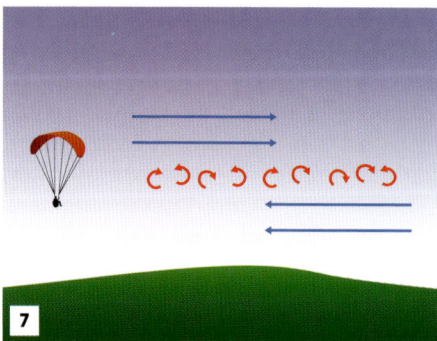

6 Wind gradient is the change in wind speed with changing altitude. Airflow decelerates due to friction with the surface, and we feel this deceleration effect from about 10m above the ground. This is an important effect to note while landing, or even to take advantage of. Especially when landing in strong winds, it may seem as if you lose all groundspeed and can't make it to the landing field. However, the wind gradient will cause the wind lower down to slacken off, allowing you to regain some forward speed and touch down on the desired field after all.

Be aware though that this sudden increase in groundspeed low down can also catch pilots out, causing pilots to land faster and harder than they would normally. This is because the glider can pitch forward when the wind suddenly decreases. With enough height you should catch this dive gently but be careful not to accidentally stall the glider or cause too much pitch-and-dive. The best way is to let the glider fly with enough speed and flare as usual.

In situations where a strong wind gradient is anticipated (looking at the windsock in the landing field will show you what the wind is doing, and if it is hanging straight down or is limp on an otherwise windy day then that is a good clue) you should adjust your approach accordingly. Approach with hands high to keep your speed up and retain energy for the flare. Flare strongly to land. If safe to do so it can be good practice to radio the wind speed in the landing field to your friends in the air.

7 Windshear is the effect of two layers of air moving against each other in different directions. The air at the boundary of the two different winds is turbulent. For example, imagine a lower-level wind is blowing from the north at 10km/h; above it is a mid-level wind blowing from the east at 15km/h. Where the two meet is the turbulent windshear layer. Flying into it, from above or below, will be bumpy.

The greater the difference between the two winds, the greater the turbulence will be. For example, the windshear created by a lower north wind blowing at 10km/h and an upper south wind blowing at 50km/h will be much greater than the first example.

Windshear can be found wherever two air masses with different wind directions meet. For pilots, that means early mornings in the mountains where cool air pools in the bottom of the valley overnight while the meteo wind continues to blow over the top of it; associated with storms and weather fronts; at temperature inversion layers; and in thermals.

Windshear can also occur when two winds have the same direction but markedly different speeds (eg south 15km/h and south 35km/h). In this respect it is like wind gradient.

8 Convergence is found where two winds meet or collide, for example where two valley winds meet; where an onshore sea breeze meets an offshore meteo wind; or in the lee of a hill where the wind meets again after splitting and flowing around it. Where the winds meet the air can go nowhere but up. Paragliders can take advantage of this rising air and use it to climb up in, and in some cases, fly along it for long distances.

Ridge lift

When wind blows against a slope or ridge it is forced up. We call this rising air **ridge lift**. Using ridge lift to stay up in the air is called **ridge soaring**, **slope soaring** or flying in **dynamic wind**. The area where the air rises is known as the **lift band** and is found above and in front of the top of the hill, slope or dune. You will find the best lift when flying in front of the hill, not right above it. The stronger the wind, the bigger the lift band and the stronger the lift – and the further out you find lift.

If you fly too far behind the lift band you will fly into what is known as the **compression zone**. Just above the top of the hill the air has a higher speed than in free space because the air is compressed as it flows over the hill.

The airflow is also not up, like in the lift band, but horizontal. This effect can be felt high above the hill and will be stronger with stronger wind. In stronger winds flying into the compression zone is to be avoided as there is a danger of being blown back in the strong wind. If you do get blown back, you will then be in the lee of the hill and subject to rotor and turbulence. It's not a good place to be.

On sunny days thermals will often form in front of the hill and will mix in with the ridge lift. This allows pilots to use both wind and thermals to climb higher – often much higher than the lift band formed by wind alone. However, it will also be more turbulent than purely laminar conditions.

▼ **RIDGE SOARING**
When soaring in ridge lift you want to stay out front of the hill. This puts you in the best lift, and keeps you away from the compression zone and the turbulence behind the hill. The size of the lift band increases with stronger wind, and gets smaller when the wind is lighter.

Lift band

Compression zone

Rotor and turbulence

Dynamic wind

All the factors described so far come together when you start to assess a potential site for paragliding. There is a lot to take in and learn, which is why it's important your learning is progressive. Here are some examples of actual flying areas.

Trees around take-off can cause turbulence. When the wind is directly on the slope you can expect turbulence behind the trees at the end of the take-off run. When launching here you want to lift off early. When the wind is from the side, eg from the right as shown here (from the pilot's point of view), expect turbulence on the right. With a fairly strong wind, you may also expect turbulence in the air when you are at tree-top height. The wind hitting the trees on the left side may also cause turbulence.

Cliffs create rotor. The stronger the wind, the larger and more turbulent the rotor will be. Some soaring cliffs will require quite a strong wind to soar and may even produce a backwind on take-off. Cliff launching in these conditions requires experience in judging the risks of the rotor.

A gully in the hill as is shown here on the dunes, will not only cause turbulence, but also a Venturi. The wind in front of and in the gully accelerates up to twice its speed. If you fly too close in front of this gully you may be blown back in strong, turbulent wind. Along the sides you can expect turbulent air. When ridge soaring like this always aim to give gullies a wide berth, adapted for the wind speed.

Obstacles and turbulence. A technical top-landing on top of a cliff. The area is large enough, but much of it is affected by rotor. Fly too low over the right side and you will be washed down towards the bushes. Additionally, the trees can cause turbulence in stronger winds from the left. Landing to the left of the trees is not advisable because of obstacles (an old building). Better to land after the trees in that case. This is a good example of why you need to take a look at the landing before you fly.

▲ **MASTERS OF THE ART**
The masters of thermalling are the birds we share the sky with. You will often see birds thermalling – watch them and learn from them. If you are lucky, they may join you in a thermal. Photo: Marcus King

▶ THERMAL FLYING

What is thermal flying?

Thermal flying is the art, skill and science of using thermals to stay up in the air, and to fly distance. If you have ever watched a bird of prey flying in circles as it climbs out from down low you have watched a master of thermal flying in action. Your goal as a paraglider pilot is to fly like that eagle. It's not impossible.

Paraglider pilots regularly fly more than 100km using thermals, often staying in the air for hours. The world record is around 600km over nearly 11 hours. Weekend pilots regularly fly two-hour flights of 50km or more. Thermals allow us paraglider pilots to stay aloft for hours and travel long distances, all without switching on an engine. Thermal flying involves harnessing the energy in the landscape and the atmosphere – and the feeling it gives you is like big-wave surfing, or swimming with wild dolphins. It is a unique experience that ties us directly to nature.

The basics

Thermals form when the sun heats the ground and the ground in turn heats the air. The land is very rarely uniform, so it heats up at different rates. A cliff that faces directly into sun for example, will heat much more than a cool hillside in shadow. A dry, brown ploughed field will heat up more quickly than a wet field full of green grass. A village or town, with all its tiles, tarmac and concrete, will warm much more quickly than a cool forest. We call these **thermal sources**.

Air can not go down into the ground, it can only go up. And warm air really wants to go up, to **release**. To release, a thermal needs a trigger. The **thermal trigger** can simply be the air getting hot enough to overcome its own inertia, or something in the landscape giving it a kickstart – for example, a break in terrain, a line of trees, or a windmill in a field.

Once triggered, the mass of warm air will rise through the surrounding air, cooling as it goes. Your job, as a paraglider pilot, is to fly in that rising air as it ascends. It can be going up slowly (0.5m/s) or very quickly (10m/s). Sometimes the air is smooth as silk, other times it is rough.

Whatever happens and whatever it's like, the game is to hang on in there and get as high as possible. This is harder than it sounds as thermals are of course invisible – you can't see the air rushing skywards. This is probably a good thing – remember the water analogy? You are in a river of air flowing to the clouds!

The way we stay in this column of rising air is to turn in circles. That's the bit that takes quite a long time to learn to do well. In fact you never really stop learning how to climb in thermals – you just have good days and bad days. The fact that no two thermals are ever the same is one of the reasons the sport is so engaging and is what keeps people in the game.

When the thermal has cooled to the same temperature as the surrounding air it stops rising. In fact it might even start to sink a little bit. Quite often as it cools

▼ **DIFFERENTIAL HEATING**

Thermals form when the sun heats the ground differentially, and the ground in turn heats the air above it. Built-up areas, ploughed fields and rocky slopes in the direct sun heat more quickly and are good thermal sources. Bodies of water, forest, and green grassy fields heat more slowly, and are not good thermal sources.

The French Alps in the morning. The sun hits the top of the hills and mountains first, while the valley is still in deep shade. Morning is a good time for still-air flights and hike-and-fly. Photo: Jérôme Maupoint

the air in it condenses to water vapour, forming a cumulus cloud. Sometimes, on what we call blue days, it doesn't.

When you have reached cloudbase it's time to go. You can either drift with the cloud as it floats slowly across the landscape, or you can turn downwind and fly to where you think the next thermal is. Congratulations, you are now flying cross country – the whole world of paragliding is about to open up in front of you.

What time is it?

However, before you get there you need to catch your first thermal. And doing that starts even before you get to the hill.

Regardless of where you are flying, flatlands, hills or mountains, thermals are all generated by the sun. And that means the first thing you need to consider is what time of day it is.

In most of the places we fly you won't find many usable thermals in the early morning or late in the evening. This is because the sun is low and it is heating the land less.

Again, depending on where you are, on a good day in the Alps thermals will typically start to form at about 10am. They grow stronger as the sun rises higher in the sky. As the sun reaches its maximum strength for the day, so the thermals reach their peak strength too. As the sun starts to set, the thermals slowly die off.

When the sun is weaker in the winter, there is less thermic activity too. Thermalling season tends to be spring to autumn.

Where are you?

Remember aspect? If you are in the hills or mountains thermalling is when aspect really matters. We'll assume we're in the northern hemisphere. If you are on a west-facing slope at 10am, then you will be standing in the shade. There will be no thermals formed on the slope as the sun will not be heating the ground.

However, on the opposite side of the valley, which is east-facing and catches the sun, the first thermals of the day will be starting to develop. You could try to launch and fly over to the east-facing valley, but in the shaded part of the valley the air will be sinking and you will descend quickly to the valley floor. Your morning will have been wasted. That is why if you want to fly thermals it is important to check what time it is, and check which direction your chosen take-off faces.

Morning sites include east and southeast-facing sites. Lunchtime and afternoon sites face south. Evening sites face southwest and west.

If you are towing in the flatlands then aspect matters less – what is important is the wind direction for the tow.

▼ AFTERNOON
By mid-afternoon the sun is high in the sky and the thermic circulation is well established. Pilots can fly the sun-baked rocks, and get high using the thermals. Cumulus clouds show how active the air is. Photo: Andy Busslinger

▶ HOW DO YOU FIND A THERMAL?

Flying thermals successfully requires you to find the rising air and stay in it. But rising air is invisible, so how do you find a thermal?

There is an old-school system called the **five-star system**, which awards one star for each of the following points.

Sunshine: Areas in the sun will be warmer than shaded areas, so sunny areas offer a better chance of creating thermals. If the area where you are looking for a thermal is in the sunshine, give it one star.

Wind: The meteo wind can create dynamic lift or can blow thermals onto the slope. If the area is sunny and in the wind, give it a second star.

Terrain: Some terrain creates better thermals than other types of terrain, for example, a dry ploughed field will be better than a green wet field. A rocky mountain slope baking in the afternoon sunshine will be better than a snowfield basking in the same sunshine. If the terrain is good, give it another star.

Clouds: Cumulus clouds are formed by rising air, so if there is a cumulus cloud above the thermal source, give it a fourth star.

Gliders: If you see something climbing, be it a bird of prey or another paraglider, then there is no doubt that there is a thermal out there. That's your fifth star. Go get it!

Photo: Marcus King

Wind
The valley wind hits this slope and goes up

Clouds
This forming cumulus cloud is a sure sign

Terrain
Steep rocky cliffs and gullies act as perfect triggers

Sunshine
This whole mountain is baking in the sun

Gliders
This pilot is not going up yet but keep an eye on them

▲ **FLYING THE FLATLANDS**
When looking for thermals in the flatlands, look for dark fields which heat up, and triggers like lines of trees, buildings or low hills. Cumulus clouds are key – they mark the tops of thermals. Watch the wind, other pilots and look out for climbing birds. Pilots have flown more than 400km from this hill in Manilla, Australia. Photo: Tex Beck

Thermal sources and triggers

As you can see from the five-star system, searching for thermals starts by identifying surfaces that are heated by the sun. Not every surface heats equally well, because of differences in **absorption** and **conduction** of **radiation**, and **evaporation** of water or moisture.

A white surface such as snow will absorb little heat, in fact it will reflect most of it. A wet surface such as damp grass will use the heat first to evaporate the water. Only then does the temperature of the surface rise. Additionally, some surfaces, such as water, conduct heat. This causes the heat to spread out to layers beneath the surface, and not radiated to the air above.

Surfaces that heat up well include dark, rocky-type surfaces like tarmac car parks, towns and villages, cliff faces, ploughed fields and quarries. These types of surfaces absorb heat, warm up quickly, and emit it. In strong sunshine these types of areas nearly always work well as **sources** for thermals.

You don't just need a source for your thermal however – you also need a **trigger**. This is a feature, or a disturbance, that causes the warm air on the ground to release from the surface.

How do you identify a trigger? You look for breaks in the landscape where air can no longer stay attached to the ground.

200

In the mountains, this could be a mountain peak, or a break in the terrain. In the flatlands it could be a line of trees, a farmhouse, working tractor or even a wind turbine in a field. Anything that is going to disturb the airflow.

The trick to working out where thermals will trigger is to identify a likely thermal source, and then look downwind of it for a trigger. That is where the thermal will be.

In the mountains this tends to be more obvious than in the flatlands. Spurs, peaks, ridges are all **breakaway points** for any rising air. Warm air rising up the mountain simply must release – it can not reverse and roll back down the other side.

In the flatlands, identifying the source and trigger can be more difficult. You must look at the rise and fall of the landscape, hedgerows, farms, rivers or streams, and work out which way the wind is blowing.

If there is no wind then the warm air will still release. A ploughed field baking in the sunshine will warm up until there is so much warm air that it just releases without a trigger. There are many flying-club tales of flatland pilots flying low over fields shouting at the sheep to get them moving in an attempt to trigger a thermal. Sometimes it has even worked! Frustratingly pilots are sometimes the sheep – lots of flatland pilots have landed

▼ **READING THE TERRAIN**
Sources and triggers are not always easy to identify, especially in complex terrain like here in the Austrian Alps. Sources include ploughed fields, villages and slopes facing the sun. Triggers include forest breaks and edges, and breaks in the landscape. Forests and rivers are not good thermal sources – they are too cool. Photo: Marcus King

in a field only to see another pilot climb out above them in the thermal triggered by them landing and stirring up the air.

Your first thermals

Assuming you are under instruction for your first day of thermal flying, you will be on the right site at the right time. Your first thermal flights will most likely be either mid-morning flights or late-afternoon flights, when thermal activity is less. This allows you to start to learn to feel what is going on in the air, and what your glider does, and how to respond correctly. It's small steps, and it's progressive.

If you are under instruction you will most likely be on radio. There will also probably be other pilots around, and you will be able to see them turning and going up in thermals. If the air is crowded your instructor might ask you to wait until it is less busy – this is for your safety and comfort as well as that of other pilots.

But let's assume everything is perfect. There are one or two other gliders thermalling in the sky and staying up, so you know you can too. Launch is easy – you've mastered those basics – and you are in the air. The aim of the game is now to find a thermal and to turn in it, staying in it so it carries you up well above take-off height.

The first thing you will notice is that thermic air is more active than non-thermic air. Especially if there is a little bit of wind – for example if you are soaring a hillside while looking for a thermal – then the air can feel quite choppy. It is like sitting in a canoe on a gently flowing river compared with floating on a calm lake.

▶ HONEY AND WATER

The simplest way to imagine where thermals will release from is to look at the landscape and mentally cover it in runny honey, or water. Turn it upside down in your head. Where the honey or water runs off is where the thermals will flow off. Some in great drips, others in small drops. For flying thermals this is one of the best mental models you will ever learn.

Active flying

Fly normally, keep your hands on the brakes, and try to feel what the glider is doing. If the glider pitches forwards, brake it a little bit to keep it overhead. If it pitches back, then let the brakes up and let the glider fly. This is called **active flying**. Keep your movements smooth and deliberate: don't jab or be aggressive and reactionary.

Stay observant – keep an eye out for other pilots and watch your position in relation to the terrain all the time. If you want to look up at the glider from time to time then do so. It might be rustling about more than you are used to and you might like to reassure yourself it is still there. Don't worry, it is. However, don't fly around constantly staring up at it, you need to look where you are going.

▲ **BRAKE POSITION**
This pilot shows good style in thermalling, with weightshift and hands held in a good position. The idea is to turn in the best lift, which means constantly reacting to what the air is doing, and what your vario is telling you
Photo: Marcus King

Your instructor might be telling you where to go over the radio, or you might have had a pre-flight briefing. Either way, let's assume you are now flying towards a thermal.

Thermals are not uniform. They have a **core** and outer regions of less strong lift. We want to get through the outer region and into the core, where the best and smoothest lift is. In the air this outer region of broken lift can feel a little like riding a bike over cobbled streets. This is a good clue that you are approaching a good thermal. If you have a vario then it will start to beep around now. The trick is not to turn immediately. You want to fly on for one, two, three seconds until you can feel and hear on the vario that you are in consistent lift.

Once you are in consistent lift, take a look in the direction you are about to turn, check it's all clear, and then make a smooth, easy turn. Adding some weightshift – leaning over in the harness to the side you want to turn – and then applying the brake will have you turning around in a smooth 360. If you have timed it right, then your full 360-degree turn will be made in smoothly rising lift, and your vario will be making a happy beeping noise.

Suddenly, you know what all the fuss is about! Compared to soaring in ridge lift, or flying top-to-bottoms, flying in thermals is like taking the pulse of the atmosphere. You can feel the power of the environment you are in. In this, paragliding is like surfing and thermals are our waves.

Keep 360-ing, keep looking around for other air traffic, pilots, the terrain, and keep climbing. That grin is going to take a long time to fade!

Centring thermals

Although they are invisible to us, it is useful to imagine the shape of thermals, both so we can get to grips with the theory of how to fly them, and also in the air so we can visualise what is happening around us. It helps to imagine the rising air as a bubble or column.

Once you have found a thermal, turning in circles is the best way to stay in the rising air. The air in the centre of the thermal, or core, rises

fastest. At the edges, the air does not rise as fast, and just outside or at the top of the thermal, the air may sink and be turbulent.

Centring means circling in the best lift. A straightforward way to centre a thermal is to listen to your vario. When the vario indicates lift – beep-beep-beeeep! – fly straight for another two seconds. Then turn towards the side you felt your canopy being lifted. If the lift increases, open your turn and fly on into the strongest lift. When the lift drops off, turn back towards the stronger lift. In this way you will work your way towards the strongest lift – the core.

If the lift remains constant over a full turn, then great, you are going up smoothly. Once established in the thermal you can explore it a bit, opening and closing your turn to see if you can find even stronger lift. Learning to thermal well can take a long time.

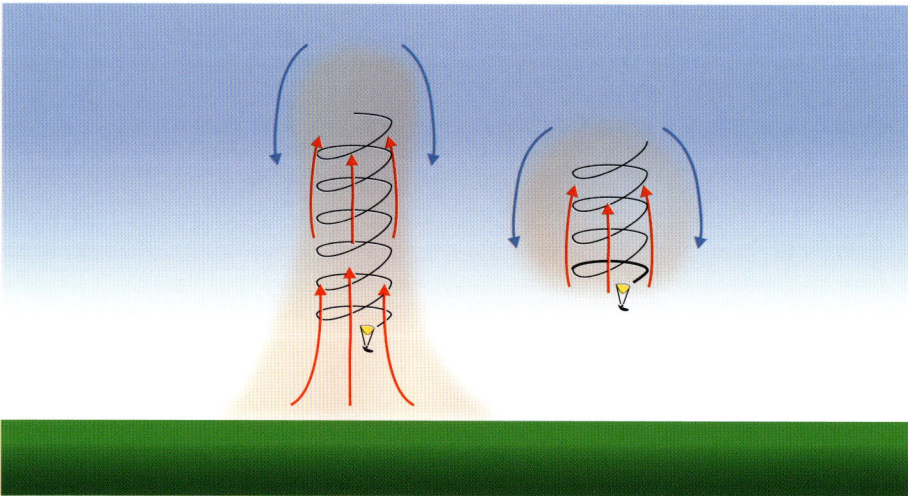

▲ **THERMAL COLUMNS AND BUBBLES**
It can be useful to imagine thermals as columns or bubbles of rising air. This allows us to visualise them in flight, creating a mental map of what they look like. Warm rising air in a thermal is often surrounded by cooler, sinking air. To thermal efficiently we must avoid the sink and stay turning circles in the lift.

▲ **THE VIEW FROM ABOVE**

Imagine looking down on a thermal from above. You enter the thermal at point (**a**), notice light lift and start to turn. You fly out of the lift (**b**), so keep turning to get back into the lift. Flying straight you feel the lift increasing (**c**), before it drops off again at (**d**). You turn back to find the stronger lift and fly all the way through a narrow area of strong lift and out again (**e**). You turn back tightly into the strongest lift in the thermal (**f**). You are in the core.

Thermal character

No one thermal is the same as the next. As discussed already, thermals in the morning and evening are generally weaker than those between 12-4pm. Even at the same site the strength of the day's thermals will also depend on what season it is, the air mass and any changes in the terrain or ground cover (whether snow has fallen, for example, or it has rained).

We tend to talk about weak, light and strong thermals. A **weak thermal** is when we go up at 0.1-1.0 metres a second (up to 60 metres a minute). A **light thermal** would be 1-3m/s; above 4m/s is a good or **strong thermal**. The terms are relative however – both to the day and your location. A pilot on a strong day in the Canadian Rockies will have a very different idea of what 'weak' and 'strong' are compared with a pilot in say, England.

Techniques for flying light and strong thermals differ. In broad, light thermals, for example, you should aim to make smooth, flat turns, losing as little height in the turn as possible. In small, strong thermals however you need to make tighter, steeper turns so you stay in the lift. The key is to recognise the air you are in and then respond appropriately and efficiently.

We also describe thermals as **rough** or **smooth**. This is not necessarily related to how strong a thermal is. You can for example get smooth 8m/s thermals, and rough and ragged 1m/s climbs.

Again, each day will be different. At the same site, yesterday might have been rough but today might be smooth. How do you know what the character of the thermals might be like before you fly?

▶ PITCH AND DIVE

When entering a thermal your glider will pitch back, causing the angle of attack to increase temporarily. This means you are closer to the glider's stall speed than when flying at trim speed. Therefore, when entering a thermal you should keep your speed up, keeping your hands up, not braking too much. If you are already flying slowly, with a higher angle of attack, the increase in angle of attack may cause the glider to stall.

Leaving a thermal the opposite happens. The canopy pitches forwards and the angle of attack decreases. It is wise to brake the dive slightly – active flying – so that the canopy does not shoot too far in front of you. The risk is a collapse, where the leading edge closes. It is not good practice to use your speed bar when leaving a thermal, as this decreases the angle of attack, making it more likely to collapse in this situation.

Wind: strength or a change in direction, wind shear, can make things rough, especially in the mountains. The thermals are blown around and become chopped up and difficult to use.

Stability: stable, hot air can make for rough flying. A high-pressure day with high temperatures can mean it is hard for the thermals to trigger. The thermals struggle to rise through the heavy, treacle-like air mass. When they do, they can be small, 'bullet-like' and demanding.

Moisture: dry or drought conditions can mean strong and rough thermals in the air. Expect dust devils and high cloudbase. After rain thermals can be milder, because the ground is damp and doesn't warm up so quickly.

Time of day: morning thermals can be light, afternoons strong, while evening thermals can be mellow and large.

Time of year: spring thermals are notoriously strong and can be spiky with sharp edges. In this case it's because of the big temperature differentials involved (cold nights, with a sudden blast of hot spring sunshine in the day). In autumn, as the sun is weaker, thermals are typically mellower and smoother.

Watching gliders in the sky will give you a clue about conditions. Are the other paragliders pitching about and having tip collapses (rough air)? Are they climbing quickly straight up (strong thermals, no wind), or are they scratching up slowly while being blown along at an angle (weak thermals, strong wind)?

These are all signs, and a pilot will develop a feel for a 'good' day versus a

When thermalling you want to be leaning into the turn, using weightshift and brake to turn circles. The aim is to tighten in on the better lift, the core, so you climb quickly. Using a vario will help you do this. Photo: Marcus King

'bad' day. Listen to that feeling, and never feel embarrassed about sitting it out if it looks rough or beyond what you know you will feel comfortable with. Equally however, it could be smoother than it looks, so try not to talk yourself out of a good day's flying. It's a balance that you learn as you develop experience as a pilot. Currency also counts for a lot. Pilots who fly twice a week will feel more at home than pilots who fly once a month.

House thermals

House thermals are thermals that are always there at a particular site. They are known about and used by pilots all the time. You might hear pilots talking about their flight plan: "I'll turn left, find the house thermal and get to cloudbase."

Sometimes house thermals will be almost never-ending columns of rising air, being fed from a source below; other times they will pulse, regularly releasing bubbles of warm air. They are regular features of the flying site, and can be depended on (usually!). Because of this they are very good places to learn the art of thermalling. However, they can also be busy as everyone who flies the site regularly will know about them.

Find out if the site you use regularly has any house thermals by asking other pilots or instructors. Tracklogs online can also show you where regular thermals are.

▲ GOING XC
A stunning landscape and a stunning day for flying cross country through the mountains. Plan for success – pack your map, charge your batteries and have an idea of how you plan to get home. Photo: Adi Geisegger

Cross-country flying

If you take off, climb in a thermal, and then fly away from the site you launched from you are flying **cross country** or **XC**. You are venturing beyond the known confines of your local site, heading off on a journey. If you have calculated things correctly and have some luck, you might find another thermal, climb to cloudbase again, and carry on. You will most likely end up landing away from your usual landing field.

This is cross-country flying – and it can be incredibly exciting and very rewarding. Working out how to extend your flight so you can fly further and travel many kilometres can become all-consuming and can seriously change your life.

Learning to fly cross country is a big topic, and is beyond the remit of this book. If you are just learning, it is also a little bit in the future for you as a pilot. Most pilots don't fly cross country until they are qualified; in some countries pilots must reach a certain level of competence and be signed off before they are allowed to fly cross country. Other countries are more informal.

Some pilots never fly cross country at all. Instead they are happy to fly their local site for their entire flying career. If that is the case, that's fine. But I encourage you to at least try flying cross country. It opens the sport up and will take you places you never imagined. There are plenty of XC courses available where, over a week or long weekend, your school, instructors or guides will help you connect the dots between thermals and then pick you up from where you land. Flying as part of a group on a dedicated XC course like that is very enjoyable, and it adds an element of security too.

Whether planning to fly XC on your own or as part of a group, you should approach it sensibly. You need to be prepared:

Know the local site rules and regulations. Flying XC from the site might not be allowed.

Know about the airspace where you plan to fly. Are paraglider pilots allowed to fly there? It could be a military zone, an airport, or a nature reserve. Check before you fly.

Have a map of where you plan to fly. Just as you would never go on a hike into the mountains without a map, you should not fly XC without an air map and ground map.

Know what is next. Are you flying into the mountains? Have you considered valley winds, turbulence, Venturi? Is there a standard route that XC pilots follow? Do you know where the next thermal is likely to be? Look at a map and plan your route.

Know the weather forecast. What is the wind direction and predicted strength for the day? Is the weather suitable for your plan? Is rain expected or will it stay dry all day?

Take the right equipment. As well as the right flying equipment (reserve parachute, vario, GPS, map) you should wear suitable clothing and have enough food and drink for a long day. You might not use it in flight, but you will if you have to walk a long way to the nearest road after landing.

Charge your batteries and take extra ones. Make sure your phone, GPS and anything else is fully charged. Take a power pack to recharge your phone.

Be ambitious, but not too ambitious. Not many people fly more than 15km or 20km on their first XC flight. Set realistic goals for yourself – and try not to make it a number. Saying, "I want to stay in the air as long as I can"; "I want to get to cloudbase and stay there"; or "I want to see what's in the next valley" are much more achievable goals early on.

Know how to get home. Look at the retrieve options before you head off on XC. Knowing there is a train, bus or road in the next valley can really take the pressure off when you are at cloudbase and deciding where to go next.

▶ **FURTHER READING**

Mastering Paragliding by Kelly Farina and *Fifty Ways to Fly Better* by Bruce Goldsmith are packed with advice on flying XC

▲ LAUNCHING WITH A HELPER
If you need a helper to launch and control your glider, then it is probably too strong to fly safely. Practise your groundhandling in a field to get better at managing your wing in strong winds. Photo: Charlie King

▶ STRONG-WIND TECHNIQUES

Strong-wind launches

Strong wind for an average paraglider pilot with a regular size glider is considered to be over 25km/h.

To manage launching in strong wind you need to have full control over a reverse launch. An incorrect launch in these conditions may see you being dragged behind the glider. The easiest way to get good at managing reverse launches in strong wind is to practise them in a flat field or on a beach – groundhandling. This minimises the risk and the stress.

Where you know that the maximum wind speed is within flyable limits, you can move down the slope to launch. The wind will be lighter there than at the top, where it is often accelerating. This works in places like dunes or low hills, but does not apply to mountain environments. Be careful with this technique, but if you do use it, then once in the air push out away from the hill into the wide lift band out front, away from any compression zone. If in doubt, hike to the top of the hill to assess the true wind speed there. If it is too strong to fly, then forget it: even if you launch low down you run the risk of launching into strong wind, going up in the lift into stronger wind, and being blown back behind the hill.

Anchors and helpers

Using a **helper** to **anchor** you in strong wind is one of those techniques that divides opinion. On the one hand, if the helper knows paragliding, and is experienced, they can add weight, provide confidence, and help the pilot stay steady in the strong wind. On the other, if they don't know what they are doing, they can get in the way, pull the wrong thing (reserve handles are not unheard of), and in the worst case scenario be pulled into the air with the pilot. There have been fatalities like this.

If you do anchor someone, or use a helper, then make sure there are no loose straps or speedbars to get tangled up in. Use open, flat hands on straps or harness. Never (never!) hook your arms around the pilot's harness. Never tie in or clip in. The idea of the helper is to help the pilot launch the wing and get it above their head, where it is much less powerful. Release your hold at that point: don't haul people backwards off the hill and into the air (the helper runs the risk of getting airborne too); instead guide them with a gentle push from behind.

Before asking someone to anchor you it is a good idea to consider whether the conditions are suitable for your abilities. If you find launching in strong wind difficult, then it is much better to practise and develop your strong-wind groundhandling skills in a safe place. That way you will grow in confidence and slowly lose the need for an anchor. If it is still too windy, then wait until conditions are better for you.

One useful and non-contentious use of a helper is to have them stand behind the centre of the wing when it is on the ground. This way they can gently lean into the wall with their knees or body and de-power it while it's on launch. This can give the pilot the confidence to manage their take-off without an anchor.

Another possibility for strong winds is to choose a smaller glider. For dynamic soaring, mini wings are popular, although smaller gliders are more dynamic in handling and require an experienced pilot.

▶ WATCH THE BIRDS

Seagulls are reliable wind meters. When the wind is just strong enough to soar, they fly with their wings outstretched (top). But if the wind is stronger, they fold their wings in a bit. For paraglider pilots, this also means strong winds. When soaring the coast they also follow the best lift, and when landing they always land into wind.

Flying in strong winds

You need to consider the effects of strong wind when you are in the air too. If you are flying into wind and the wind is greater than your trim speed you will fly backwards with respect to the ground. This is obvious when you fly close to the ground, but since your airspeed is always constant (so long as you don't apply brakes or use your speed bar), you may not notice your low groundspeed when flying high.

This is where a GPS is useful as it tells you your groundspeed. Although a GPS will not indicate a negative speed, it will tell you when your groundspeed is close to zero. That is a good time to push the speed bar or open the trimmers so you go faster. If that is still not enough to penetrate into wind and you are not above a suitable landing zone, then it may be a good idea to turn around and fly downwind – but only if you have enough height, and of course it depends on the terrain. By flying downwind, you can fly a much greater distance over the ground, increasing your chances of finding a good landing field (or the next area of lift).

When flying turns in strong winds, you will notice a drift in the turn. A 360-degree turn when flying downwind is very small; a turn when flying upwind is large. During the turn, you must correct for this **drift**, especially when flying near obstacles or other gliders. When you are following a set course, you must also correct for the drift caused by the wind by **crabbing** (more on this on p286).

▼ **TURNING WITH THE WIND**
In nil wind the pilot turns an even circle
Flying a 360 while flying downwind results in a small, tight circle
Flying a 360 while flying into wind results in an elongated circle, with a longer downwind leg
Flying a 360 while flying crosswind is like flying downwind, but with a crabbing, sideways, component

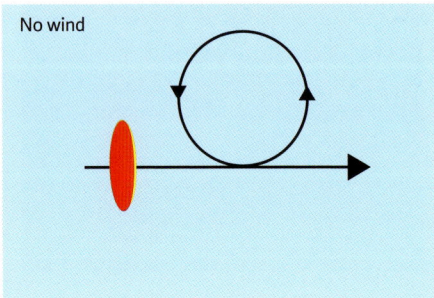

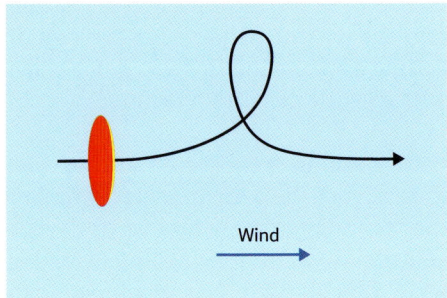

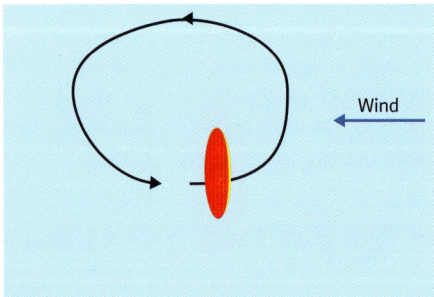

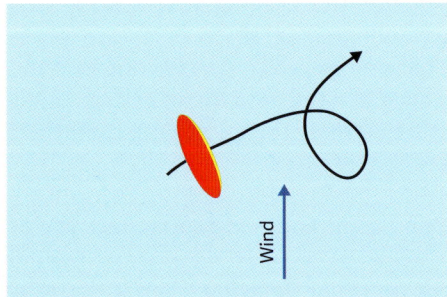

No wind

Wind

Wind

Wind

▲ **FLYING IN A CROSSWIND**
When flying in a strong crosswind you keep your course by adjusting upwind. This is called crabbing.

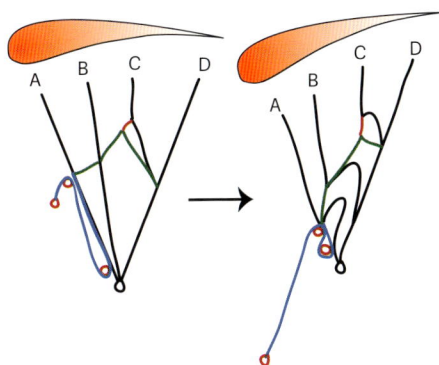

▲ **THE SPEED SYSTEM**
The glider and speed system at trim (hands up), and the glider with its speed system fully engaged (exaggerated for clarity). Pushing the speed bar causes the A- and B-risers to be shortened. The angle of incidence changes so that the paraglider flies faster.

Using the speed bar

The **speed system** is useful in strong wind conditions. How does it work? A line runs from the A-risers through a series of pulleys to the **speed bar** attached to the bottom of your harness. By putting your feet on this bar and slowly stretching your legs, the A-risers are pulled down by up to about 15cm, usually taking the B-risers and sometimes the Cs down a bit as well. The effect is that the angle of incidence of the wing changes, and with it, the angle of attack and the glide angle: the wing points down a bit more, which increases the trim speed of the glider by a maximum of around 15km/h.

The speed system must be adapted to the length of your legs before you take off. Typically you will set it once when you first start to fly your chosen wing and harness combination. The right length is when the speed bar is fully extended with your legs at full, comfortable stretch. When the speed bar is fully engaged the pulleys of the speed system on the risers should be touching or just overlapping.

If you need to adjust the length of the speed bar – it is too long or too short – then land and adjust it by a centimetre or two on each side at a time. Fly and try until you have set the correct length.

On launch as part of your pre-flight checks remember to hook up the speed system so it is connected properly. Many models use Brummel hooks; others use small maillon rapides.

To use the speed bar in flight, put one or both feet on the bar and stretch your legs slowly. You will notice that the wind in your face increases, indicating that your speed is increasing. In level flight engage and release the speed bar smoothly. The wing may start to pitch if you move too quickly. An exception is if you experience a collapse or incident in flight: in that

▲ **TRIMMERS**
Trimmers have an influence on the profile of the wing. Left you see the neutral, 'slow' setting of the trimmers. Right is the profile with the trimmers fully open. Note the length of the lines at the back has increased. With the trimmers open airspeed is higher, but at the same time the wing has less lift and reacts more dynamically to control inputs.

instance, release the bar quickly and then manage the collapse. Return to steady flight before applying the speed bar again.

Beyond holding them lightly, do not pull down on the brakes while flying on speed bar. That would be like driving a car with the acceleration and brake pedals depressed simultaneously. It can also be dangerous and lead to a front collapse. You can steer using weightshift or by lightly pulling on the rear risers.

Your glider manual will include information on the speed system that is specific to that model. You should definitely make time to read it.

Trimmers

Trimmers also change the angle of incidence of the wing, and with it the angle of attack and the glide angle, and consequently the trim speed of the glider. On most wings, the neutral position of the trimmers is fully closed. When you open the trimmers, the rear risers are lengthened. This changes the profile of the canopy, reducing drag and increasing the speed. Lift also decreases, causing a slight increase in descent rate.

Additionally, the change of the profile of the canopy causes the lift to be generated by a smaller portion of the aerofoil, more towards the front. In effect, the canopy will behave like a wing with a higher aspect ratio. It is therefore more sensitive to brake inputs and the flying characteristics are more dynamic.

Be aware that you need to adapt your flying techniques when flying with the trimmers open. Always start by opening the trimmers by one or two centimetres, before going further. Note that not all gliders have trimmers. If yours does, your glider manual will include important information on the trimmer system that is specific to that model and it is important to read this.

214

Strong-wind dune soaring

Soaring in strong winds at low **dunes** is fun but requires some specific preparation. Analyse the situation when you arrive at the dunes. The wind may feel strong, but you need a fair amount of wind to be able to soar. Look at the waves: if you see white caps, the wind is probably more than 20km/h. If sand dust flies over the beach, the wind is more than 25km/h. Finally, look at the seagulls. If these birds soar without flapping, a paraglider can soar as well. Normally, these birds fly with their wings stretched. In strong winds, they fold their wings a bit, so that you see a bend in the middle.

In all of these cases, the wind may be too strong to fly with your regular wing: the one you fly in the hills, mountains or flatlands may be too big. The most important danger is that your trim speed will be too low for the wind speed and you may be blown back over the dunes. Make sure you have a working speed system in place or your trimmers are in the right position.

Secondly, look at the wind direction. With a strong crosswind you need to fly into wind after launch. If you fly downwind, groundspeed can easily reach 50km/h. Since you are still low, this may pose considerable risk. A paraglider's tolerance for crosswind on low dunes is a lot lower during take-off than in the mountains. A crosswind of just 10 degrees requires you to fly away into wind.

In low dunes with strong wind a forward launch is almost never suitable because you risk being blown backwards. You need a good command of the reverse launch. Inflate the glider at the foot of the dune. Once it is under control, you can walk in the direction of the dune

▼ **HIGH-WIND SOARING AT THE BEACH**
Soaring in strong wind at the beach, like here in the Netherlands, needs some special skills, including the ability to manage your glider very well. Look for wind indicators that show the changing strength of the wind, including birds, white caps approaching on the sea, and clouds and rain on the horizon. Photo: Leonard Bik

until you have enough lift to fly away. This is called **kiting**.

When soaring in strong winds, a real risk is being blown back over the top, especially if you get caught in the compression zone or the wind picks up. If you have used up your supply of extra speed by flying with full speed bar or trimmers fully open, and you are still flying backwards, then your options rapidly diminish.

In general the advice is: do not turn around if low. If you do, you will very quickly find yourself flying fast – 50km/h or more – downwind and low. If you land downwind at these speeds you will likely injure yourself. (If this ever does happen, flare very strongly and try to run it out or PLF. If landing on snow or sand you can 'surf' it out downwind, but it's not recommended.)

Instead, continue to fly into wind with your hands up. Keep your hands on your brakes but don't apply brake; get your legs out of your harness and prepare for touchdown. Once you are blown back, you are in the rotor zone and you will be washed down fairly quickly. Manage the glider as you descend, try to land on your feet, do not flare but de-power the glider if necessary.

If you have height however, then turning downwind and making a run for it is a possibility. It depends on the situation – and you will have to think quickly and make decisions. Pilots can often get very high in strong wind at the coast. When they get blown back – perhaps by increasing wind or by flying into the compression at the back of a bowl – then they may well have the option of turning

and making a dash inland to a suitable, open landing area out of the compression zone. Flying downwind at 60km/h for 30 seconds means you will cover 500m across the ground. However, the pilot in that situation must still turn into wind before landing.

Suffice to say the best answer is to avoid this situation in the first place. Maintain larger safety margins in strong wind and fly out at the front of the hill, not on top of it. You will notice that the lift band is much further out front in strong wind anyway. Also, before you take off, make sure that you choose the right wing and set the speed system and trimmers.

Landing in wind

Will I make it to the landing field? If you have a strong headwind this issue may come up. To help answer the question, you can **gauge your height** with respect to objects in the surroundings.

Assume the landing field is behind a row of trees and before a house. While flying towards the landing, check the position of the house with respect to the row of trees. Fly further, check again. Did the house move up with respect to the trees? If it did, this means you will fly over the trees. Did it move down? This means you will not make it over the trees.

If you have established you can't make it to your landing field, look around for other options on the downwind side of the landing field. Remember to look behind you too. If you have enough height, you can turn around and fly downwind. With a strong tailwind you will fly much faster, giving you more options to land. Turn around in time to land into wind.

The best option for landing in a strong wind is to fly a U-circuit. That means you stay upwind of the landing field at all times, while losing your excess height and making sure you can always reach the landing. Another option is to fly figure-of-eights upwind of the landing field while drifting slowly backwards in the direction of the landing. The large disadvantage of this method is that you are not facing your direction of travel.

In strong winds, obstacles cause turbulence over large distances behind them. Exactly how far depends on the shape of the object (sharp edges are bad) and the strength of the wind. Pay particular attention to turbulence and your glider close to the ground. Wind gradient is where the wind speed decreases close to the ground. This may work to your advantage, giving you some forward groundspeed at the last moment when you thought you were going to be landing backwards. But it may also catch you out and cause the glider to suddenly pitch forward when close to the ground. Face into wind and keep your hands high before touching down.

Flaring in strong wind is different to flaring in light or medium winds. If you land gently in a strong wind and then apply a full flare the glider is likely to act like a kite and pull you off your feet backwards. Keep your hands up and turn around quickly while walking towards the wing. Then grab the rear risers and pull the canopy down with these; this requires a bit of practice.

▼ CAN I MAKE IT?
The landing field is over the trees in front of the house. During your approach, this is what you see from the three different positions: A Gauge the position of the house behind the trees. B The house has moved up relative to the trees: you will make the landing. C The house has moved down and disappeared behind the trees. You will not make it over the trees. Best to find a different landing.

217

▲ **BIG EARS AND BIG BIG-EARS**
Test pilot Russell Ogden demonstrates big ears and big big-ears. Big ears is the most basic descent technique you will learn. You simply fold in the wingtips by pulling on the outer A-lines. Photo: Marcus King

▶ DESCENT TECHNIQUES

You may find yourself in a situation where you want to descend quickly. For example, you might be high in a valley when you see a rainstorm approaching and it seems wise to land before you get caught. Or you might find yourself in strong lift under a cloud just going up and up (we call this 'cloud suck').

There are several techniques that you can employ to get down quickly. In all cases it is important to remember that you are piloting your glider through the manoeuvre. You are not a passenger. You decide how to fly your wing, how to descend, and how quickly to come down.

Not all the **descent techniques** described will be suitable for every situation, pilot or glider, but the more techniques you master the more choice you have. This is of course not a do-it-yourself guide, so it is important to get proper instruction in these techniques. Apart from the basic ones, these descent techniques are all taught post-qualification on a **safety course** – called a **manoeuvres course** or **SIV course**, from the French term Simulation d'Incident en Vol which means Simulation of Incidents in Flight. Carried out over water while wearing a life vest, with a safety boat and instructor on hand, these are run by experienced SIV instructors and usually take three to five days to complete.

Big ears

In steady flight in still air most paragliders have a descent rate of about 1m/s. To increase this descent rate to about 2-3m/s the easiest and safest technique is to apply **big ears**. This is usually taught in schools and you will learn it before you qualify as a pilot.

It's called big ears because the pilot folds in both wing tips of the glider, which then flap about and look a bit like ears on the side of the wing.

By pulling big ears you decrease the surface area of the canopy by folding back the tips. The drag of the wing increases and the descent rate of the paraglider increases to about 2-3m/s.

Many wings have separate outer A-lines to facilitate pulling big ears. You should read your paraglider manual for specific advice on this technique as they do differ, but typically a pilot will reach up to the dedicated A-line and pull it down. It is good practice to do one ear and then the next. After the wing has stabilised you can steer by weightshifting.

The advantage of this technique is that you continue to fly forwards, away from the strong lift or the rainstorm. You also maintain directional control and can fly relatively normally. With experience, you can even land with your big ears in.

To reset, simply let go of the A-lines and wait. The big ears on most gliders will pop out or slowly unfurl. If they don't, give each side a pump on the brakes, first one then the other, to encourage them.

Big big-ears

Pulling **big big-ears** involves reaching up higher and pulling down more A-line. The descent rate is about 4m/s. Always do one first and then the other. If you pull both down at the same time you increase the risk of creating a frontal collapse.

▼ **BIG EARS ONBOARD VIEW**
Pulling in big ears and big big-ears on the same glider. You can pull in big big-ears by reaching higher on the outer A-line, or like the pilot has done here, pull in the two outer A-lines, thus collapsing more of the wing tip.
Photos: Russell Ogden

▶ B-LINE STALL

A **B-line stall** is a way of deforming the paraglider so it turns into a parachute. You do this by pulling straight down on the B-risers, which pulls in a crease over the full span of the canopy. The result is a descent rate straight down of about 7-8m/s.

Many instructors consider it an out-dated technique and don't like it, because modern wings have fewer lines and more plastic inserts than they used to, but it is still discussed and taught. It is possible you will only ever do one on an SIV course.

To B-line, you hold both B-risers at the maillons and pull them down slowly, evenly and symmetrically. The glider will crease along the span and your airspeed will reduce drastically. Then you just sit and hold it in as you descend. If the glider starts to snake or rosette you have pulled too deep. To release, you let the B-risers up, the crease disappears, and the glider starts to fly again.

B-line stalls can be useful for pilots who are not comfortable with spiral dives. However, because there is no option to steer and there is no forward speed instructors will tell you that big big-ears and speedbar is a better way of getting down quickly. Not all gliders are suitable for B-line stall, so read your glider manual to find out.

You can also apply big big-ears by pulling down the outer two A-lines on each side. You obviously need a wing that has at least three A-lines to execute this technique, otherwise you will simply collapse the entire leading edge of the glider. Some gliders have only two A-lines, which makes this method of pulling big big-ears unsuitable. However, in that case standard big ears will already be quite big.

Big ears and bar

Once your big ears are in you can also apply the speed bar. Most gliders sink faster, about 1m/s extra, when the speed bar is fully applied. Once big ears are in and the canopy is stable, slowly push the speed bar while keeping your hands high (brakes off). This increases your forward speed and decreases the tendency for a stall.

To release, slowly release the speed bar again, then let go of the A-lines and wait until the ears inflate. **Big big-ears with speed** may result in a descent rate of around 4-5m/s, while maintaining an increased forward speed. This is a good technique to use when trying to escape the influence of a large cloud as it allows you to descend and also cover a lot of ground while flying forwards. Only apply the bar when the big big-ears are in and stable, and never try to pull the ears with the speed bar engaged. If you can not remember whether to apply speed bar before or after applying big ears, then remember it this way: "That pilot friend of yours? He always goes to the bar last!"

Spiral dive

The **spiral dive** is a series of tight 360-turns. It is an extremely effective way to lose height quickly but involves speed and **G-force**. A series of steep 360s (-6m/s to -8m/s) will usually be enough.

◄ **SPIRAL DIVE**

A test pilot, executes a perfect spiral dive on an intermediate glider. Descent rates can reach 18m/s or more in a strong spiral dive. They can be a lot of fun but they need proper training
Photo: Marcus King

▲ A SPIRAL TO THE RIGHT
The pilot has applied right brake and is also weightshifting to the right. In a spiral dive you can see your glider – to avoid getting dizzy focus on the inner wingtip. Always be aware of your height and speed. Photo: Russell Ogden

A moderate spiral will see you descend at 10m/s; strong **nose-down spiral** dives (where the leading edge is pointing directly at the ground) will see you descend at 15-20m/s. One point to note is that the spiral dive takes you straight down. So although you regularly hear tales of pilots "spiralling down out of cloudsuck", this is rarely a good technique as all the pilot is doing is spiralling down in strong lift while staying in the same region of strong lift. As soon as they stop spiralling they will get sucked back up.

A better approach if caught by strong lift may be to use big big-ears and speed bar (-4-5m/s) to fly away from the lift into less strong lift or even sinking air. Then, fly tight 360s or a mild spiral to get down.

The harness and harness settings can also influence how a glider behaves in a spiral. Your glider manual will have specific advice on this for spiral dives. Moving outside of manufacturer tolerances can create unpredictable results, such as **spiral neutrality** where the turn remains constant or even **spiral instability** where the spiral actually accelerates after releasing the brakes. Always be prepared to fly out of a spiral dive using opposite weightshift and outside brake.

Spiral dives also come with a warning. They can be easy to do, and fun. But they are also an advanced manoeuvre, need appropriate training, and should not be flown low. In untrained hands a spiral dive can go wrong; pilots can lose consciousness or freeze, overwhelmed by the forces and sensory experience. In these cases, tragically, the results are often fatal. Always remember, you pilot *in* to a spiral dive and you must pilot *out*.

That said, once properly taught and mastered spiral dives give you a real get-out-of-jail card for getting down quickly. It is beyond this book to teach you how to spiral: train progressively with an instructor, preferably over water. Here, we describe what the steps might be that they will teach you.

Your first spiral is a tight 360 where you gradually apply a bit more inside brake. The speed can build quickly: within two turns you will feel the G-force pushing you into your harness. Modulate speed with outside brake. Maintain situational awareness; monitor height and speed.

To stop the spiral, give yourself plenty of height (300m above ground or more), centre yourself, pull a little bit of outside brake and slowly release the inside brake. The glider should start to slow down and by flying a few 360s you will be able to bleed off the energy. Manage any pitch on exit, and return to level flight. Don't just suddenly release a spiral dive: you'll get big pitches and collapses. Pilot out of the turn. You can gradually start to build stronger spirals but only if you master the exit and manage the pitch.

Be aware! In strong (greater-than 14m/s) nose-down spiral dives (also known as '**over the nose**' spiral dives) it is possible for some gliders, including beginner wings, to **lock in**. That means that even when you release the brakes the glider continues to spiral, often increasing in speed. Locking-in is why this manoeuvre

can be dangerous, because it is here that the pilot, who was expecting the spiral to slow down, can be taken by surprise and freeze. G-forces quickly increase to over 5G. Everything happens fast and 300m of height is suddenly less than 20 seconds.

The correct thing to do if this happens would be to pull the outside brake and also try to weightshift that way. This slows down the glider to a normal spiral, which is exited as usual. In a locked-in spiral dive you are likely to be completely disoriented, and might not know what is inside or outside. As an emergency reset, pull both brakes progressively until you slow down, then bleed off the energy.

Approach spiral dives with care. Learn progressively, and build up to stronger spirals. That way tolerance and experience build too.

▶ G-LOC

G-LOC is G-force induced loss of consciousness. It happens when the blood drains from your brain, causing **blackout**. The first sign is your vision 'greying out' and narrowing. If this happens stop and return to level flight. Paraglider pilots can train for G-force on the **G-Force Trainer**, a mechanical spinning arm with a paraglider harness at the end of it. *gforce-trainer.com*

Wingovers

Wingovers are an elegant series of left and right turns, getting higher as you progress until you fly over the wing. It seems easy enough to connect left and right turns together, but in reality, perfectly performed high wingovers in a long series are one of the hardest manoeuvres to master.

Wingovers are no descent technique, nor an emergency manoeuvre. Rather, besides being a lot of fun, wingovers teach you perfect control of the three axes around which a paraglider moves: pitch, roll and yaw, and how to connect these three together fluently.

Mastering wingovers starts by weight-shifting in the right rhythm. Keeping your hands high, move your full body weight to one side, wait for the glider to turn, then shift fully to the opposite side.

As you reach the top of each turn and start to dive back the other way, shift your weight fully to the opposite side. Push down on your seatplate on the high side, swing the other way, and repeat.

Next, you can start adding a small amount of inside brake: just when the glider accelerates in the turn, help it around the corner with a bit of brake. Be ready to slow down the outside with the brake, as your wingovers are now getting high to the point of collapse. Release both brakes when you start to travel down, and repeat.

When starting to add brake, wingovers can get messy when executed wrongly. Practise with an instructor, over water, with a life vest and a rescue boat at hand.

Photo: Marcus King

225

▲ KNOT IN THE LINES
A glider in Australia with a knot in the lines on the right-hand side. A knot can pull in the glider, deform it and disrupt the airflow over the wing. If it doesn't come out, the best advice is to head to the landing field. Photo: Tex Beck

▶ INCIDENTS IN FLIGHT

Knots in the lines

Sometimes gliders will get a **knot** or a twig stuck in their lines. Pre-flight checks should eliminate this, and you should spot it and abort before you take off.

If you do launch with a knot then the first thing you know about it may be that the canopy seems to pull in one direction.

If this happens, it is important to maintain your heading safely. Don't panic. Use weightshift, and if safe to do so the controls, to steer away from the hill into clear air, avoiding obstacles and other pilots.

Once you are in free space, look up at the knot. If it is a small knot in one of the rear lines or brake lines, this will not usually cause a lot of trouble other than the need to apply a continuous course correction.

You can try to clear the knot by pulling a big ear on the side with the knot and pumping it out. Or try a short sharp pull on the riser line which attaches to the knot. If the knot stays in, then you should go to land – further attempts will most likely be futile and will often just tighten the knot.

Head towards the landing field, use weightshift to stay on course and stay light on any brake inputs. Your glider will have a natural turn towards the side with the knot. You can use this to your advantage, turning towards the knotted side as you approach the landing field. Turning against the pull of the knot may result in a stall or spin.

A knot in the A or B-lines is potentially more serious than a knot in the C or D-lines. Your descent rate may be high or you might need a lot of correction to keep your course. More experienced pilots might try to clear the knot by inducing a side collapse, but this is an advanced manoeuvre – only try it if you are confident. Check whether you can make it to your landing field. If you won't, start looking for an alternative.

Knots and twigs in lines should always be treated with caution. Check your glider for them before you take off, and abort the launch if you have one.

Broken lines

Not all take-offs are from smooth grassy surfaces. If a line gets stuck on a rock or branch during inflation, it may break. A **broken line** is unwanted but not usually a problem.

First, keep your course, avoid obstacles and other pilots and fly away from the hill. Then look up and identify the problem. Weightshift is your friend here – use it to maintain course.

If your brake line is broken you can still steer, brake and land with the rear risers: cup the riser in your hand at the maillon, and pull gently towards you, not down.

If one of the C or D-lines is broken, treat it in the same way as a knot and head for the landing field.

A broken A or B-line is rare. This is because it is usually the rear lines that get stuck during take-off. If you do break an A or B-line be aware that the glider may react violently. Maintain your course, identify the problem and the behaviour of the glider and find a safe place to land.

▶ **WET GLIDER**

If your glider gets wet in the air, by flying in rain for example, then land safely and soon. Don't apply big ears as this adds drag and increases the risk of going into deep stall. The wet wing can also stick to itself, making it hard to exit big ears. Simply fly down, hands high, and land normally.

For experienced pilots a good tip is to apply half speedbar as you fly to the landing zone. Keep the bar applied and hands high all the way down until you are ready to flare. With a **wet glider** there is a danger that when you release the speed bar the glider goes into deep stall. If that happens on your landing approach at 30m then you won't have time to sort it out – that's why you keep the speed bar on all the way to the moment you flare. If you are high and your glider gets wet but you fly into clear air, then you can apply speed bar and fly fast so the wing dries out. After a few minutes you will be ok.

▲ **DEEP STALL**
In a deep stall the glider loses all lift because the air is not flowing fluidly over the canopy anymore. The wing has no forward speed and descends like a parachute. The pilot will feel and hear no wind and the glider is sensitive to stall and spin. Put your hands up and wait four seconds to recover normal flight. Photo: NOVA / Marcus King

Deep stall

A **deep stall** is a situation in which the glider looks like it is flying but in fact has no forward airspeed and instead acts like a parachute. It is also called a **parachutal stall**.

The descent rate is about 5-8 m/s, but a deep stall is not a suitable descent technique because of the instability of the canopy.

In a deep stall the chances that you will **spin** the wing (make one side turn backwards quickly) are high. Using the brakes to try to control the wing in the normal way also won't work – the glider is likely to react to brake input by stalling.

A tell-tale sign of a deep stall is the absence of wind in your face and a lack of wind noise. In some countries beginner pilots must fly with a streamer or ribbon tied to their risers. If this streamer ever floats upwards instead of backwards but the canopy still looks inflated, you are most likely in deep stall.

Ways that a pilot can enter a deep stall by mistake include:

A pilot can induce a deep stall by braking too much and flying too slowly. It can also occur after a slowly released B-stall.

A wet glider is also susceptible to deep stall. Water droplets on the top surface

228

of the glider disrupt the airflow over the canopy (**flow separation**), causing a decrease in lift. The forward speed decreases to zero and you enter a deep stall. New gliders with shiny new fabric seem particularly susceptible to this – the water seems to bead more easily, rather than be absorbed into the fabric. This is why flying in rain (or fog, mist, drizzle, snow or cloud) is never a good idea.

Cold air causes a deep stall to occur at higher airspeed. This can be an issue when tow-launching on a cold winter's day, because the angle of attack is already fairly large while connected to the tow.

Pilots used to think old gliders would enter deep stall because the cloth had become porous with age. While this is a possibility, the main reason old canopies can be susceptible to entering deep stall is likely to be because they are out of trim (their lines are not the right length, through shrinkage or stretching). This means they can have a higher stall speed and can enter a deep stall more easily.

Recover from a deep stall by keeping your hands up for four seconds to give the glider time to fly. A modern beginner or intermediate glider should recover by itself. If this doesn't work, then push the speed bar. This reduces the glider's angle of attack, pushes the nose down a little, and it reconnects with the airflow and starts to fly again. You can also push on the A-risers; it does the same thing.

The key is to wait those four seconds. In cases where pilots in deep stall get into trouble they have usually reacted too early and started to pull on the brakes. The result is the glider can enter a full stall and react violently.

▶ YOUR FIRST SIV COURSE

Going on an **SIV course**, also known as an advanced manoeuvres course, is a good way to gain skills and confidence in your glider. Over three to five days an instructor will guide you through some or all of the exercises described here, from pitch exercises to full stall and spiral dive.

They take place over water, and pilots are equipped with a life vest and radio. The instructor is below, in a boat, talking you through the exercises over the radio. Depending on how big the site is, you will have two or three flights a day. Each will include a thorough briefing and your flights may be filmed, so you can talk them through later at a debrief.

Popular sites for SIV include Ölüdeniz in Turkey, Lake Annecy in France and Lake Garda in Italy. Tow launch SIV courses above lakes are also popular.

▲ **SIDE COLLAPSE AND RECOVERY**
The glider on the left has a 70% side collapse, or asymmetric collapse. Almost immediately the collapse starts to roll out with no pilot input and the glider recovers. Beginner and intermediate paragliders typically behave well following side collapses. Photo: Marcus King

Side collapse

Also known as an **asymmetric collapse** a **side-collapse** is where one side of the canopy collapses: the leading edge closes and the tip folds backwards. It does this because the airflow is turbulent or has been disrupted, usually because you are flying downwind of something creating turbulence, in thermic air or flying through a shear layer.

Paragliders are designed to do this and as a result, in typical recreational flying conditions, a side collapse is usually not a problem. Beginner (EN-A) and intermediate (EN-B) paragliders are designed to recover automatically. You simply need to put your hands up so

there is no brake applied and allow the glider to re-inflate.

However, that doesn't mean you should just sit there and do nothing. You should think about and monitor three things:

1. Maintaining a clear course
2. Avoiding obstacles
3. Clearing the collapse

The glider will start to turn towards the collapsed side, so you may need to counter the turn by weightshifting to the other side and applying some opposite brake to steer away from any present dangers, for example other pilots or terrain. The aim is to establish level flight again.

230

Often you will feel a collapse and hear it open again with a rustle or bang before you have time to look up and see it. By the time you do look up there is nothing to see.

But sometimes a collapse can be slower to clear. In this case you can apply a smooth pump of the brake on the collapsed side. It's not a stab, it's a pump. This pushes air from the back of the glider to the front, and will open the collapsed cells.

There are different degrees of side collapse. Pilots talk about **tip collapses** where just a few cells in the tip fold in before unfolding again quickly. Larger collapses are discussed in percentage terms: a 25% or 50% collapse. These are the ones that will be discussed (and sometimes exaggerated!) over post-flight beers or coffees. Anything over 50% is considered large and is unusual.

Side collapses are dangerous when they happen close to the ground, perhaps in turbulent or thermic conditions, and the pilot is turned suddenly and unexpectedly towards the terrain. This is one of the leading causes of accidents in paragliding, and is why recovery from side collapses is taught on SIV courses where pilots learn to maintain course and stay calm and collected.

Another danger following a side collapse is that a glider gets a **cravat**, in which case that will need to be dealt with as outlined in the box on the right.

Note that all collapses will be more aggressive if they happen when the speed bar is applied. If you get a collapse while on bar, release the speed bar.

▶ CRAVATS

If glider fabric gets folded through the lines, this is a **cravat**. Typically they happen during recovery from a stall or spin. When the glider recovers some of the fabric gets caught in the lines. As the wing re-inflates everything gets tied up tightly. While you will not fall out of the sky, the danger is the glider will start to turn towards the cravat. If not stopped this can result in an unwanted spiral or a sharp turn into terrain.

If you get a cravat, first maintain your course. Use weightshift and lean away from the cravat. There are then several ways you can try to clear a cravat. First, a deep full pump (or series of pumps) on the brake on the cravatted side to empty the air from the tip. Second, look up at the cravat and find the stabilo line (the line that goes to the very wingtip, do not confuse it with your outer A-line). Pull on it until you feel tension. This will often help the cravat work loose. Third, pull in a big ear sharply; this can release the tension enough. Finally, a full stall will usually clear it (experts only).

It is ok to land with a cravat. Think of it as a large knot. Use weightshift and small control inputs to reach a safe landing. Use the natural turn of the cravatted wing, rather than flying with lots of opposite brake. If you start to spiral, don't hesitate to deploy your reserve before you lose control.

▲**FRONT COLLAPSE**
A big front collapse. The leading edge of the paraglider has lost pressure and folded under itself. With no input from the pilot the glider will recover within four seconds. Photo: Marcus King

Front collapse

Also known as a **symmetric collapse** or a front tuck, a **front collapse** occurs when the centre of the leading edge collapses. The leading edge tucks under the glider, leading to an immediate loss of lift.

This makes the glider pitch back. It then starts to re-inflate from the centre almost immediately and will pitch forwards as it regains normal flight. If the collapse is a big one this recovery can be quite forceful and fast.

Failing to control the pitch of your glider as it dives forward is the most common cause of a front collapse. As with a side collapse, front collapses usually happen in strongly turbulent air: flying in thermals, in the lee of obstacles or through a shear layer.

Again, like side collapses, your glider is designed to collapse like this and is tested for it as part of the certification process. Beginner (EN-A) and intermediate (EN-B) gliders are designed to recover automatically. In theory you simply need to put your hands up, and allow the glider to re-inflate.

However, gliders are tested in still air, and in real-world flying in active air putting your hands up does not mean you simply sit there and rock about until your glider steadies itself. You need to think about:

1. Maintaining a clear course
2. Clearing any secondary side collapses
3. Returning to level flight

If the collapse does not clear automatically after a few seconds, you can help push air through the cells of the glider by applying a short pump on both brakes.

However, if you do this too strongly or in a panicky way you can stall the glider, leading to a cascade of further events. This is why it is better to try to be calm and smooth and wait, monitor and then clear the collapse.

As the glider recovers it will pitch and surge forward as it gathers speed for normal flight. Allow the glider to do this – don't try to drag the glider back under control with a lot of brake, let it fly.

Paragliders are more sensitive to front collapses when you fly with the speed bar applied. This is because the glider has a lower angle of attack – the nose is pointed down more – so it is more susceptible to taking a whack from turbulent air. If you have a front collapse at full speed you can expect it to be more dynamic than having a front collapse without speed bar.

A common scenario for front collapses is leaving a thermal with full speed bar applied. In this instance you will fly through descending and possibly turbulent air at the edge of the thermal.

When leaving thermals it is best practice to leave them at trim speed, and then apply the speed bar when getting established on glide. If you have a front collapse while the speed bar is applied – release it!

An SIV course is the best place to learn how to deal with front collapses. With instruction and with height over water you will learn how to handle them and yourself. Learning about collapses in this controlled environment means if or when you experience one in flight it can be managed safely.

▲ **SPIN**
In a spin half the glider is stalled while the other half keeps flying. The glider spins on its yaw axis, above the pilot.
The danger of a spin is that it may be followed by a twist – where the risers start to twist up. With twists, the pilot
loses control of the glider. Photo: Marcus King

Spin

A **spin** is where one side of the paraglider is stalled while the other half continues to fly. This causes the glider to rotate – to spin – on its vertical axis very quickly. In some cases, the spin is so quick that the pilot does not follow, causing the risers to **twist**.

Spins are usually induced by mistake, if you brake too deeply on one side. This can happen if you are flying slowly when thermalling, for example, or when ridge soaring with lots of brake on. Pilots flying close to the ground while soaring with a crosswind often find they fly with lots of brake on while on the downwind leg. This is because they feel they are flying too fast. When it comes to turning back into wind they apply more brake on one side, and spin the wing. Because they are low this can mean a strong impact with the terrain.

Given clear air and time a spin will stop when the pilot puts their hands up and allows the stalled side to recover. Be prepared to check any dive. The danger with a spin is with a twist: the risers and lines can twist together so tightly that you lose control of the brakes and brake lines.

If there is one twist and the glider is recovering you can try to swing your legs and rotate out of the twist, but if you have lots of twists and the glider is not recovering then there is a problem. Twists are a common cause of pilots throwing their reserve as having twists makes it very hard to regain control of the glider. If you are twisted and out of control, do not hesitate to throw your reserve.

In general, spins are not something that you will practise outside of an SIV course. On an SIV course you will practise recognising the point at which the glider starts to spin, and recovering from it. The onset of a spin is recognisable because you feel the brake pressure suddenly drop: bring your hands up quickly and let the glider gather airspeed and fly.

Note that in some countries a spin is also called a **negative spiral**, since you are turning backwards.

▶CASCADE AND AUTO-ROTATION

Given the right mix of circumstances, usually involving mis-timed or incorrect pilot inputs (also known as **over-control**), a combination of multiple collapses can occur, one after the other. We call this a **cascade**, after cascade of events. As cascades are often caused by over-control, often the answer to solving them is to stop trying to control the glider so much: if you have enough height put your hands up and allow the glider to recover and fly.

Conversely, if you are unable to control your wing after a collapse, perhaps because of twists (pictured), you can enter **auto-rotation**. This is where the glider spirals out of control on its own with little or no pilot input. In this situation, with no control over the glider, often the best course of action is to deploy your reserve.

The good thing is that situations like this can be anticipated and trained for as part of an advanced pilot's progression. This is what SIV courses are for. They introduce the pilot to difficult situations in a controlled and safe way, so the pilot can learn what they feel and look like. That way, if something does happen in flight, then the pilot is ready to deal with it, stopping a single incident from developing into an uncontrolled event.

Full stall

A **full stall** is where you fully apply both brakes in flight. This slows the glider down, airflow over the glider is disrupted, the wing stops flying and falls back behind you. It is like flaring when you come in to land, but you're doing it in flight.

There are a few different ways to full stall a glider, but they all follow the same principles. The first is you want to be compact and stable in your harness, so you don't flail about or twist. The second is that the exit is important: there is a lot of energy in a full stall and the glider will 'pulse' because it wants to fly. The critical part is to not release the full stall immediately, or if the glider is behind you. Allow the rocking back motion, hold the brakes down until the wing has come back above the head or is in front, then you can the release the brakes.

The third is that learning to full stall is part of a progression towards learning about back fly. **Back fly** is the stable, narrow position between full stall and deep stall. You get there from full stall by raising your hands slowly until the glider stops pulsing and is in a stable position.

Full stalls, searching for back fly, and back fly are advanced manoeuvres and should be approached step-by-step. Learning is best done on an SIV course, above water and with radio instruction.

Separately, knowing where the stall point is on your glider is extremely useful, as it allows you to be confident in using the full range of the brakes. Groundhandling is a good place to start.

Outside of acro and SIV the full stall is useful in flight as a 're-set' when other things have failed, eg to clear a cravat. If you want to fly acro, it is also a foundation manoeuvre. Acro pilots will train the full stall 300-400 times to become proficient.

▲**WATER LANDING**
Splashdown! This pilot threw his reserve during an SIV course and came down safely to land in the lake. The rescue boat was on hand to recover him within seconds. As it is fresh water the gear just needs to be dried out and the reserve repacked – then he can go and do it all again. Photo: Andy Busslinger

Tree landings

It's unfortunate but true that pilots do land in trees. If you ever get caught out and have to **land in a tree**, then pick your tree and land in it properly. Choose a young tree with lots of leaves and small branches. Coniferous trees are said to be softer than deciduous trees, but the latter usually have a denser canopy. Fly straight towards it: if you snag a wingtip on a tree you may be flung around and into it at speed.

Prepare for impact and land purposefully in the tree. Release your flare so that the glider flies over the top of the tree, preventing you from falling down one side. Protect your face.

Hang on to the largest branches and secure yourself to the tree; some pilots who fly in forested areas carry a sling and karabiner exactly for this purpose. Your biggest danger is now falling out.

Call for help (phone, radio, tracker, whistle) and accept a rescue. Far more people are injured trying to climb down out of trees than are ever injured landing in them. It can be embarrassing, but it needn't be damaging or life threatening. Do not try to climb down on your own.

When flying in forested areas it can pay to make sure you have your radio or phone within reach and know where you are and how to transmit GPS coordinates or your What3Words location (W3W is a location app). One tip is to carry a roll of dental floss or fishing line: that way if you land in a tree you can drop it and then pull up a climbing rope.

Landing in still water

Water landings are a risky business. But if you are unable to reach land because of a strong headwind (look behind you – how close is the shore downwind?) then landing in still water like a lake is not the worst option. The largest risk is getting tangled in your lines or equipment.

Because it is very hard to judge height above flat water, it is not advisable to unclip and jump out before you land in the lake. Pilots have drowned when they have jumped from what they thought was a safe distance, only to discover too late they were 30m above the water.

If you have time, prepare for the landing. Tell people on the radio what is happening or shout out to people on the shore or in boats; loosen straps; get your **hook-knife** to hand; work out which shore is closest before you are in the water.

If you land into wind release the brakes so the glider overshoots you. You can also land downwind, so the glider falls overhead and pulls the lines taut and clear, keeping air in the glider. Unbuckle in the water. Depending on your harness it may help you float, or conversely, it may push you face down in the water as it floats. Your helmet may also float. If you are wearing a **life jacket**, inflate it.

If you swim for shore forget about trying to drag your glider with you, it will be far too heavy.

If you are in a populated area then someone will hopefully have seen you land in the lake and will be on their way to rescue you and your equipment.

Landing in moving water

Landing in a fast-flowing river, strong swell or in the surf zone of the sea is extremely dangerous for paraglider pilots. The glider will fill with water and will drag you underwater or out to sea very quickly.

This has the potential to be a critical emergency and you must act to save your life. Choose landing in the open sea over landing in the surf zone – turn and fly towards it if necessary (but choose the beach first, obviously). Unbuckle quickly – perhaps even before landing although make that decision at the time – and have your hook-knife ready to cut yourself free of lines and straps. Separate yourself from the glider quickly.

If you see someone else land in the surf-zone or in a river, do not follow them in. Land somewhere safe and call for help and the emergency services. Mark their location and start a rescue operation immediately.

▶ WEAR A LIFE VEST

Every year there are avoidable tragedies where pilots drown. If you regularly fly near or above water, especially where tides can limit bottom landing, then consider making a life vest part of your kit. Combined with a hook-knife it means you can separate yourself from heavy equipment and float. Always wear a life vest if flying SIV over water.

▲ **RESERVE THROW**
A real-world reserve deployment during an SIV course. The paraglider has a cravat, which initiated a strong spiral dive, and the pilot lost control. He has thrown his reserve into clear air. To pass certification a reserve parachute must open fully in less than five seconds. Photo: Andy Busslinger

Throwing your reserve

Reserve parachutes save lives – but only if they are used in time. It's important to keep your **reserve** in good condition, to have it checked and packed regularly (once a year at least) and to know how to use it.

Some clubs hold reserve demo days, where you can practise throwing your reserve on an aerial runway, and these are good things to go to. Flight incidents can be disorientating, so knowing what to do next when it comes to deploying your reserve can save you precious seconds.

Most pilots will never need to throw their reserve parachute. However, reasons you might need to include:

- **Mid-air collisions** where two pilots collide. Unless you separate and can fly away safely, throw your reserve

- An unrecoverable situation like having a cravat or collapse followed by auto-rotation with twisted risers

- An uncontrolled high-G situation where you are at risk of blacking out

- Equipment failure. An unchecked and open maillon fails or there is a catastrophic line failure

- You are low and you have no time to recover from an incident.

There is a process to throwing your reserve successfully. It is not simply grab, chuck and hope for the best.

1. **Decide** you are going to deploy your reserve. This is an active piloting decision and is easily made when the time comes.

2. **Look and locate**. Find your reserve handle. In each flight it is good practice to reach out and touch your reserve handle. This way you know where it is. Use your eyes to look for the handle as well as your hands to feel for it.

3. **Pull your reserve handle**. The parachute will come out in its container.

4. **Look at where you are going to throw it**. You want to see some clear space, to avoid throwing it into the glider or even your lap (it happens).

5. **Throw it**. This is a positive action, throwing the parachute away from your body. If you are disorientated, throw it towards your feet. Don't forget to let it go!

6. **Check the reserve**. All being well your reserve will have deployed and you will now be descending under it.

7. **Disable your paraglider**. Your main glider now has the potential to act against your reserve, so pull in a line until you can get hold of some fabric, then haul in the fabric. Stuff it between your legs and into your lap to get it out of the way.

8. **Prepare to land**. You are now a parachutist and should land like one. Paraglider parachutes are designed to descend at around 5.5m/s or less. That's like jumping off a 1.5m wall. So prepare to make a **parachute landing fall**: legs together and slightly bent; roll like a banana on impact. Don't try to land standing up, you might break something.

9. **Report back**. Tell your friends you are safe and sound, and let them know if you need any help. Signal to others in the air that you are ok by walking around and quickly packing away your equipment. Don't sit there taking selfies with your glider spread out as this is a sign you need help. A parachute landing is adrenaline-fuelled, but it will not necessarily prompt an emergency call-out.

10. **File a report**. Some clubs, associations and countries ask you to fill out an incident report if you throw your reserve. These are often anonymous and are there to help other pilots learn from your incident.

▶**PLF**

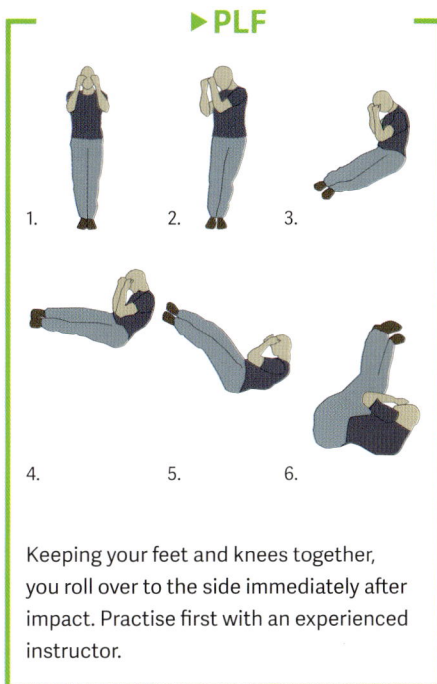

1.   2.   3.

4.   5.   6.

Keeping your feet and knees together, you roll over to the side immediately after impact. Practise first with an experienced instructor.

▲ EMERGENCY PROCEDURES
If an emergency helicopter is called clear the air quickly. Land if safe, or fly clearly away from the scene. An emergency helicopter will not approach a hill of soaring paragliders. If on the ground, secure your equipment
Photo: Bastienne Wentzel

▶ MANAGING EMERGENCIES

This section is written with and approved by Dr Matt Wilkes, a paraglider pilot and expedition medic

Accidents can and do happen in paragliding – ankle and back injuries are the most common. Prevention is better than cure, which is why adequate back protection and familiarity with your reserve system is important. Having general overall sporting fitness, suitable for what you are doing, can also help you avoid accidents. However, if an accident does happen it is important to be prepared and know what to do.

In case of an accident

Your priority following an incident you have witnessed is to swiftly transform the immediate chaos into a safe, coordinated **rescue effort**. You may be somewhere remote from help, so this will require more judgement than in an urban environment.

Your actions may be determined by the number of rescuers, by experience, equipment or environmental threats. However, while caring for a casualty in the outdoors is challenging, even situations that seem desperate can be improved.

Keep the safety of the group uppermost in your mind, act within your limits and treat the casualty as you would like to be treated under similar circumstances.

Controlling the scene

Nominate a coordinator. The coordinator stands back, delegates when possible and allows others to care for the casualty. Thinking out loud helps the group follow the train of thought. Followers should be supportive and minimise the demands on the controller's 'bandwidth': accompany questions with potential solutions and close the 'loop of communication', actively confirming when tasks have been understood or completed.

Ensure the safety of the group. Before approaching the casualty, always think, "could the same accident happen to us?"

Secure the casualty. Move a casualty only if their present position risks further injury. You may need to tie them to something secure, pack away their glider or shelter them from the elements.

Prepare the scene for rescue. Secure loose gear. Clear airspace and put up a wind indicator if anticipating a helicopter. Helicopters are hazardous: approach them from the front and only advance once the pilot has signalled you directly to do so.

Calling for help

Use the local **emergency number** (Australia 000, Europe 112, UK 999, USA 911, New Zealand 111, South Africa 112) or emergency radio frequency. Before calling, note your location, key details (what happened, the casualty's current condition) and any anticipated difficulties for rescuers. Most importantly, think about what you might need before you call: mountain rescue? An ambulance?

A helicopter? Preparation before calling will allow you to communicate fluently, to be connected to the right people and will minimise the impact of poor phone reception.

Assessing the casualty

Look, listen and feel for **injuries**. Whether you go from head-to-toe or system-to-system (i.e. airway, breathing, circulation) doesn't matter, it is more important that you are systematic and thorough. Casualty assessment is a continuous process. If you find a problem, try to fix it but then reassess once more.

Key interventions

Airway. Listen to the casualty's breathing. If it sounds clear or they are talking, the airway is open. If they are snoring or gurgling, it is partially obstructed. If you hear nothing, or see 'see-saw' movements of the chest and abdomen, it is likely closed. If there is anything obvious in the mouth obstructing the airway, then remove it. Open an airway with a 'head tilt, chin lift' manoeuvre or by pushing the jaw forwards from the face 'jaw thrust' or both, then reassess the casualty's breathing. Be gentle, particularly if you have concerns about the casualty's cervical spine, but their airway takes priority. Remove a full-face helmet if a casualty is not talking to you normally, or if you have any other concerns about the airway.

Haemorrhage control. Look for, and then try hard to stop any **bleeding** through 1) Direct pressure (the most important), 2) Splinting broken limbs, 3) Tourniquets. This sequence may have to be followed in quick succession. Do not apply tourniquets unnecessarily, but equally don't be inhibited if bleeding

243

cannot be stopped by other means. The tourniquet must be tight enough to stop arterial and venous bleeding. Once a tourniquet has been applied, do not loosen it until hospital. Make sure the emergency services are aware a tourniquet has been used. Tie a binder around the pelvis and ankles following all heavy crashes.

The first clot the body makes is the strongest so try not to disrupt it. Do not remove dressings or tourniquets once applied, handle the casualty gently and avoid moving them unnecessarily. Stopping a casualty getting cold, even in warm weather, is essential to reduce bleeding.

Compassionate care. Reassure the casualty: talk to them kindly, directly and in terms they understand. Protect them from the elements, pad pressure areas and be mindful of their dignity. Give pain relief, food and water.

Aftermath and reporting

Make notes about the incident, timings, injuries or treatments given. Write on the casualty if necessary. Take photos to help with future investigations. Report any incident to the national paragliding association, aviation authority or police, depending on its severity.

Practise

Consider running an incident simulation in your club. These are great opportunities to practise working together and to make a future rescue slicker. For example, can you effectively communicate the location of your local take-off to a third party? Consider a Wilderness First Responder course to take your knowledge further.

Health in extreme conditions

Above about 3,000m the oxygen content of the air is reduced to a level where most people are affected. Symptoms of low oxygen (hypoxia) are most notable in organs that need a lot of oxygen, such as the heart, brain and eyes. A shortage of oxygen may cause you to think less clearly, cause mood changes, diminished coordination and deteriorating sight. **Hypoxia** usually occurs when you climb above 3,000m quickly, because your body has no time to adapt to the lower oxygen content. Be aware of this when you fly in the mountains and to high altitudes. In particular, be careful top-landing at high altitudes, as the extra oxygen required when you run to take off again may use up the little oxygen your body has in reserve and lead to an accident.

If you remain at higher altitudes for a prolonged period, overnight during a hike-and-fly trip for example, you can develop altitude illness. **Acute mountain sickness** (AMS) is characterised by headaches, dizziness, poor appetite, nausea and fatigue. In up to 5% of cases, altitude illness may progress to high altitude pulmonary or cerebral oedema, both of which can be fatal. Build in rest days during ascent to let your body acclimatise. Try to sleep no more than 500 vertical metres higher each night. Descent is the key treatment for all altitude illnesses.

At high altitudes it can be extremely cold, leading to **hypothermia**, frostbite or non-freezing cold injury. Keep your hands protected by keeping them dry, your core warm, wearing good gloves and sheltering them from the wind whenever possible.

▶ LEARN MORE

- **Fifty Ways to Fly Better, by Bruce Goldsmith,** xcmag.com/50/en.html

- **Mastering Paragliding, by Kelly Farina**
  xcmag.com/masteringparagliding

- **Security in Flight & Master Acro**
  tinyurl.com/paraglidingfilms

- **Thermal Flying & Cross Country Flying, by B Martens**, tinyurl.com/burkibooks

- **Jocky Sanderson's YouTube channel**
  tinyurl.com/jocky-xc

- **Cloudbase Mayhem, podcasts**,
  cloudbasemayhem.com

- **Paragliding Forum, online community**
  paraglidingforum.com

- **Just Acro, website and community**
  justacro.com

- **Adventure medicine**
  theadventuremedic.com

- **Free Flight Physiology Project**
  freeflightphysiology.org

REGULATIONS AND RULES

#7

▶ **RULES OF THE AIR**

▶ **AIRSPACE AND AIR LAW**

▶ **LICENCES AND ASSOCIATIONS**

Staying safe with other air users

Rules of the air, air law and airspace regulations are important because they keep pilots safe in the air. They give structure to situations where you are flying with others, and allow pilots to fly close to each other without colliding.

Every paragliding exam has a section that deals with rules and regulations, and it is important to know the specific rules and regulations that apply for wherever you are sitting your exam.

However, much of what follows is internationally understood and observed and will apply, with some local differences, wherever you are. Note that airspace is often updated or changed, so stay abreast of any changes in your local area as they can affect us.

The rules and regulations are especially important when you travel internationally or compete. We might not speak the same language on the ground, but in the air it is vital we can all be understood. Sticking to the rules is the best way of doing that and keeping ourselves and others safe in the air.

▲ **RULES OF THE AIR**
Simple rules help keep us safely apart from others in the air
Photo: Ed Ewing

◄ **BALLOONS**
Flying with a hot air balloon can be an amazing experience. As they can not steer, it is up to us to stay clear
Photo: Ronald ten Berge

248

▶ RULES OF THE AIR

Whatever the letter of the **law** actually says, the main thing when flying with others is that pilots have an obligation to avoid problems. This means following the **rules of the air**, flying in a responsible and coordinated way and **giving way** to other pilots when needed.

This makes sense: there is no point in having the law on your side if you fail to avoid a potentially dangerous situation. If you or another pilot don't know what to do, or someone else fails to give way where they should, then the rule is always to move apart, avoid each other and stay safe. Keep your margins comfortable.

Here are some important ways to help you do that:

- Maintain **situational awareness**. Keep an eye on your surroundings so you know what is going on. Look up, down and all around during take-off, the flight and landing. You can only avoid what you see coming, whether it's a hillside, tree or another pilot.

- Fly predictably and with intent. Show others what you are about to do. When flying close to other pilots, indicate with your hand or body where you are going. Let others know that you have seen them, and acknowledge other people's signals. Shouting at others is not considered good etiquette and can be confusing, so only use your voice if you have to.

- Keep your distance from other paraglider pilots. Not only to avoid the turbulence of their tip vortices, but also because other pilots may

need to diverge from their course for something you might not be able to see. If you fly too close you will not have enough time to react. How far sufficient distance is depends on the situation.

- Keep your distance from other air traffic, especially larger and motorised aircraft. They are required by law to give way to you, but they fly faster and may not see you in time. Their wake may also create turbulence.

Rules of the air

Rules of the air apply to all aircraft in flight. The rules that govern paragliders are part of a much wider set of rules that govern aviation as a whole.

In the EU, the European rules of the air are established by EU regulation and known as **SERA – Standardised European Rules of the Air**. SERA rules are based on **ICAO (International Civil Aviation Organisation)** recommendations and in particular ICAO Annex 2 (Rules of the Air). They apply to all airspace users and aircraft operating in the EU. Individual countries within the EU, and those countries that are geographically part of Europe but not members of the EU, can and will have local regulations that also apply.

In the United States the rules that govern flying paragliders come under the **Federal Aviation Regulations (FAR)** Part 103 (Ultralight Vehicles). The primary right-of-way convention is that all pilots must '**See and Avoid**' as set out in FAR Part 103.13. In Australia the rules and regulations of the air are set by the Civil Aviation Safety Authority and administered by the Sports Aviation Federation of Australia.

Regardless of which country you are in or from, the foundation for all the rules of the air for paraglider pilots is that pilots give way to each other.

1. **Head-on approach**. When two paragliders are approaching each other head-on and at similar altitude, then both pilots must give way and turn right. This avoids any chance of **collision**. It is not a game of chicken.

2. **Head-on approach when ridge-soaring**. When paragliders are approaching head-on and one has the ridge to the right and cannot safely give way to the right, that paraglider has right of way. The pilot with the ridge on their left should give way by turning right.

3. **Converging course**. When two paragliders are on a converging course then the pilot "on the right is in the right". The pilot on the left should give way, usually by turning either right or left.

4. **Overtaking**. In clear air a paraglider pilot can overtake another paraglider pilot on either side. Leave a margin and don't crowd the other pilot or box them in.

5. **Overtaking on a ridge**. When over-taking another pilot flying in the same direction as you on a ridge, pass between the pilot and the ridge where practical. This avoids boxing the other pilot in. Consider

turning around early instead of passing if it will put you too close to the other glider or ridge. Some countries have a rule against over-taking on the ridge, so if you are unsure do check.

6. **Turning in thermals**. The first pilot to enter a thermal and start turning sets the turn direction, regardless of altitude. That means pilots who join a thermal lower down, above or at the same height should turn in the same direction as the other pilots already in the thermal. The simplest way to join a thermal is to slot in when you can see the back of the other pilot's head. This way you don't disrupt the flow or collide. When established in a thermal the normal right-of-way rules apply – the pilot on the left gives way to someone coming from the right, for example.

7. **Giving way to pilots below**. US pilots are taught that the higher pilot should give way to lower pilots In the EU, UK and other countries this rule is less firmly adopted. It is definitely useful when landing. When thermalling the idea behind it is that traditionally the higher pilot can see better what is going on below, but in reality, paraglider pilots often have a restricted view below them as they are in a supine position. They may have a better view above than below. The point of the rule is to avoid the other pilot, so if you see someone coming up from below, then give way. Similarly, if you can see you are climbing into the path of another paraglider, then take action to avoid a collision.

▶ RULES OF THE AIR

All pilots should understand the rules of the air – they exist to help all of us stay safe

1. Head-on approach in clear air. Both pilots divert to the right, to avoid a collision.

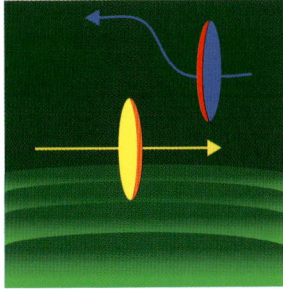

2. Head-on while ridge-soaring. The pilot with the hill on their right has the right of way. The other pilot gives way.

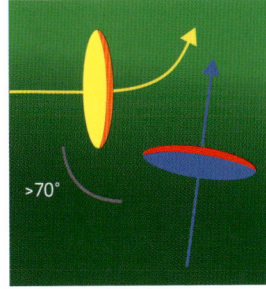

3. Converging course. Give way to an aircraft coming from the right. "On the right, in the right."

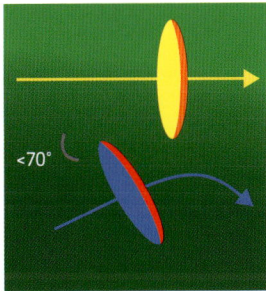

4. In clear air overtaking can be done on either the right-hand side or the left-hand side.

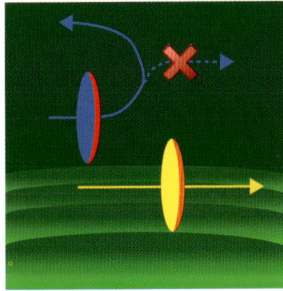

5. On a hill, overtake on the ridge-side. Don't overtake if it will put either of you in an uncomfortable position.

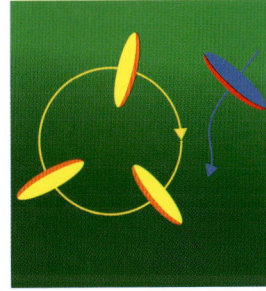

6. When joining a thermal always turn in the same direction as pilots already in the thermal.

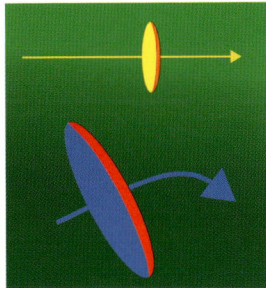

7 and 8. Give way to pilots below you to avoid a collision. When landing, let the lower pilot land first.

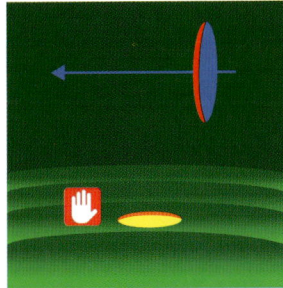

9. Pilots on the ground should give way to pilots in the air, especially when taking off and landing

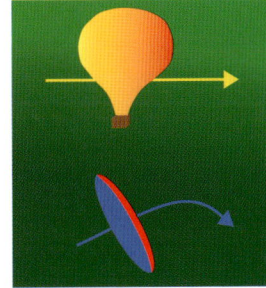

10. When flying with other aircraft that are not gliders the most manoeuvrable aircraft gives way to others.

8. **Giving way when landing**. Higher pilots should give way to lower pilots. The lower pilot therefore lands first. If you are coming down faster than the other pilot, then make it clear you will pass them, for example, by pulling big ears. Don't wait until the last moment to do this, and leave others plenty of space for their approach.

9. **Pilots on the ground**. Pilots ready to launch should wait for clear airspace. If a glider is flying in front of launch, pilots on the ground should wait for them to clear the area. If a pilot is about to top-land, then pilots on the ground should wait until they have landed before launching. When a pilot lands they should clear the landing zone promptly, moving to the side of the field to pack up.

10. **Other aircraft**. The above rules apply for all gliders – sailplanes, hang gliders and paragliders are all treated equally as '**gliders**'. Therefore, a hang glider gives way to a paraglider coming from the right for example. If two different types of aircraft are involved, then the basic rule is that the most **manoeuvrable aircraft** gives way to the less manoeuvrable aircraft. So:

   • **Powered aircraft** give way to **airships**, gliders and **balloons**

   • Airships give way to gliders and balloons

   • Gliders give way to hot air balloons and gas balloons.

Emergency helicopters

An exception to the final point 10 is that gliders should give way to **helicopters** on a rescue mission. This can be a common occurrence in busy areas of the Alps like the Annecy and Chamonix region or the Italian Dolomites. Helicopters rescue climbers, hikers, mountaineers and, yes, even paraglider pilots every day in these busy regions.

Unfortunately, in recent years there have been a handful of high-profile incidents where pilots have not given way to rescue helicopters, leading to the rescue helicopter aborting its mission. This is not only unfortunate for the person needing to be rescued, it also reflects badly on all of us.

Giving way to an emergency helicopter means gliding clearly away from the scene of any incident. In the mountains, it means leaving the mountain. If soaring a ridge, then it means landing. A helicopter pilot will not attempt to approach a hill, or make a landing in the hills, where paraglider pilots are soaring along or thermalling above the hill.

Signs that paraglider pilots use to signal to other paraglider pilots that a helicopter is on its way include pilots on the ground rotating their arm above their head; smoke to show the wind direction for the landing helicopter; and other pilots suddenly putting in big ears and making their way to land.

Do not linger, seconds save lives. If in doubt, please give way and go to land safely. Our friends in the emergency services do an amazing job and we should aim to help, not hinder, them.

Known as aeronautical charts, air charts, air maps or aviation maps, they are all designed to do the same thing – help you know where you are in the sky and navigate a course. They contain information about the airspace you are in and also what is below you. They are available as laminated maps and digitally. Photo: Marcus King

▶ AIR LAW & AIRSPACE

Paragliding and other gliding sports are often referred to as **free flight**. The 'free' refers to being free of regulation, as much as engine-free. However, a paraglider is a glider and an **aircraft**. This means we have to obey the laws that govern the air wherever we are flying, and all rules and regulations connected to those laws.

This can be a complicated web of regulations and exceptions, and each country will have their own. Even within countries, there will be exceptions and changes, with daily updates on where you can and cannot fly. The aim of this section is to introduce you to some of the concepts and language that applies. Some will be relevant for you, others less so. Either way, it is a good idea to get to grips with understanding the basics of air law and airspace.

The paraglider

In most countries paragliders are unregulated aircraft. That is, they do not need an annual service or to have a **licence number**. Some countries do demand this however. Other countries demand that all aircraft must carry a **transponder** – a kind of beacon that alerts other air users of your presence – but make exceptions for hang gliders and paragliders.

253

With the ever-increasing number of drones, there are calls for everything in the air to be digitally 'visible', but we are not there yet.

However, rules and regulations around paragliders do change, so if in doubt, search out the correct information that you need for where you fly. Your first port of call should be the website of the national paragliding or sports aviation association website. A good source of information is provided by the Aeronautical Information Services (AIS) governed by ICAO. Most countries have their own AIS website with information on NOTAMs, aerodromes, VFR, air charts and rules and regulations.

Airspace

Airspace is the space above the surface of the Earth used by **air traffic**. Air traffic can range from drones to jumbo jets. The world's airspace is divided up into **flight information regions** (**FIR**) – specified regions of airspace. Smaller countries' airspace is encompassed by a single FIR; larger countries have national airspace subdivided into a number of FIRs.

Air charts

To make sense of each FIR you need a map. **Aeronautical charts**, air maps, are categorised according to their scale. World aeronautical charts have a scale of 1:1,000,000 and cover large areas. (Note that world aeronautical charts have been discontinued in the USA). Sectional charts typically cover an area of about 500km x 500km at a scale of 1:500,000 – they are like motorway maps of the sky.

A third series of air maps at 1:250,000 scale feature more topographic features and are useful for pilots flying visually as you can more easily relate what you see on the ground to the map. You can buy laminated printed maps, or digital maps to download to a flight instrument.

Height and altitude

To use a map, you need to know where you are. Not only with respect to a place on the ground, but also to how high you are. Many airspace rules only apply when you reach a certain altitude. **Altitude** normally means the vertical distance **above mean sea level**, abbreviated as **AMSL**. **Height** indicates the vertical distance **above ground level** (**AGL**). **Ground level** is abbreviated as **GND**.

It is a quirk of aviation that although pilots might talk about kilometres flown or how many hundreds of metres it is to the landing zone, altitude and heights are often given in feet. One foot is 0.3048 metres (roughly three feet to one metre). It is important to know which unit you are talking about when comparing vertical distances. The difference between 3,000ft and 3,000m is considerable!

Q-codes or altimeter settings

We measure our altitude using an **altimeter**, which works based on changes in air pressure. Air pressure is highest at sea level, and decreases with height. Air pressure at the summit of Mount Everest (8,848m) for example, is one third of that at sea level.

Air pressure on Earth however, is not constant. Therefore, to get a useful and accurate altitude reading you need to have a known baseline air pressure. In aviation we use three baseline air pressures: measured against standard air pressure; our height against real sea-level; and our height above a

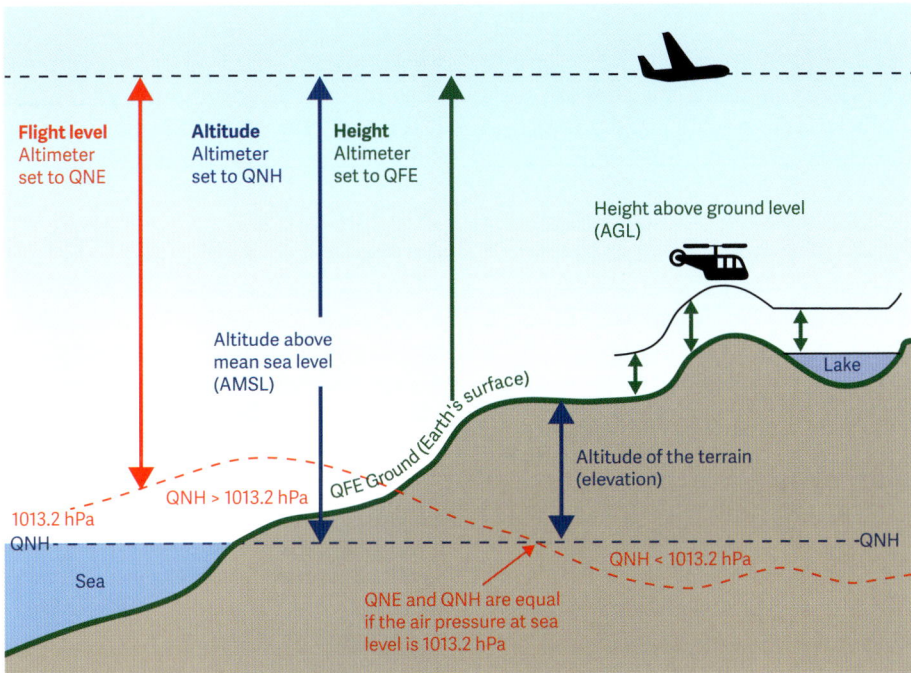

▲ FLIGHT LEVELS, ALTITUDE AND HEIGHT
Green text relates to concepts that involve height above the ground. Blue text is concepts that involve the altitude at which we fly, indicated on an altimeter that is set to a certain air pressure. Red shows concepts related to Flight Level. This is where the altimeter is set to the standard air pressure 1013.2 hPa.

chosen point, for example launch or the landing.

In aviation we use altimeter settings or 'Q-codes' to refer to those three different baseline air pressures. **Q-codes** are standardised three-letter codes, which all start with the letter Q. They are assigned by the International Civil Aviation Organisation (ICAO) and were developed when pilots and the world communicated using morse code over radio. Note that Q-codes are not used in the USA – they are just called '**altimeter settings**'. However, the concept of measuring your altitude from a known baseline air pressure is the same.

The three important Q-codes that paraglider pilots need to know about, especially for exams, are:

QNH (mnemonic: Query nautical height): Current air pressure at sea level. An altimeter set to QNH will indicate the altitude above mean sea level (AMSL).

QFE (Query field elevation): Current air pressure at a specific location. For example, launch: an altimeter set to QFE will indicate the height above launch. On launch the altimeter reading will be zero, provided that the air pressure has not changed in the mean time.

QNE (Query normal elevation): An aircraft's altitude assuming standard air pressure at sea level, defined as 1013.2 hPa. This is also called an aircraft's flight level (FL). That is, an aircraft's altitude at standard air pressure expressed in hundreds of feet.

255

Flight level

In aviation **Flight Level** (**FL**) is an aircraft's altitude at standard air pressure – the altimeter set to QNE. Flight levels are used in aviation above a certain altitude to ensure safe vertical separation between aircraft, despite natural local variations in atmospheric air pressure.

FL is indicated in hundreds of feet, ie in feet with the last two zeros omitted. For example, at standard air pressure FL095 indicates a flying altitude of 9,500ft.

This standardisation means that all aircraft can determine their relative altitudes, wherever they have taken off from. This prevents accidents as it means they all know where they are relative to each other. If each aircraft set their altimeter to a different air pressure in a different location, for example, then the altimeters would all indicate different flying altitudes, even if two aircraft were flying next to each other.

Aircraft only set their altimeter to Flight Level above a certain altitude. This is called the **transition altitude**. The transition altitude varies between countries. In the US and Canada the transition altitude is 18,000ft, while in some parts of Europe it can be as low as 3,000ft.

The **transition level** is the lowest usable FL above the transition altitude. This is important because there can be many FL, but not all usable, perhaps because of airspace. When descending below the transition level, the pilot starts to refer to altitude of the aircraft by setting the altimeter to the QNH for the region or airfield. Between the two is the **transition layer** – a band of airspace typically 500ft to 1,000ft thick. If you fly in an area where the Flight Level starts low, and are legally allowed to enter it, then you will need to know how to switch your flight instrument between QNH and QNE as you fly through the transition layer.

VFR and IFR

Air traffic can be divided into two groups. Aircraft that are operated with instruments can fly under **instrument meteorological conditions** (**IMC**) and can use **instrument flight rules** (**IFR**).

Aircraft flying under IFR must have radio communication with the local **Air Traffic Control** (**ATC**). In most cases they need permission – Air Traffic Control clearance (**ATC clearance**) – to enter controlled airspace.

The second group is aircraft without instruments, where the aircraft is operated by sight alone. They must fly under **visual meteorological conditions** (**VMC**) and operate under **visual flight rules** (**VFR**). Paragliders come into this group – we fly without instruments or contact with ATC.

Paraglider pilots don't normally carry the type of radio needed to talk to ATC and so don't have to pass a radio exam (**flight radio telephony operator's licence**, **FRTOL**), which is needed to talk to Air Traffic Control. Also, the nature of a glider means it cannot be effectively directed by ATC. Hence, we stay out of controlled airspace. This keeps us and other air users separated and thus safe in busy airspace.

VMC and VFR

Paraglider pilots are required by law to fly only in weather conditions with good **visibility**. This is known as observing

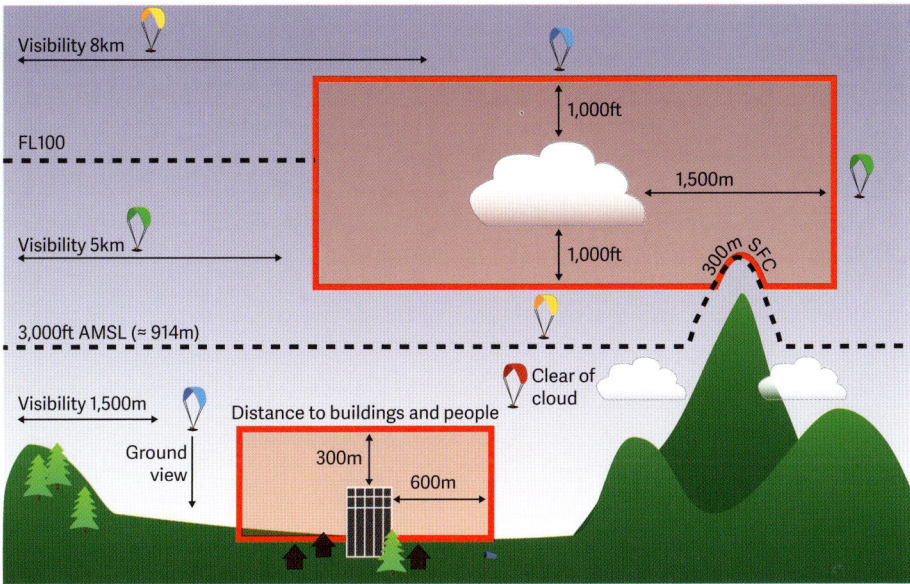

▲ **VISUAL METEOROLOGICAL CONDITIONS**
Visual meteorological conditions (VMC) are the minimum weather requirements needed for an aircraft to fly under visual flight rules (VFR). The rules around VMC do change from country to country, but this is a typical example of VMC in open airspace. Pilots must stay clear of cloud, keep the ground in sight and not fly close to built-up areas. As glider pilots we are often granted exemptions to fly up to cloudbase, soar close to terrain, and take off and land.

visual meteorological conditions (VMC). Flying under VMC ensures that all aircraft flying without instruments stay clear of cloud, only fly when they have a clear view, and don't fly in the dark. Aircraft that fly under VMC need to follow the accompanying visual flight rules (VFR). VMC and VFR are set by ICAO and can vary by country.

The most important VFR rule to know about is that you need to keep a horizontal and vertical distance to clouds to ensure good visibility. In short, we often say that the rule is '1,000ft **clear of cloud**', but in practice, the rules are a bit more complicated (see the illustration above).

In most countries, when flying in uncontrolled airspace between 3,000ft-10,000ft pilots must have at least 5km visibility and must stay 1,500m horizontally from cloud and 1,000ft (approximately 300m) vertically from cloud. Below 3,000ft the rule is 1,500m visibility, clear of cloud and in sight of the surface.

In the USA the rule is that between 1,200ft-10,000ft pilots must have three miles visibility and stay 500ft below, 1,000ft above, and 2,000ft horizontally from cloud. Below 1,200ft it is 1 statute mile visibility and clear of clouds.

When we fly cross country however, it is often difficult for us to keep sufficient vertical distance from clouds as the whole point of the sport is to reach cloudbase before flying on to the next cloud. What this means is as soon as you are close to cloudbase you are automatically flying in Instrument Meteorological Conditions. Because we are slow flying and the chance of collision is low, all this means is we must stay clear of cloud and keep the ground in sight – as well as keep a very good lookout for other air traffic. It is important to 'see and avoid' and don't simply rely on others to see and avoid you. It also means you should not fly into the cloud.

The other key VFR rule is that you must keep a minimum height above built-up areas and crowds, and always be able to see the ground. In Europe, the rule is a minimum height of 300m above the largest obstacle within a radius of 600m of the aircraft. In practice this means you shouldn't fly low over towns or villages, for example. Exceptions to this are when you are landing, taking off, or ridge-soaring. In the USA you are not allowed to fly over any congested areas at any altitude.

This rule ensures that pilots land well clear of these obstacles, even in an emergency. In mountainous regions there are minimum distances to keep with respect to ski lifts, pistes and cable cars and some countries have rules against flying low over railways and motorways.

It is important to know how VMC and VFR work where you fly. In Europe, the VMC and VFR rules are outlined in detail in Section 5 of the Easy Access Rules for Standardised European Rules of the Air (SERA). This 200-page document can be downloaded from easa.europa.eu. Be aware that a country's local laws always overrule SERA.

Airspace classification

Airspace is divided into three-dimensional segments, called classes.

Most countries use the classification specified by ICAO, although they might not use all of the classes. The ICAO **airspace classification** system runs from Class A to Class G. Classes A-E are controlled airspace – that is, overseen by ATC. Classes F and G are **uncontrolled airspace**.

Areas of controlled airspace typically have a floor and a ceiling. For example, the airspace might start at 2,500ft AMSL and extend up to FL095 (at QNH 1013.2, FL095 = 9,500ft). If the airspace below 2,500ft is uncontrolled then paragliders can fly there – but they must not enter the airspace above 2,500ft AMSL.

International airspace classes

Airspace is a dry and involved subject and it can become confusing. What follows is a brief look at the ICAO classifications for airspace classes A-G. In general Class A is the most restricted airspace, the classes then become progressively less restricted until Class G, which is uncontrolled, open airspace.

As paraglider pilots the main information we need to know is this: we can not fly in airspace Classes A-D. To fly there you need ATC clearance, a radio licence and airband radio, sometimes additional equipment, and also the ability to be vectored (controlled) by ATC.

Most of our flying is done in uncontrolled airspace, Classes F and G. In the USA much of the airspace you will fly in is Class E, which is controlled airspace, but you don't need a radio or to talk to ATC.

Exceptions do occur, and airspace also changes, so keep airspace files up to date.

Classes A, B, C and D: Controlled airspace. All aircraft that enter this airspace must be in radio contact with ATC. Found around and on approach to airfields and major and minor airports. We are not allowed to fly in this airspace.

Class E: Controlled airspace, but flights under Visual Flight Rules are allowed and are not subject to ATC clearance. Paragliders can enter and fly through this airspace without being in radio contact with ATC, subject to observing Visual Meteorological Conditions. A large amount of the airspace over the USA is designated as Class E airspace, starting at 1,200 ft AGL and extending up to 17,999 ft AMSL.

Class F: Uncontrolled airspace. Operations may be conducted under IFR or VFR. Air Traffic Control separation will be provided, so far as practical, to aircraft operating under IFR. This keeps the IFR and VFR air traffic apart. Paragliders can fly here, subject to observing Visual Meteorological Conditions.

Class G: Uncontrolled airspace. Operations may be conducted under IFR or VFR. Air Traffic Control has no authority but pilots need to know about and observe the Visual Flight Rules minima – that is, how much distance we must keep from things like built-up areas, crowds and cloud. This is open airspace and we can fly here happily knowing we are not about to upset a control tower.

Air Traffic Control areas

As well as the seven classes of airspace, there are a number of different areas that are overseen by ATC. Paragliders are not allowed in this airspace, because they have no means of communicating with ATC. These are some of the most important ATC areas.

CTR (**Controlled Traffic Region** or **Control Zone**). The space around an airfield where the control tower can see air traffic. Typically covers from ground level up to a certain height, for example 3,000ft. A paraglider is allowed to fly over CTRs, but you must have enough height to make it across, otherwise you run the risk of sinking into the CTR from above. This may put you or others in danger.

TMA (**Terminal Manoeuvring Area**) or **TCA** (**Terminal Control Area**). The designated area around a major airport where incoming traffic arrives. A TMA is usually above a CTR and sometimes envelops it. The classification is found on the ICAO map and is usually marked as controlled airspace, but VFR traffic is sometimes allowed. The minimum and maximum heights of the TMA are also found on the map.

CTA (**Control Area**). This is a fairly extensive ATC area over and around some TMAs. It is controlled airspace. The class and heights of a CTA are again given on the ICAO map.

Special Airspace

In addition to Classes A-G, national authorities may designate special areas of airspace, for example, around an airport, power station or danger zone. Some are time dependent, active only during the week or around a special event like an air show, sporting event or military manoeuvres. Some examples follow, but note that not all of them apply internationally. You can find them on the ICAO map.

TMZ (**Transponder Mandatory Zone**): Airspace where carrying a transponder is required. Paragliders generally do not carry one, and are therefore not allowed.

RMZ (**Radio Mandatory Zone**): Airspace where it is obligatory to carry a radio to communicate with the local Air Traffic Control. You need to notify ATC by radio before flying.

Prohibited airspace: This is a type of segregated airspace that is often depicted on charts with the letter P, followed by a serial number. No aircraft can enter. They are usually there for security reasons.

Restricted airspace: Segregated airspace that is typically used by institutions like prisons. Shown on charts with the letter R followed by a serial number. They might not always be active.

Danger areas: Usually operated by the military. For example, live firing ranges, military parachuting, areas of radiation.

Parachute dropzones: These are not always a special class of airspace, but may appear on your air chart as a circle. Skydivers jump from 3,000-12,000ft and travel at 200km/h; best avoided.

Temporary Restricted Areas (**TRA**s): These are activated by NOTAM and are used during active search and rescue operations and other large incidents. Can be activated day or night, often in mountains or on the coast.

Nature reserves and national parks: restrictions can change depending on time of year, eg nesting season. National parks often have blanket bans on launch or landing, but can often be flown over.

UK airspace

The UK has a few classes of airspace that do not fall within the ICAO classes:

AIAA (**Areas of intense aerial activity**): UK specific. Can be military or civilian. For example, a site for helicopter low-flying or ballooning. Paragliders are allowed to enter, but keep a lookout.

ATZ (**Aerodrome Traffic Zone**): This is airspace established around an aerodrome for the protection of aerodrome traffic. They typically extend up a few thousand feet with a radius of a few kilometres. They can be controlled by a control tower, or uncontrolled.

MATZ (**Military Aerodrome Traffic Zone**): Like the ATZ, but established around a military aerodrome. The main airspace is a zone five nautical miles in radius, from GND to 3,000ft AGL. One or two stubs may extend from the main airspace.

Legally paragliders are allowed to fly through MATZs in Class G airspace, but not through the inner part that contains the ATZ. In the UK ATZ are 2NM radius and 2,000ft AGL. However, MATZs are usually very busy with military air traffic, especially mid-week. Best avoided.

USA airspace

In the USA airspace is categorised as regulatory and non-regulatory. Classes A, B, C, D and E are controlled airspace. Class G is uncontrolled. Class F is not used. Other types of airspace include Special Use and Other Airspace.

Special Use airspace includes: Alert areas, eg pilot training zones; Warning areas, which extend three nautical miles

▶ NOTAMS

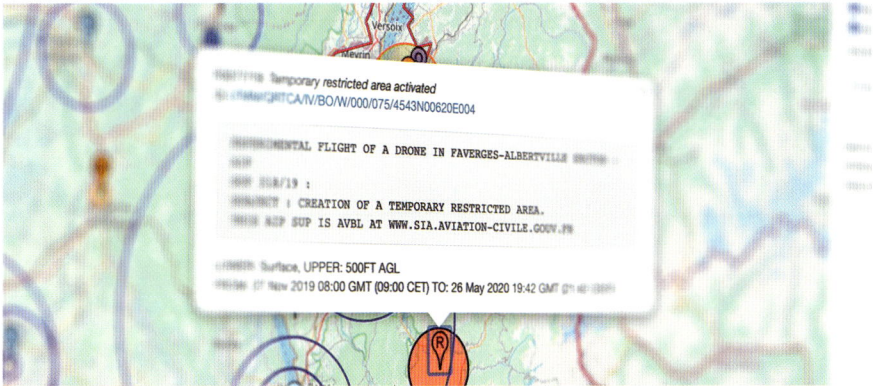

There are new demands on airspace use every day, from many different airspace users. For example, air shows which happen over a week, an afternoon drone race, or even rocket-firing from a university. While you will find permanent airspace information on an up-to-date air chart, you also need to be aware of these daily changes and alerts.

These extra rules always prevail over any other rules and regulations. They are published daily in a NOTAM (Notice to AirMen). NOTAMs contain important information about what is due to happen in a particular part of airspace that day. This information is in addition to any temporary or permanent change of the rules.

NOTAMs are issued by the local aviation authority, and are accessible online. However, to the uninitiated they can look unintelligible, so it's important to get to grips with them before you start to fly cross country regularly. NOTAMs are issued in English, and contain:

- Location information
- Who it applies to
- Dates and times it is valid
- A message about the airspace use

ICAO, the International Civil Aviation Organisation, have issued a standard way of coding NOTAMs, but not all countries comply to this standard. Therefore it is important to get to know your own local NOTAM language.

For a cross-country pilot who flies regularly, checking local NOTAMs should become as routine as checking the weather forecast. Pilots planning to fly cross country, hold a competition, fly midweek or at an unusual site can also issue a NOTAM to tell other air traffic what they are doing.

Check for NOTAMs using these websites:

USA
pilotweb.nas.faa.gov/PilotWeb
www.notams.faa.gov

EUROPEAN UNION (EU)
notaminfo.com/international

UK
notaminfo.com/ukmap

AUSTRALIA
airservicesaustralia.com
xcaustralia.org

from the coast of the USA; Restricted airspace, eg firing ranges; Prohibited airspace, eg the White House; Military operation areas (MOAs); Controlled firing areas; and National security areas (NSAs).

With the exception of Temporary Flight Restrictions, Other Airspace areas are used to draw special attention to an unusual activity or hazard, or to provide additional services to pilots.

Airport advisory/information service area: Local Airport Advisory service is provided within 10 miles of an airport where a Flight Service Station is located and a control tower is not operating.

Terminal Radar Service Area (TRSA): General controlled airspace where air traffic control provides radar vectoring.

Temporary Flight Restriction: designated by NOTAM and used to clear airspace for air shows, search and rescue, forest fires or the President, for example.

Military training route: special zones dedicated for high-speed, low-level military flight.

Parachute jump areas: the FAA maintains a list of all the designated active dropzones in the US.

Australian airspace

Australia's airspace system is based on the US system. Class E is used along populated coastal areas, from 8,500ft AGL. Additional classes include: P (prohibited, and usually temporary); R (restricted, typically used by military operations); and D (Danger, caution required).

▼ **THE KEY**

Like ground maps, air charts have a key which explains the icons, shading, numbers and lines used on the chart. Getting to know the ones on the map you use is useful. Note that air charts do go out of date – they are re-issued regularly with changes added, so keep yours up to date. Photo: Marcus King

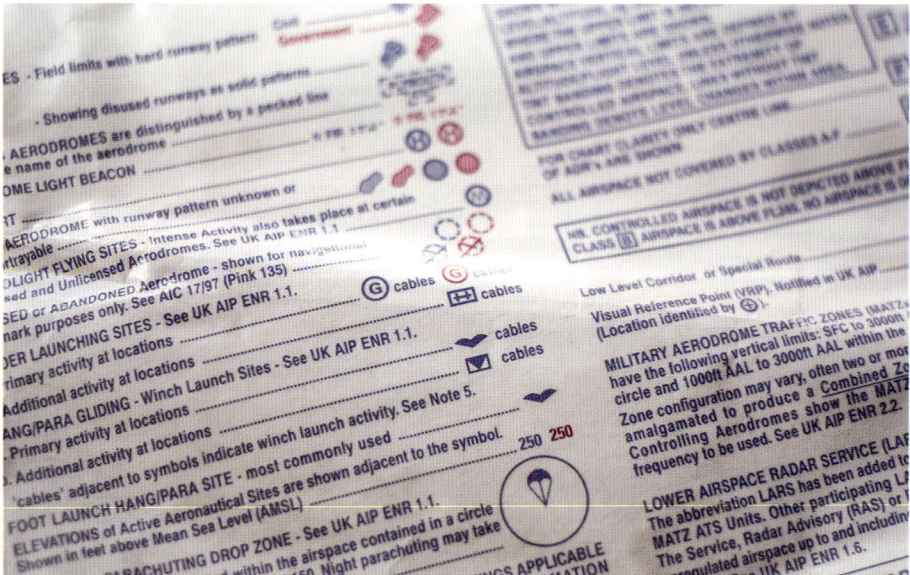

▶ LICENCES AND ASSOCIATIONS

National **paragliding associations** exist in many countries and work hard to communicate with other civilian, commercial and military air organisations. They have often been around for decades, and focus on issues that affect all pilots in their country: air law, safety, insurance, training, accident investigations, sites and competition.

Many national associations cover both hang gliding and paragliding. The largest associations in the world are the French and German ones, with between 25-35,000 members each.

National associations are the best place to start when you want to find out more about the sport or to find a reputable school. They carry lists of approved instructors and schools, and give a good overview of the sport in their country.

When you join a national association you will have to pay an annual fee. In return you get **third-party liability insurance** and a national magazine or access to the association website.

Getting a licence often means becoming a member of the association. It is always a good idea to join the national association in the country where you live – going 'rogue' to save some money and paperwork can seem attractive but may leave you uninsured and, in the long run, only harms the sport and your progression in it. In some countries a membership is required by law and you will be asked to show your flying licence and membership card when you fly a new site. For visiting pilots, most associations offer a visiting membership too, meaning you can buy a short-term pass to fly in that country legally and easily.

Why do I need a licence?

Just like a driving licence, a **paragliding licence** is generally accepted as proof of the knowledge and skills of the pilot who owns it. It shows to others that the holder has sufficient capacity to fly a paraglider without causing danger to themselves or others.

Additionally, in many countries pilots need to have adequate third-party liability insurance. Most national associations offer this insurance cover as standard. Some countries, for example Germany, ask for proof of your insurance before you are allowed to fly there. Again, membership of your paragliding association will help with this.

▶ NATIONAL ASSOCIATIONS

Free-flight associations typically look after training, licences, insurance and sites. They also represent the sport in the wider aviation ecosystem. Many are run partly or in full by volunteers. Some examples:

ABVL (Brazil, abvl.net)
BHPA (UK, bhpa.co.uk)
FIVL (Italy, fivl.it)
FFVL (France, ffvl.fr)
DHV (Germany, dhv.de)
HKPF (Hong Kong, hkpa.net)
HPAC (Canada, hpac.ca)
NZHGPA (New Zealand, nzhgpa.org.nz)
PAI (Paraglidingassociationofindia.org)
SAFA (Australia, safa.asn.au)
SAHPA (South Africa, sahpa.co.za)
SHV (Switzerland, shv-fsvl.ch/en)
USHPA (United States, ushpa.org)

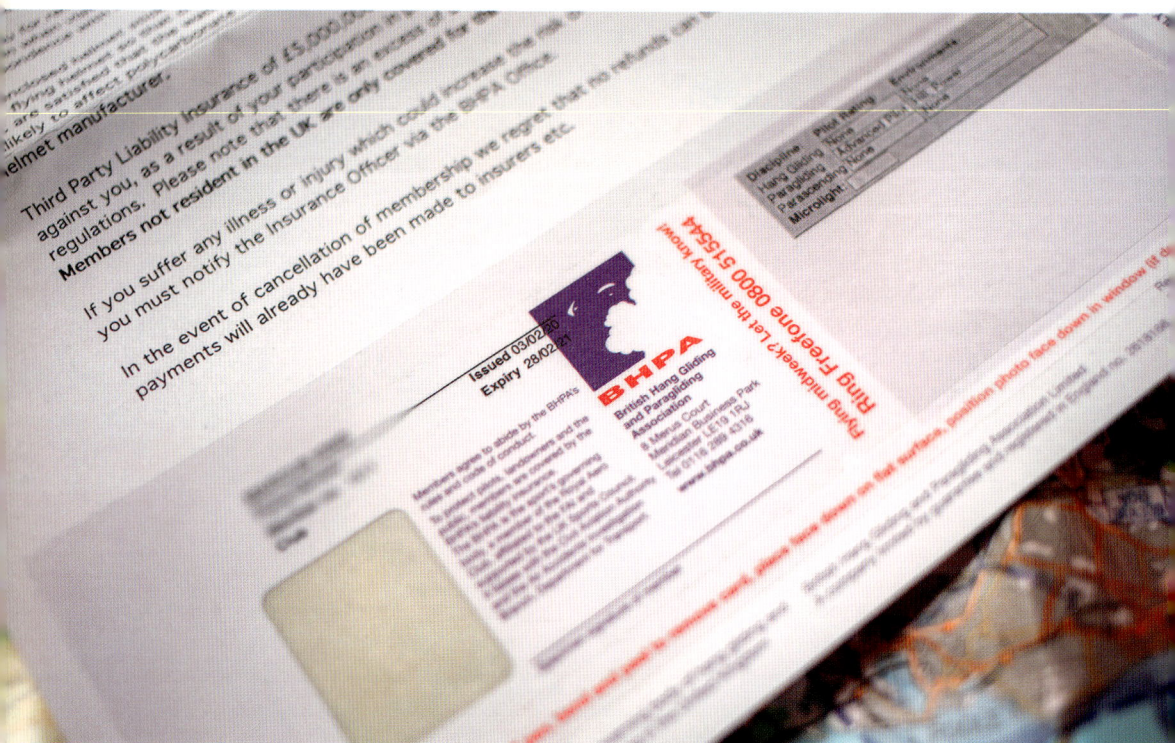

▲ **LICENCE TO THRILL**
A BHPA paragliding licence. Issued once a year this licence is proof that the holder can fly a paraglider and shows what level they are at. Each country operates its own system, but the idea is the same – to show clubs, site wardens and others in the sport that you are qualified. Photo: Marcus King

Pilot training

To obtain your paragliding **licence**, you follow a training programme with a local paragliding school. The school will be a member of the national association that issues the licences.

Qualified paragliding instructors will teach you practical skills and theoretical knowledge. In most countries you can start your training at 14 years old, although you might have to wait until you are 16 before you can qualify for your licence.

In most countries, paragliding training is divided into several stages. A typical training programme looks like this:

Stage 1. Trainee pilot. In this first stage you will get familiar with the equipment, learn some basic theory and make your first solo flights. You might have a tandem flight with an instructor, then make short 'bunny hops' before graduating onto bigger solo flights. At the end of the first stage you will sit a short exam, and get a basic licence. You are not experienced enough to fly alone and still need more training, but the basics are over. Given good weather you can complete this stage in three or four days.

Stage 2. Qualified pilot. The purpose of this second stage is to teach you more skills and then to reinforce those skills so you become a proficient, independent pilot who can fly without instructor oversight. You will learn lots more theory, and how to stay up and have longer flights. At the end of this stage, you will be assessed and have to sit a theory test. Once you pass you will be granted a paragliding licence so you can fly as an independent pilot. There is still a lot to learn, but you will be doing it outside the school environment, perhaps by joining a club or going on advanced training courses. Given good weather you can complete this with 10-15 days' training.

Stage 3. Becoming an advanced pilot. The responsibility lies with you to progress in the sport. You can do this by flying lots and staying current, by continuing to learn, by joining a local club, and training in advanced skills. Courses can include thermalling clinics, cross-country courses, SIV (manoeuvres) courses and theory lessons. You will want to learn more about the weather, and the skills of flying XC. You can continue to work your way through your national pilot rating scheme. Pilots typically need at least three seasons to become proficient cross-country pilots.

Stage 4. Specialising. Paragliding is a very deep and broad sport. You can choose to specialise in XC flying, and log every flight you do in an online league. Or you can become an acro pilot and tumble upside down all summer long. You can take up hike-and-fly, train to become an instructor, become a professional tandem pilot, learn about winching, travel the world, pursue adventure racing with your paraglider, or simply spend your evenings after work soaring by the beach. Whatever you do, you will never forget your basic training, so it is important to spend time working on these crucial foundation skills.

▼ **TRAINING RUN**
Learning to fly under the watchful eye of an instructor. You can easily learn the basics of paragliding in a few days and get a basic licence after a week. From there, progression can be as quick or slow as you like. Photo: Mac Para

The US System

The United States Hang Gliding and Paragliding Association (**USHPA** *ushpa.org*) has a five-level rating programme.

- **P1 Beginner**: Can take off, fly straight and land under direct supervision. Understands the basics of glider setup and breakdown.

- **P2 Novice**: Knows how to turn and to land. Has flown from higher ground under supervision and demonstrated confident handling. Can fly on their own within operating limits.

- **P3 Intermediate Pilot**: Fully trained and skilled enough to make decisions in moderate soaring conditions.

- **P4 Advanced Pilot**: Has accumulated the experience and judgment necessary to handle technically demanding conditions at a wide range of flying sites. Can pursue instructor and tandem training.

- **P5 Master Pilot**: Has demonstrated outstanding skill and maturity over a long period of time. Has a long track record of safety.

The UK system

The British Hang Gliding and Paragliding Association (**BHPA,** *bhpa.co.uk*) has a four-level rating system.

- **Elementary Pilot**: A three- to four-day beginners' course. The pilot demonstrates they can take off, fly straight, make turns and land. They understand the basics of how to set up their glider and to pack it away. Qualified to fly under instructor supervision.

- **Club Pilot**: A further 5-10 days of training. The pilot learns to soar, to fly actively, manage small collapses and top-landing theory. Once qualified as a Club Pilot they are ready to join a club and fly independently.

- **Pilot**: Understands air law, can read an air chart, and is qualified to fly cross country. Has logged at least 50 flights and 25 hours.

- **Advanced Pilot**: Experienced cross-country pilot with at least 100 hours, including a 30km XC flight and a 20km out-and-return.

The Australian system

The Sports Aviation Federation of Australia (**SAFA** *safa.asn.au*) has a four-level rating programme.

- **PG2**: Pilots complete the supervised pilot certificate. A nine-day training course sees pilots learn to soar and thermal. Typically 6/7 days are spent training, with extra days spent logging flights and hours. The newly qualified PG2 pilot is licensed to fly solo, in the club environment, as a new pilot.

- **PG3**: After at least 15 flying hours over 60 successful flights the pilot is eligible to graduate to limited unsupervised flying.

- **PG4**: With at least 30 hours' flying time on at least 25 flying days the pilot can be certified for flying at more difficult flying sites. Trained in the use of VHF radio.

- **PG5**: The top-rated pilot certification, this requires additional flying hours as well as navigational certification, allowing you to fly as far as you can. Advanced XC pilot.

The New Zealand system

The NZ Hang Gliding and Paragliding Association (**NZHGPA** *nzhgpa.org.nz*) has a three-level rating programme.

- **PG1**: A beginner course that teaches the basics of paragliding. Consists of a minimum of six flights over two or three days and forms the first part of the PG2 course.

- **PG2**: Teaches pilots to become independent pilots who can fly unsupervised. Pilots must log a total of 150 minutes in 10 flights or less, and complete at least 40 flights. Must have flown in light wind and strong wind conditions and flown from at least four different launches, including an inland site.

- **PG3**: Advanced Pilot level. Pilots must have held a PG2 for a year and logged a further 50 hours and 250 flights. Pilots must have flown at least 20km XC, have completed an SIV course and hold a first aid certificate. They must also demonstrate the ability to fly in the mountains, assess an unknown landing site and determine the wind direction while in the air.

The South African system

The South African Hang Gliding and Paragliding Association (**SAHPA,** *sahpa. co.za*) has a two-level rating system.

- **Basic Licence**: Students complete a week to nine days of training and flying and graduate as qualified pilots. They must complete at least 35 flights, with at least 10 high flights and a total of four hours' flight time, including flying at two different mountain sites. At least two flights must be thermalling flights. Five of the 35 flights can be as a tandem passenger under instruction.

- **Sport Licence**: Pilots must have held the Basic license for at least 12 months and logged at least 50 hours airtime. They must have completed 200 flights, of which 50 must be thermalling flights, including one 20km XC. They need to have flown at least six sites, achieved 500m height gain and spot landed three out of three times. They must have a good knowledge of theory and weather, and understand cliff launches, spirals, stalls and spins. They must complete formal SIV training.

The Canadian system

The Hang Gliding and Paragliding Association of Canada (**HPAC,** *hpac.ca*) has a five-level rating system.

- **P1 Student**: Six flights and a test.

- **P2 Novice**: Minimum 25 flights, pass a written test, be able to give an accurate site assessment and fly independently without instructor.

- **P3 Intermediate**: Trained in both coastal/ridge flying and thermalling. Must log a minimum 60 hours and minimum 90 flights over a minimum of 30 days. Must pass a written test and Transport Canada-mandated Canadian Airspace Regulations Exam.

- **P4 Advanced**: Must complete an SIV course and have flown a minimum of 250 flights over 80 flying days. Must fly a variety of different sites, and have flown a minimum of five different models of wing. Written exam.

- **Master**: For pilots who have made a major contribution. Must show at least 250 hours logged plus significant service to the sport/association.

APPI

In countries where there is no national association, you may come across **APPI**, the Association of Paragliding Pilots and Instructors (*appifly.org*). Much like PADI offers a uniform approach to teaching scuba diving around the world, APPI offers the same for paragliding. Note that APPI is not the same as the FAI's IPPI system, described overleaf.

- **APPI 1 Discover**: Beginners' course. Launch, landing and first solo flights.

- **APPI 2 Explore**: improving skills and knowledge under instruction. Must complete at least 10 high flights.

- **APPI 3 Pilot**: Must make a minimum of 30 flights, and have learnt the basics of thermalling or soaring. They can then fly without supervision.

- **APPI 4**: 50 flights, 30 hours, on three different sites.

- **APPI 5 Advanced pilot**: Must have held APPI 3 for one year minimum and have 100 hours across 10 flying sites. Must complete SIV training.

▼ **PROGRESSIVE LEARNING**
Wherever you learn the process will follow a similar structure. Your easy low flights will be followed by longer and higher flights, where you gradually learn to be an independent pilot. Photo: Mac Para

The IPPI system

The International Pilot Proficiency Identification (**IPPI**) system is a standard reference for pilots who travel outside their own country.

An IPPI card is issued by your own national association and is only valid in combination with your own, valid, national paragliding licence. The system was developed by the World Air Sports Federation (**FAI**, *fai.org*) and **CIVL**, the International Commission for Free Flight.

The five IPPI stages, with their descriptions from CIVL are:

- **Stage 1**: **Ground skimming**. Ground skimming is gliding near the ground over smooth terrain, below a few metres (not higher than you would care to fall).

- **Stage 2**: **Altitude gliding**. Altitude gliding is gliding with enough height and distance from the terrain to be able to manoeuvre relatively freely.

- **Stage 3**: **Active flying**. Active flying is maintaining the normal flying mode

in turbulent air. It includes keeping the angle of attack within the limits, managing pitch and roll movements, preventing and recovering from collapses, tucks and stalls, and quick descent techniques.

- **Stage 4**: **Soaring**. Soaring is using updraughts to extend the flight duration, be it flying on a ridge facing wind or in thermals, or even in wave.

- **Stage 4a**: **Landing accuracy**. This additional rating shows that the pilot has mastered the specific skills needed to practise landing accuracy, including in competitions. This rating can be qualifying to enter competitions.

- **Stage 5**: **Senior pilot**. The senior pilot is fully autonomous and shows good flying experience. They are able to take care of their own and others' safety while flying. They are able to operate their paraglider in a wide range of terrains and conditions.

- **Stage 5b**: **Cross country**. This additional rating shows that the pilot has mastered the specific skills needed to fly cross country

- **Stage 5c**: **Racing**. This additional rating shows that the pilot has mastered the specific skills needed to fly racing competitions with a large number of pilots in challenging and directed tasks.

- **Stage 5d**: **Aerobatics**. This additional rating shows that the pilot has mastered the specific skills needed to fly aerobatics, including in competitions.

A competition pilot at the FAI Paragliding World Championships. World championships are held every two years in a different country each time. Pilots compete for their country, and can win individual and nation medals
Photo: Marcus King

Competitions and records

The **FAI** is the World Air Sports Federation (*fai.org*). Based in Lausanne, Switzerland, it is an international umbrella organisation for 40 air sports disciplines, including paragliding.

The FAI is made up of more than 100 member nations and is recognised by the IOC, the International Olympic Commission. Paragliding and hang gliding are represented within the FAI by **CIVL**, the International Free Flight Commission.

Both CIVL and the FAI are involved in sanctioning international **competitions** and approving continental **records**

(European, Asian, North and South Americas) and world records.

If you want to take part in a high-level competition, for example a national paragliding championships, you will need to apply for an FAI Sporting Licence beforehand. This is done through your national association, not the FAI. There is usually a small fee.

The FAI classifies competitions into **Category 1** or Category 2 competitions. **FAI Cat. 1 competitions** are the most prestigious and are world or continental championships such as the FAI Paragliding World Championships, or the FAI European Paragliding

Championships. Cat. 2 competitions are all the other competitions that are sanctioned by the FAI throughout the year. For example, a national paragliding championships will be Cat. 2. There is a calendar of all sanctioned paragliding competitions around the world on the FAI website.

The FAI also approves all paragliding world records. If you want to claim a world record you need to submit your tracklog and paperwork in order and in time. The claim is assessed by the FAI and approved or not. The rules about how to claim a world record are on the FAI website.

▶ LEARN MORE

- **The World Air Sports Federation (FAI)** fai.org

- **FAI Paragliding Commission (CIVL)** fai.org/commission/civl

- **IPPI scheme**, fai.org/page/civl-ippi-card

- **APPI**, appifly.org

- **Airtribune, competition calendar** airtribune.com

- **Paragliding World Cup**, pwca.org

- **World records**, fai.org/records

▼ NATIONAL COMPETITIONS
Competing at the Swiss Cup in Engelberg, Switzerland. National competitions see a country's best pilots compete against each other over a week. Each day, depending on the weather, a different task of around 40-120km is set, and pilots race to be the quickest around the course. Photo: Martin Scheel

▲ TOP OF THE STACK
Looking down from the top of a competition gaggle in Brazil. The best competition pilots in the world compete in the Paragliding World Cup, an international series of competitions at different sites around the world throughout the year. Each competition lasts one week, with a two-week Superfinal to crown the year's overall champion. Photo: Harry Bloxham

GPS Speed

40 km/h

Altitude GNSS

1,678 m

Glide ratio

28.66 :1

Glide to: XCP003

1.98 :1

Dist Opt to XCP003

875 m

Alt. over: XCP003

81

C08

Altitude Gdsn

0.

1706

Edit Screen	Route Management	ADD WayPoint	SetQNH

NAVIGATION #8

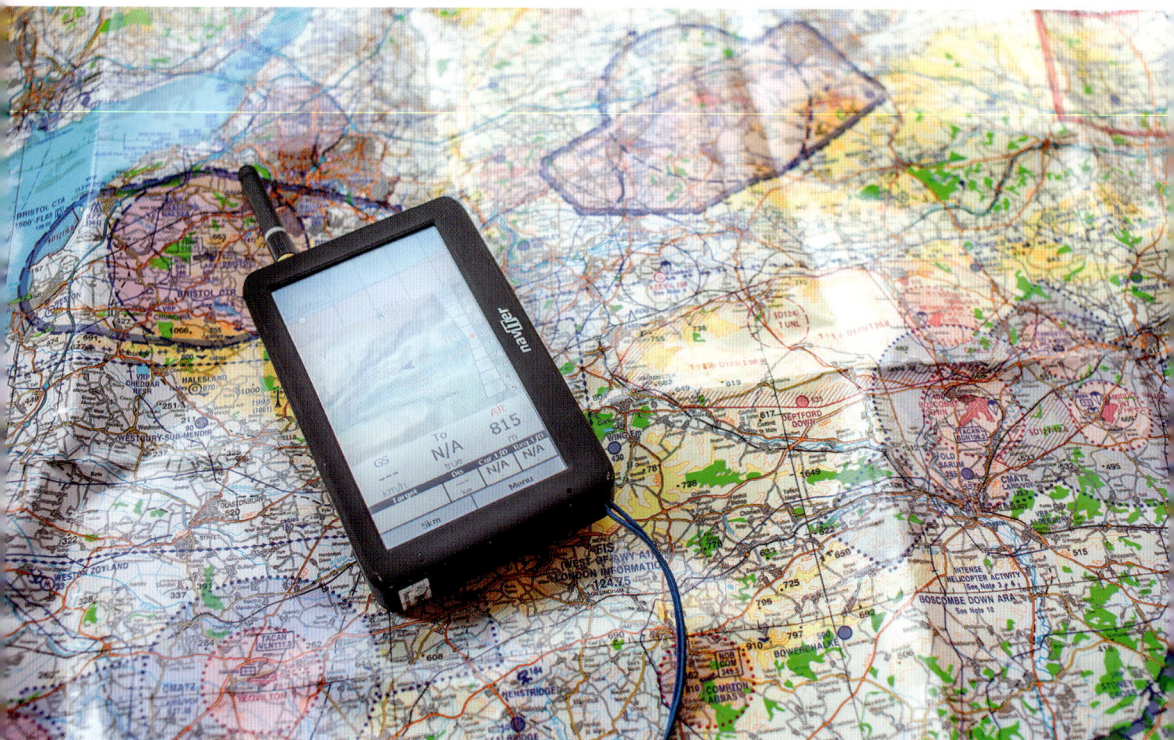

▲ **OLD AND THE NEW**
A laminated air chart for busy airspace in the south of England, and a flight instrument with moving-map display
Photo: Marcus King

How to find your way in the sky

You probably carry a navigation system in your car or even on your bike. This device will tell you where you are and how to get to where you want to be. That's the essence of navigation.

Reading maps is an important part of it, but not the whole story. To navigate with a paraglider you need to determine your course based on a map, compass or GPS. You must take wind and terrain into account. The course that you've set must be checked regularly during your flight, and possibly adapted according to the conditions.

In this chapter, we cover the factors that allow you to safely navigate a paraglider through airspace. We also take a look at anti-collision and avoidance technology. Increasingly airspace is also used by unmanned aircraft – drones, big and small. They use electronic systems to alert other air traffic to their presence, and these are being integrated into our own flight instruments.

▶ PLANET EARTH

Planet **Earth** is a sphere that rotates around its axis once every 24 hours. Half the time we face the **Sun**; we call this daytime. The other half is night. The two points where the imaginary axis penetrates the Earth's surface are called the **Geographic North Pole** and the **Geographic South Pole**, also called the **true North Pole** and **true South Pole**. The Earth rotates to the left, or anticlockwise, as seen from the north pole.

As well as rotating around its axis, the Earth orbits the Sun. A complete orbit takes a little over 365 days. The axis of the Earth is not exactly perpendicular to the plane of rotation around the sun; it's 23° off. This means day and night are not always the same length. It also gives rise to the various seasons.

Circles

The Earth is almost a perfect sphere, but not quite. It's flattened slightly at the poles. For most purposes, it's perfectly acceptable to think of the Earth as a sphere. But for navigation, a more accurate model is needed. For GPS, for example, calculations are done using a mathematical ellipsoid model called **WGS84**. To put the flattening into perspective: the circumference of the Earth at the equator is 40,075km. That's just 67km longer than the circumference via the north and south poles.

However you dissect a sphere, the intersection is a **circle**. If you dissect the Earth exactly through the centre, the circle has the largest circumference. This is called a **great circle** or an **orthodrome**.

If you were to dissect it exactly on the **equator**, the intersection would also be a great circle. This intersection divides the Earth into the N and S hemispheres. Every other intersection that doesn't cut through the centre of the Earth results in a **small circle** – that is, having a smaller circumference than a great circle.

ROTATION OF THE EARTH
The axis of rotation of the Earth is just over 23° tilted with respect to the Earth's orbit around the sun. This causes the differences in the length of day and night, and also gives rise to the seasons

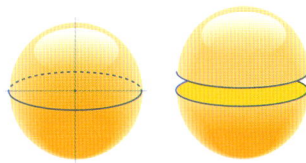

GREAT CIRCLE
The circumference of the intersection of a sphere through the centre is called a great circle

SMALL CIRCLE
The circumference of an arbitrary intersection of a sphere (not through the centre) is called a small circle

277

▶CIRCLES ON EARTH

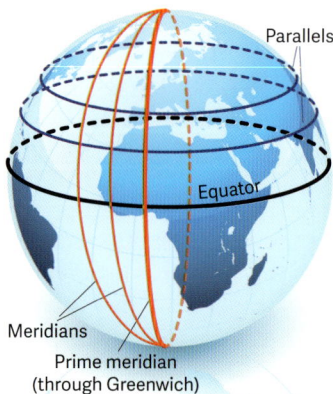

Parallels

Equator

Meridians

Prime meridian
(through Greenwich)

Parallel: a small circle running parallel to the equator; a line of equal latitude

Meridian: a great circle joining the North and South Poles; a line of equal longtitude

Equator: a great circle that divides the Earth into the N and S hemispheres

Prime meridian: a great circle that divides the Earth into the W and E hemispheres, starting at Greenwich (UK)

Arctic circle: a parallel at latitude 66° 33′ north, to the north of which there is 24 hours daylight at about 21 June and 24 hours of darkness at about 21 December

Antarctic circle: a parallel at latitude 66°33′ south, to the south of which there is 24 hours of daylight at about 21 December and 24 hours of darkness at about 21 June

Tropic of Cancer: a parallel at latitude 23°26′ north, where the sun is directly overhead at about 21 June

Tropic of Capricorn: a parallel at latitude 23°26′ south, where the sun is directly overhead at about 21 December.

If you were to dissect the Earth parallel to the equator, a small circle would result that would itself be parallel to the equator. These small circles are therefore called **parallels**.

If you were to dissect the Earth with a plane that passed through the North Pole and the South Pole, you'd end up with a **meridian**. A meridian is a great circle that connects the North and the South Poles.

A place on the globe

To represent a place on the globe by a set of numbers, a system of **coordinates** is developed, similar to the X and Y axes of a graph. The coordinate system of a sphere consists of two circles that are perpendicular to each other. On Earth, these circles are the parallels and the meridians, which you can regard as an X-axis and a Y-axis. A point on a graph is represented by values on the X and the Y axes. Similarly, coordinates on a sphere are represented by values on the meridians and parallels. These values are given in **degrees**.

A circle is divided into degrees which are represented with the symbol °. Because every circle is divided into 360° by definition, parallels and meridians are as well. For both, a starting point is defined. The starting point for parallels is the equator. Parallels run from 0° to 90° to the north or the south. The number of degrees along a parallel is called **latitude**. For example, London is at 51° north latitude.

The starting point for meridians is the **prime meridian** that runs through Greenwich in England. From there, we count from 0° to 180° to the east or to the west. On the opposite side of the planet – exactly – we find the 180° meridian. That is the **dateline** or **anti-meridian**. The number of degrees counted from the prime meridian is called **longitude**. For example, New York can be found at a longitude of 74° west, Singapore at a longitude of 103° east.

The intersection of a meridian and a parallel will give you the exact position of any point in the world. For example, Paris is 48°N, 2°E.

For a more accurate indication of a position, degrees are divided into 60 **minutes** (indicated by ') and minutes are divided into 60 **seconds** ("). The central railway station in Amsterdam can be accurately found at the coordinates 52°22'43"N 4°54'02"E.

Note that we do not need the full 360° of the meridians or parallels, because of the addition of east or west and north or south. Parallels therefore run from 0 to 90° north or south. Meridians run from 0 to 180° east or west.

Distance

Using degrees, minutes and seconds to partition meridians and parallels enables us to determine distances when travelling or flying over the Earth. The shortest distance between two points on a sphere always runs via a great circle. Try it out with a football and string.

As we have seen, each circle is divided into 360°. The circumference of a great circle on Earth is obviously equal to the circumference of the Earth, which is approximately 40,000km. Therefore, one degree over a meridian is equal to 40,000/360 = 111.111km.

Again, we divide degrees into minutes. One meridian minute or minute of latitude is therefore: 111,111/60 = 1,852 metres. By definition, this is a **nautical mile** (**NM**). A **knot** is a quantity of speed that is based on the nautical mile: 1kn = 1NM/h.

Finally, to be even more precise we use seconds of latitude, which represent a distance of 1852/60 = almost 31 metres.

These quantities apply to any meridian and to any other great circle on Earth, but not to small circles. It follows that minutes of latitude are always of equal length because all meridians are great circles. However, the length of a minute over a parallel (a minute of longitude) can differ greatly depending on its position on the Earth. A minute of longitude at the mid latitudes is a much shorter distance than a minute of longitude at the equator. For example, a minute of longitude in London is only 1,154m; at the equator it is 1,852m.

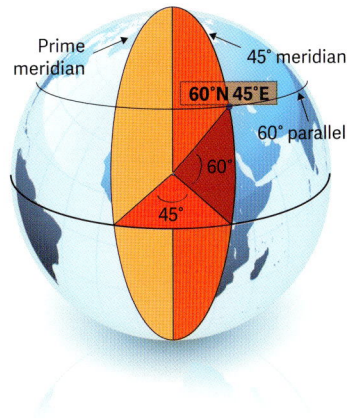

MERIDIANS AND PARALLELS
The intersection of a meridian and a parallel is a coordinate of a position on Earth, for example 60° N 45° E. That is the intersection of the 60° parallel on the northern hemisphere and the 45° meridian east of Greenwich.

279

▶ DIRECTION & COURSE

Understanding how a compass works

The easiest – and most traditional – way to determine a **course** is by using a **compass**. A compass works because the Earth has a magnetic field generated by the core of molten iron. This effectively makes the Earth a giant magnet with one pole at the position of the North Pole and the other on the South Pole. A compass has a magnetic needle that always points to the **magnetic north** of the Earth.

Unfortunately, things are a little more complicated. On maps, true north is usually indicated. But several disturbances cause the compass needle not to point exactly to the true north. It's essential to take these disturbances into account when navigating with a map and compass. The most important are variation and deviation.

THE MAGNETIC NORTH
The Earth's magnetic north is not in the same location as the Earth's true north. The difference between these two is called the variation

The first problem with a compass is the difference between the magnetic North and South Poles and the true North and South Poles. This difference is called (magnetic) **variation** or **magnetic declination**. To complicate things, the magnetic North Pole changes its position over time because the molten iron core moves. The magnetic North Pole is at present found in Canada, and moves by several tens of kilometres a year in the direction of Russia. The variation therefore depends on location and changes over time.

On sea charts and air charts, information on variation is indicated with **isogonic lines**, contour lines which represent a fixed variation. One of these lines indicates a variation of zero and is called the **agonic line**. As variation changes over time, maps or charts with isogons should be updated fairly frequently. Close to the poles, the variation is so large that a compass is of no use.

The second issue to take into account is **deviation**, the difference between magnetic north and compass north, to which the compass needle points. Deviation is caused by disruption of the compass, for example by iron objects.

The total **compass error** is equal to the variation plus the deviation. Compass error indicates how many degrees the 'north' that your compass needle points to is different from true north on the map.

Because of compass error, you need to recalculate your compass course to a course drawn on your map, because on the map true north is indicated.

Finally, a compass has an **inclination**. This means that the compass needle is not balanced exactly horizontally, but with its north pole (the red end) tilted downward a bit in the northern hemisphere.

This is compensated for during the manufacture of the compass, for example by making the other end of the needle a bit heavier. But because of this correction, a compass is only suitable for use in one hemisphere. If you travel to the other hemisphere, you'll need a different compass.

▶ MAPS

Trying to represent a sphere such as the Earth, which is three-dimensional, on to a flat surface such as a map presents a problem. This transition is called a projection. Try cutting up an old football and spreading it on a flat surface. The result is not flat but wrinkled. You'll get the best result by cutting the seams between the pentagons and hexagons.

If the football were the Earth and the map were the separated pentagons and hexagons, we would have a fairly good **projection** of the curved surface of the Earth. But pentagons and hexagons are not particularly practicable as maps. We prefer a rectangular map.

Projections

There are a number of different solutions to this problem, each with its pros and cons. The ideal map has all three of the following properties:

Conformal projections preserve angles on a small scale, which enables you to set a course. All parallels and meridians intersect at right angles (90° angles).

▶ CALCULATING A COMPASS COURSE

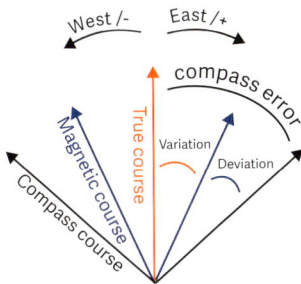

Variation is the difference between true north and magnetic north. Deviation is caused by disruption of the compass by iron objects. The compass error is the sum of variation and deviation.

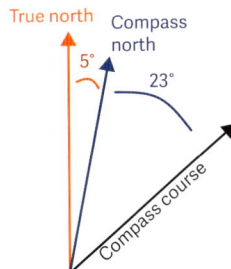

Example a. Let's say you want to set course to true north. Your compass points to 23° and you know the compass error is 5° east. Which course should you fly?
(The answer is 28°)

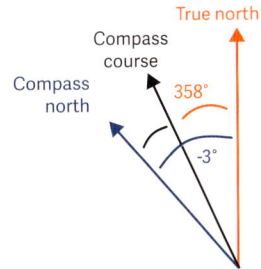

Example b. Let's say you want to set course to true north. Your compass points to 001° and the compass error is -3° (3 degrees west). Which course should you fly? (The answer is 358°)

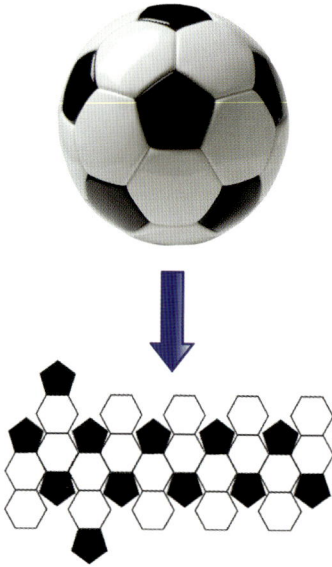

PROJECTION
It is difficult to represent a three-dimensional object such as a sphere on a flat surface. If you were to cut a football along the pentagons and hexagons, you end up with such a plane. But for a map of the Earth, this method is not very suitable

Equidistant projections preserve distances, scaled down, on the map, allowing you to determine the length of a route.

Equivalent projections or equal-area projections preserve areas at scale on the map, so that you can determine the area of a country for example. It usually distorts the shape of a country.

Unfortunately, the ideal map does not exist. The map designer must choose which of these properties are most important, because some exclude the others. For example, an equivalent map is by definition never equidistant or conformal. Therefore, an equivalent map is rarely used for navigation.

One of the most common projections for aviation is the **Lambert conformal conic projection**, abbreviated to **LCC**. This projection preserves angles. A compass course or a GPS course on an LCC map is a straight line. To obtain a Lambert conformal conic projection, an imaginary cone is seated over the sphere of the Earth on to which the surface is projected. Then the cone is cut open and unrolled, resulting in a flat map. The cone dissects two parallels, called **standard parallels**. The standards differ per map and are always indicated.

Note that the parallels (the semi-circles) and the meridians (the straight lines) on the LCC map cross each other at 90° angles. That's how you recognise a Lambert conformal conic projection. The LCC is not only conformal but also almost equidistant between the two standard parallels. Distances measured to scale on an LCC map are very close to actual distances.

The ICAO aeronautical chart

The International Civil Aviation Organisation or **ICAO**, a UN agency, organises navigation in international airspace, for example by adopting standards and recommended practices for international civil aviation. Among its publications are international **aeronautical charts** that contain fewer roads and cities than ordinary maps, but instead show all relevant airspace.

Most countries have their own aeronautical maps. Their **scale** differs between countries; some are at 1:500,000. That means one centimetre on the map represents 500,000 centimetres in reality, which is 5km. Others are at 1:250,000 or 1:1,000,000. The ICAO map is also a Lambert conformal conic projection.

That results in a map that's almost equidistant, which means the scale of the map changes toward the edges. This must be accounted for when planning a route on the map.

At first sight, an ICAO map is packed with symbols, lines and text. The way to bring order into this chaos is by learning to recognise the most important of these. Memorising all the symbols is not necessary; the legend or key of the map lists all of them. ICAO maps are similar between countries, although some details vary.

On the map you'll see horizontal lines with small divisions. Those are the parallels. The distance between two lines is exactly one degree. The divisions indicate minutes. The vertical lines with divisions are meridians. The distance between two lines is again one degree and the divisions indicate minutes and therefore also nautical miles (NM). Note that a minute on a parallel is always shorter than a meridian minute because parallels are small circles (except on the equator).

Using coordinates on a map

A location can be indicated by coordinates, as we have seen. If a set of coordinates is available, you can find the location on the map. Conversely, you can read the coordinates of a location on the map and use them, for example in your GPS.

To find a location on a map using coordinates, follow the steps below. You will need: an ICAO map, a pencil and a protractor. A typical pilot exam question could be: *What is the name of the flying site at the location with given coordinates 051°22'45"N 001°51'20"W?*

The latitude is given by the first number. Those are the parallels. Find the 51° parallel and the 52° parallel on the map. Move up from the 51° parallel by 22'45" in the direction of the 52° parallel (45" is equal to three-quarters of a minute).

▶ LAMBERT CONFORMAL CONIC PROJECTION

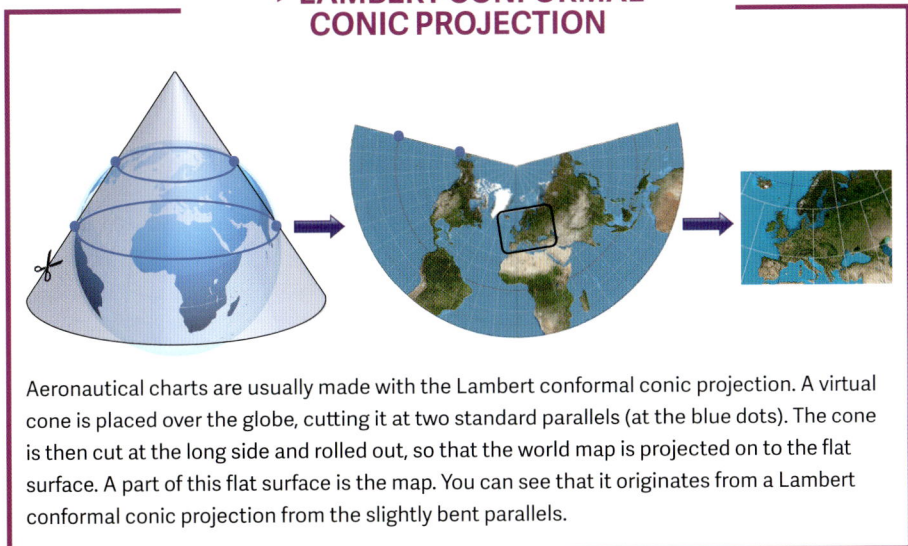

Aeronautical charts are usually made with the Lambert conformal conic projection. A virtual cone is placed over the globe, cutting it at two standard parallels (at the blue dots). The cone is then cut at the long side and rolled out, so that the world map is projected on to the flat surface. A part of this flat surface is the map. You can see that it originates from a Lambert conformal conic projection from the slightly bent parallels.

▲ OLD SCHOOL RULES
Learning to navigate using a paper map and the old-school methods is good training, plus it crops up in pilot exams and on cross-country courses. Using a large map is also helpful for seeing all the sky at once, rather than just a part of it on a small screen. Photo: Marcus King

▶ GPS COORDINATES

A GPS renders your position in coordinates. These are usually displayed as we've seen in the text: degrees, minutes and seconds. This is the most accurate representation, and is used in aviation. But there are other notations. It's important to know which notation your GPS is using, especially when exchanging coordinates. If you use the wrong format, you could end up in an entirely different spot. The most important:

Degrees in decimals: D.ddddd°
Degrees and minutes in decimals:
DD°MM.mmm'
Degrees, minutes and seconds in decimals:
DD°MM'SS.s"

Put a mark here with your pencil. The longitude is given by the second number. Those are the meridians. Find the 1° and the 2° meridians on the map. Move from the 1° meridian to the left (westward) by 51'15". Put another mark here with your pencil.

Put the protractor with its straight edge on the last mark exactly parallel to the nearest meridian. Draw a vertical line. Then, put the protractor with its straight edge on the first mark and exactly parallel to the nearest parallel. Draw a horizontal line. The location of the given coordinates is found where the two lines cross. In this case, it is Milk Hill, a flying site in the UK and marked on the air chart.

Bearing and distance

From your position on the map you can set a course to your next position, for example your goal. You need to calculate the bearing and the distance to the goal in a straight line. You need the same instruments plus a compass for drawing.

A typical exam question could be: *From Milk Hill you want to fly 12.1 NM on a bearing of 63°. What is your destination?*

Place the protractor with the centre of its straight edge on the coordinates of Milk Hill. The 0° line of the protractor should point exactly true north. Place a mark on the map at the 63° mark of the protractor. Draw a line from Milk Hill through this mark. This is your **bearing**.

Now you need to measure 12.1 NM along the bearing. On the UK 1:250,000 airmap we are using, each minute dash of longtitude equals one nautical mile (1 NM), so measure 12.1 dashes. Use the drawing compass for this. Put the needle on the map on an arbitrary meridian and put the drawing point 12.1 dashes further. Keep the arms of the compass at this length and move the compass. Put the needle on Milk Hill and draw a circle around it. (If you don't have a compass drawing tool, another method is to measure 12.1 NM with a ruler in the direction of your bearing.)

The place where the circle crosses the line of your bearing is your goal. This is the minor airfield at Membury.

▼**DESTINATION MEMBURY**
Using a technical drawing compass to measure distance, in this case the 12.1 NM (nautical miles) between launch at Milk Hill and landing at Membury is equivalent to 22.4km. That's about an hour's cross-country flying.
Photo: Marcus King

▶ KEEPING COURSE IN WIND

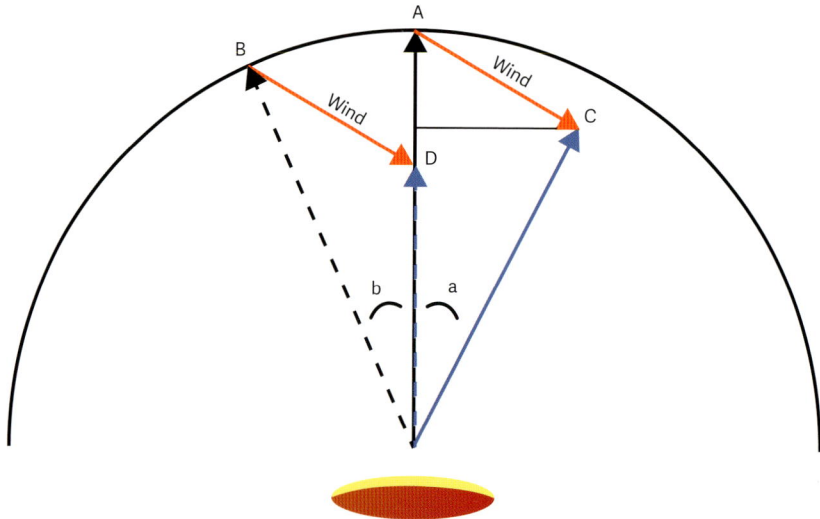

→ Course of the paraglider (without wind)
----▶ Corrected course of the paraglider in a crosswind
→ Course of the paraglider without correction
----▶ Course of the paraglider after correction by crabbing
→ Wind speed and direction
a   Leeway angle
b   Corrective angle
A   Destination of the paraglider without wind
B   Goal toward which the paraglider is headed using crabbing in a crosswind.
C   Destination of the paraglider with a crosswind but without crabbing.
D   Destination of the paraglider after a correction for the crosswind.

Imagine you've set a course to goal at point A, but during your flight you notice a crosswind. You're drifting off course towards point C if you don't act. In order to get to your goal you must shift your course. The departure from your original course is called the **leeway angle**.

Compensating your course for the crosswind is done by **crabbing** into wind. It seems obvious that you need to correct your course into wind with the same angle as the leeway angle, but, things are not that simple. The corrective angle is slightly smaller than the leeway angle and also depends on the wind speed. Therefore you must correct your course, but not by as much as you might expect.

In the illustration, you can see that to arrive at the set destination A, the corrective angle b is slightly smaller than the leeway angle a. You have to set course to point B. Also, the groundspeed with crabbing (arrow D) is lower than without crabbing (arrow C). Therefore, with a crosswind you can't fly as far as without wind (assuming the same speed).

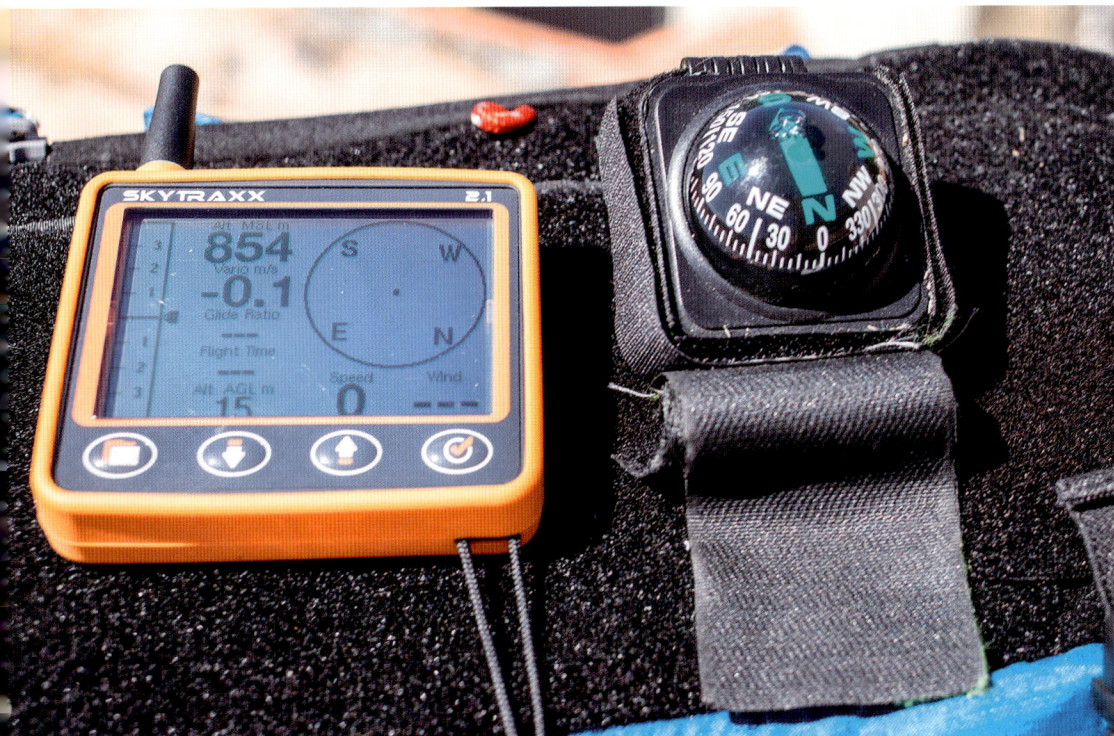

▲ A DIGITAL COMPASS AND A TRADITIONAL BALL COMPASS
Most pilots today will use a flight instrument to help them navigate, but that doesn't mean compasses have been binned. Quite the opposite: ball compasses are an essential piece of kit. In cloud they offer a horizon and an easy way to navigate. They also never get damp and malfunction, or run out of batteries. Photo: Marcus King

▶ NAVIGATING USING INSTRUMENTS

Even for paraglider pilots, instruments are all but indispensable. As soon as you leave your home hill, you need to know where you are and where you are going. The options are endless and we will discuss the most used below.

But also remember that flying is about staying up. By focusing too intently on your heading (unless it's dangerous to do otherwise) you may just end up missing the good stuff and bombing out. Whatever device you have, fly the skies and the terrain ahead of you. Don't get fixated on your instrument.

Ball compass

If you're navigating with a map on terra firma, a flat, baseplate **compass** will do the job. But what happens to the compass when you start moving around? Paragliders don't fly level: they pitch, roll and yaw, especially in turbulent air. And if you're using a flat compass, these movements can cause the needle to stick or show a misleading heading.

The solution is a **ball compass**. In a ball compass, the disk floats in a (usually, liquid-filled) globe, which allows it to stay level even as you're moving. Ensure it is big enough to see clearly, but small enough to mount on your flight deck. Ideally, it will also work up to a tilt of 45 degrees. Also remember that compasses can be affected by your other instruments. See if yours is – and allow for it – before you need it.

Using a ball compass in cloud

You might well be thinking "Why use a compass at all?" After all, we have GPS, smartphones and numerous other navigation devices at our disposal. The one word answer is: cloud. You may not need to rely on your compass to navigate from A to B, but if you ever find yourself in cloud, unable to tell up from down and being jostled around by turbulence, you'll be grateful for an easy way to maintain your heading.

This is particularly important if you're near terrain – if you're in a cloud, it's surprisingly easy to turn 180 degrees without knowing it and fly straight into the hill. So be prepared. If you are flying near cloudbase take the time to check your compass and note the bearing that will take you into clear air if you find yourself suddenly engulfed.

Navigating with a GPS

If you have a **GPS** instrument, it can calculate (among other things) your location, speed and heading. Whether or not it has a map, this allows you to use it for navigation, much like a compass. Indeed, many such devices will have a compass feature with an arrow, which can be added to your home screen.

Following a precise bearing can be difficult in flight though. You'll drift with the wind in thermals, make countless small corrections and, ultimately, aim for where the lift is. Consequently, even if you want to make a huge straight-line flight, it's often counterproductive to

stick too precisely to a bearing. Flying south(ish) will often serve you as well as sticking religiously to a 180-degree heading.

Many instruments will also allow you to input **waypoints** along your proposed route. You could make these known thermal trigger points, or landings with good road or rail links. You can then use the device to navigate between them (most will calculate an optimised route to the next one).

Using digital maps in flight

Reading a **map** on the ground is straightforward, but don't assume it's the same in the air. You'll soon discover that you can't study a map in detail, and fly a paraglider safely, at the same time. Fortunately, many flight instruments come with **digital maps** – from the rudimentary to the highly detailed.

There's plenty of choice. Some instruments only show airspace relative to your position. Others offer full-colour, topographical maps, while others still show the terrain ahead in 3D. You can also use **smartphone apps** to navigate in the air, but mobile screens can be hard to see when the sun is shining on them, and they will drain your battery fast. Many pilots fly with extra battery packs for just this reason.

A key consideration is how useful the map will be in flight, when the going gets tough, the air is turbulent and you have to make good decisions quickly. A highly detailed map may seem ideal on the ground, but how handy will it be when you can only give it the occasional quick glance? Could it even become an unwanted distraction?

▲ ROUTE PLANNING
Using a dedicated online flight-planning tool to research and plan your flying day can be extremely useful. They often show the tracklogs of other pilots, and can be adjusted for speed and time. Once you have planned your flight you can download the route to your flight instrument. Photo: Marcus King

Think about the sat-nav in your car. Rarely can you stare at it for too long – without risking a collision. In flight, you need to be even more focused on what's ahead. As well as flying the glider, you need to look to the horizon to assess conditions, plan your route, keep an eye out for other aircraft and spot potential landing spots. To spend too much time switching your attention from the far distance to the instrument right in front of you can be tiring and disruptive.

Some of the work you can do at home. If you plan your potential routes and familiarise yourself with the main features and towns on Google Earth before you set off, for example, you will be able to

read the map on your flight instrument far more easily and instinctively. Key landmarks will be quickly recognisable, saving you time and energy.

But you should also think about the ergonomics of your cockpit and flight deck. Once in your harness, does the tilt of your flight deck make the instruments hard to see? If so, it's time to make some adjustments. Try putting your instruments in different places to see where they are most visible and useful. And don't forget how the sun might make them difficult to see.

If you like flying with a moving map, consider using a second instrument for indicators such as groundspeed, climb rate and wind speed. Having everything on one screen can be distracting and unclear. And if you have to use a touchscreen to switch between screens, think about how you will do this in flight? If the air's choppy and your hands are cold, are you really going to be able to get cleanly from one screen to the next, or are you just going to end up accidentally restoring the factory settings at the crucial moment?

Also consider the environment you're flying in. If you're regularly flying your home sites and challenging yourself along familiar cross-country routes, you probably don't need a detailed map at all.

If you're flying a new range of mountains, however, it's likely an essential.

But however you choose to navigate, give it some thought in advance. Planning your route and establishing what's most useful when you're actually flying is the best route to success.

Navigating airspace

As well as our position relative to the ground, we also need to know our position in the air – what height we are at, and where we are in relation to any important airspace.

Paper **airspace maps** are widely available, but airspace can also easily be uploaded onto many instruments and smartphones.

▼ **MOVING MAP**
Digital maps must be clear enough to read quickly in flight, with a non-reflective screen so they can be viewed in bright sunshine. This instrument, a Naviter Oudie, is a fully functioning flight instrument with a colour screen. It has air charts and ground maps pre-installed for the whole of Europe. Photo: Marcus King

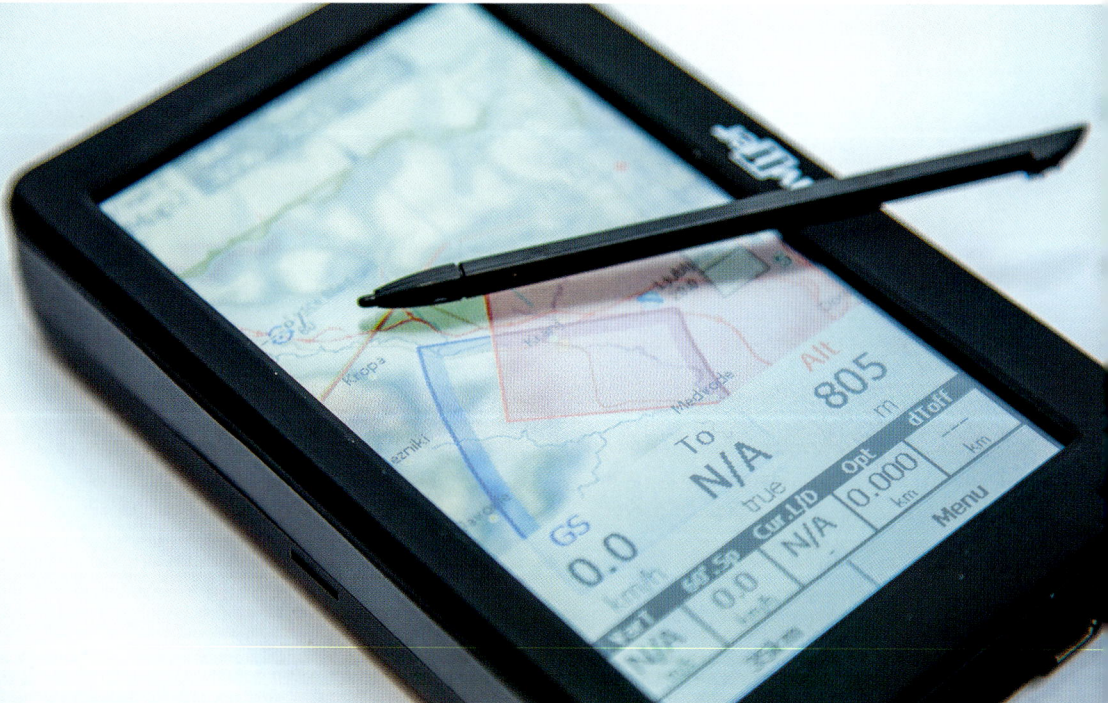

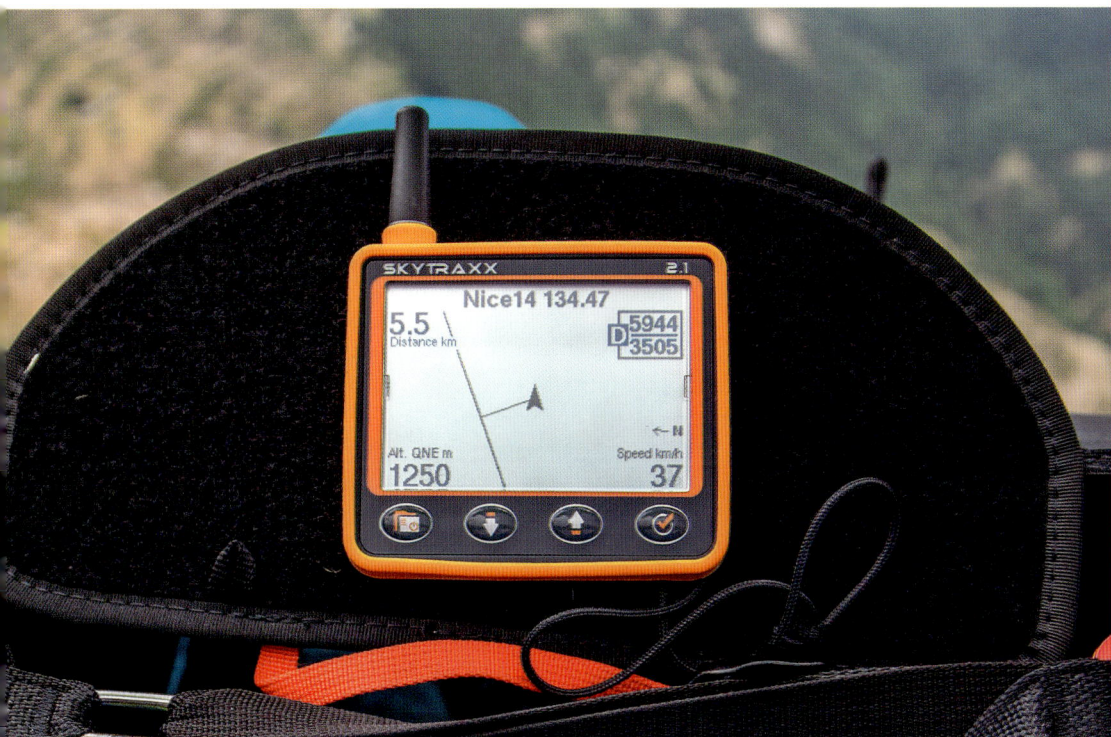

When choosing a flight instrument, especially at the start of your flying career, go for something with a big, clear screen. Instruments with black and white screens are fine, work well in bright sunlight, and have a long battery life. This instrument is only displaying information about the airspace the pilot is in. Photo: Marcus King

Either way, take some time before you fly to study the airspace along your proposed route. When you see it on your instrument later, you will then be far more familiar with its dimensions and restrictions.

You should also take some time to check for NOTAMs (p261) and other temporary airspace restrictions that may not be recorded by your instrument. And whether you use paper or digital maps, always ensure they are up to date – airspace changes.

Most instruments that show airspace will also allow you to change the settings related to it. First, consider whether you want it to sound an alarm when you reach

prohibited areas. When this alert sounds can also be changed. Perhaps you want it to beep 400m before you reach the airspace, either vertically or horizontally.

Some instruments and apps will give you detailed information about the airspace ahead – exactly what it is and at what altitude it comes into operation. Others will merely warn you when you are approaching it. Again, familiarising yourself with airspace in advance reduces the amount of time you will have to spend deciphering it in flight.

If you have airspace on a map, you should also think about scale. If you're flying in an area with complex airspace, you'll want a magnified map, so you can see your position in relation to it precisely.

But if you're flying a long cross country, you also need to be able to see and plan for the airspace many kilometres ahead, taking into account your drift and other variables. If you want to fly big distances, you need to plan your course far in advance or you could end up boxing yourself in with airspace. Use non-flying days to practise changing the scale of your map and switching between functions in flight.

If you don't always want to fly with the airspace on a digital map, consider what you include on your vario's home screen (many devices allow you to customise

this). At the very least, it's worth including your distance to the next airspace on it. You can read this with a quick glance.

You must also understand how your instrument is calculating your altitude. Is the reading in feet or metres? And is it calculated by GPS or by using barometric pressure? The aviation industry uses barometric pressure rather than GPS to calculate altitude and the two systems can produce significantly different results.

Remember, flying into prohibited airspace is illegal and potentially dangerous. But not understanding it can also force you to land. No one wants to abandon a 100km flight simply because they don't know what the airspace is.

▼ TERRAIN MAPS
This instrument is displaying a map of the terrain the pilot is flying through. This can be useful when flying through new or unfamiliar terrain, especially in the mountains. Like ground maps, the contours show the rise and fall of the hills and mountains, allowing you to 'see' beyond the horizon. Photo: Marcus King

▶GPS AND BAROMETRIC ALTITUDE

How high are you? The answer your instrument gives you might depend on whether it is showing your **GPS altitude** or **barometric altitude**. Your GPS position is calculated by your device relative to the system's orbiting satellites and then mapped onto its model (or **datum**) of the Earth – in paragliding, this is usually the World Geodetic System established in 1984 (**WGS84**). But while it generally is an excellent approximation of the planet, it is not perfect and, in some parts of the world, there are errors in its calculation of mean sea level, which in turn may result in an inaccurate altitude reading. Other factors, such as poor satellite reception, shifts in the satellites' orbits and clock errors, may also affect your GPS reading. Different datums will also give variable positions, which may compound into major discrepancies over big distances. These inaccuracies are rarely more than tens of metres, but you should be aware of them.

Rather than GPS, the aviation industry uses barometric pressure to calculate altitude. The system assumes that pressure drops at a standard rate as altitude increases. In paragliding, we deal with altitude above ground level (AGL), above mean sea level (AMSL) and with respect to the standard reference of 1013 hectopascals (hPa), otherwise known as **Pressure Altitude** or **PA**.

Your GPS and barometric vario/altimeter can give you different altitude readings, which is significant if you're using your altitude reading to avoid airspace. Because it is the aviation industry standard, using barometric pressure to calculate your altitude is the preferable option for avoiding airspace during cross-country flying. Most importantly, however, you should be aware of what your instrument is showing – and how it is calculating it.

▼WHY YOU SHOULD SET YOUR ALTIMETER
A change in air pressure will affect the reading from your barometric altimeter, but not your GPS.

On Day 1, with standard air pressure at 1013 hPa, you are flying a site with an airspace limit of FL065. Because QNH = QNE (standard air pressure), FL065 = 6,500ft. You are happy to fly to 6,000ft using your GPS altitude, confident you will not enter airspace. In fact you have a buffer of 500ft.

On Day 2, standard air pressure has dropped significantly to 973 hPa. FL065 is now at 5,300ft. If you climb to 6,000ft GPS altitude, you will actually be 700ft inside airspace.

This is why, if you are flying where there is a flight level ceiling, you should fly using barometric altitude first, and set it at launch before you take off. If there is no airspace ceiling where you fly, then you don't need to worry.

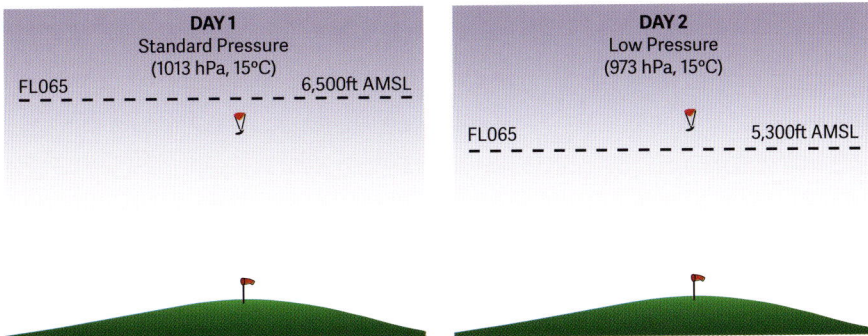

DAY 1
Standard Pressure
(1013 hPa, 15°C)
FL065 - - - - - - - - - - - - - - - 6,500ft AMSL

DAY 2
Low Pressure
(973 hPa, 15°C)
FL065 - - - - - - - - - - - - - - - 5,300ft AMSL

▲ **SAY HELLO TO THE DRONES**
Drones (also called UAVs, unmanned aviation vehicles) are part of the aviation ecosystem. Unlike manned aircraft they can not see-and-avoid. They rely on electronic anti-collision systems to keep them from bumping into things. It's down to us to make sure we are electronically visible to them. Photo: Marcus King

▶ ELECTRONIC VISIBILITY

The sky can be a busy place, and with the rising use of drones, both recreational and commercial, the ability to see and be seen is becoming increasingly important. Aircraft carry **transponders** but these are heavy, expensive and power hungry and are not suitable for us. There are, however, suitable alternatives for paragliding.

Live tracking

Many instruments now feature **live tracking** functionality. By using an internet connection, either an internal GSM chip or connected to your phone, your position can be sent to a central server. A website or app then shows your position on a map. For areas without a mobile phone network there are satellite trackers available: the two systems we typically use are either SPOT Satellite Messenger or Garmin InReach.

Live tracking is great for safety as your friends can know where you are flying. On some instruments you can also receive the position of your friends to help you fly together. Live-tracking data can also be ingested into air traffic systems, helping other air users avoid you.

FLARM

The **FLARM** system (FLight alARM) is a system that helps make us electronically-visible to other aircraft for the purpose of collision avoidance. It has a working range of about 20km and is particularly useful if you fly in an area with a lot of sailplane traffic, such as in the Alps. All sailplanes use it in Switzerland, Germany and France, and the Flarm website claims that more than 50% of general aviation air traffic, including planes and helicopters, have it in Europe (including the UK). More than 20,000 drones also use Flarm, according to flarm.com.

Flarm does away with the need for transponders, allows us to be seen by our fellow pilots, and goes some way to future-proofing ourselves against the rise of the drones.

The FANET System

FANET (Flying Ad-hoc NETwork) meanwhile is an open-source network designed to pass data between instruments over a low-power radio connection. The way the system is designed each instrument acts as a relay, so information can be passed much further by bouncing through intermediate instruments.

As well as positional data the system can be used to send messages between instruments, for example status updates. By adding ground stations into the network they can act as gateways to the internet, so you can receive up-to-

▼ HOW FANET+ WORKS
Pilots with Fanet+ transmit their information over the Flarm network (blue lines), which is received by the Flarm-equipped sailplanes and light aircraft. The paraglider pilots can also send and receive information to each other (black lines), the Fanet-equipped sailplane, and the ground station, which can also act as a relay to the internet. Even though C is out of range of A, information can be sent automatically between the two by using B as a relay.

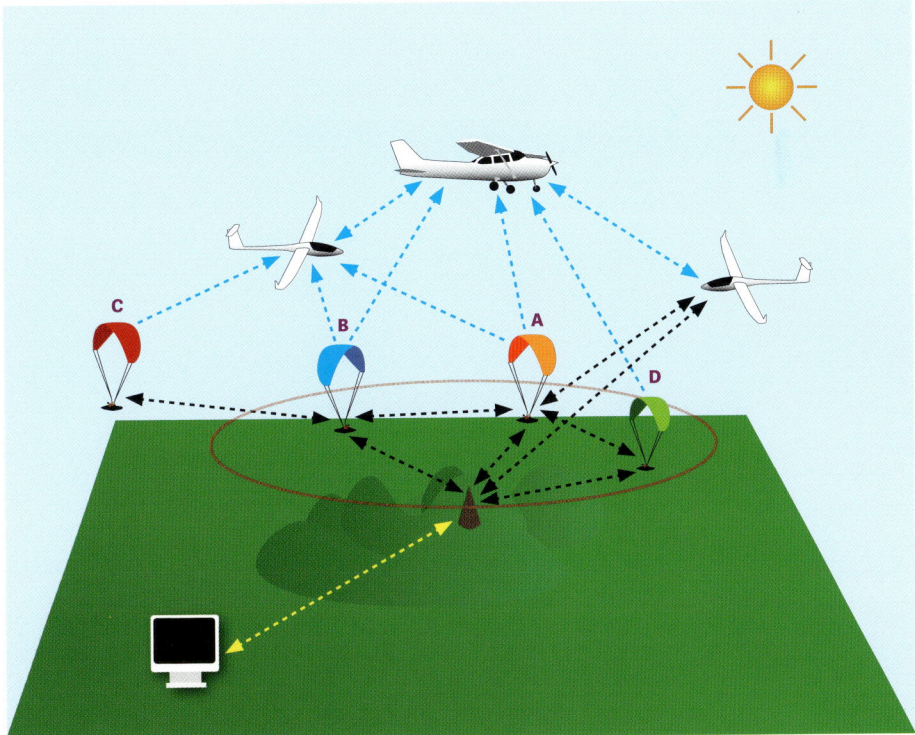

date weather information, or send your live-tracking position without needing a mobile or satellite internet connection.

FANET+

The **Fanet+** module was developed by a flight instrument manufacturer (Skytraxx) and is used in several other instruments. It combines Flarm and Fanet in one module. The module only transmits on Flarm and cannot receive using the Flarm protocol, relying instead on Fanet for receiving information. The Fanet+ module allows instruments also equipped with Fanet+ to communicate with each other and the ground stations, regardless of manufacturer. It also transmits your position to other air users in the region.

Future-proofing

The technology in this area is always developing and changing rapidly. It is important to stay up to date with new developments so you and others stay safe. It is a good idea to get into the habit of reading the new technology news and reviews, to sign up to any manufacturer email newsletters, and to take advantage of any software upgrades available for your flight instrument. Be aware too the systems described above are not universal. Different countries and organisations are developing their own collision-avoidance and awareness systems. This means it is always wise to check the flight instrument you want to buy will work and be effective in the country you want to use it in.

▼ **AIR BUDDIES**
If you and your friends have the same instrument, or instruments that can use the same technology, you can see each other's position on your screen. Here the pilot is flying with 'Charlie' – Charlie King – a short distance away just to his right. Photo: Marcus King

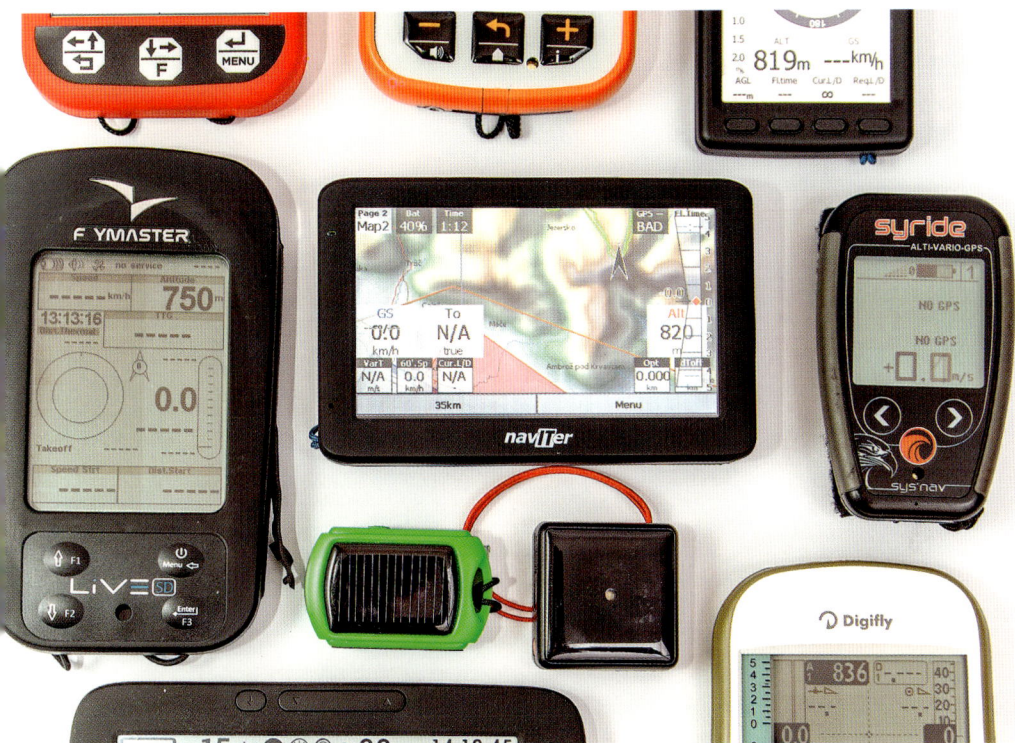

▶ CHOOSING THE RIGHT FLIGHT INSTRUMENT

When choosing an **instrument**, start with 'you'. What are your skills? What are your goals? What would best help you to improve and achieve them? Will a lot of information distract you, or give you the leg-up you need to get to the next level? The key is to do your research and find the instrument best suited to your style of flying. Here are a few pointers.

Beginner

When you're starting out, begin with the basics: ease of use, audio vario, groundspeed and altitude. You won't want to spend too long trying to decipher

the readings in the air, so ensure you can make sense of it at a glance. Get used to changing the settings (it's not helpful when the sink alarm starts screaming every time you start going down or you hate the tone of the beep) and ensure you know what it's showing you before you start flying. But consider your ambitions, too. If you want to start flying cross country, for example, make sure your instrument can show airspace if you need it to.

Intermediate

Aiming to fly far? Then navigation is key – at the very least, opt for something that shows airspace. Some instruments also come with an easy-to-read colour map –

although a number of free smartphone apps, such as XCTrack, fulfil the same function. But there's no need to get too technical. Being bombarded with complex data may just distract you from the fun bit: flying.

Technical

If you're into polar curves and technically savvy there are plenty of instruments for you. Go top-end and fully configurable, but devote some serious time to truly understanding what your device is telling you. If you don't get it, you'll just end up confused.

Competition

Managing the task and waypoints and optimising your route become key factors here, as do the specific requirements of the competition you're entering. A number of instruments are aimed specifically at competition pilots, but you may want to consider a back-up instrument, too. As well as giving you peace of mind, you can set the instruments to display different features in flight, saving you from switching between screens.

Adventurer

Something lightweight and tough that's simple to use and doesn't use a lot of power is key for off-the-beaten-track and vol-bivouac missions. You'll also want it for navigation, so look for an instrument that can store offline maps and airspace.

Minimalist

Sometimes all you want is a beep. If you're willing to do without everything but a vario, you can find plenty of miniature, solar-powered devices that will do the job. It can be liberating, but if you've been relying on a more complex

instrument to tell you your wind speed and direction, be prepared to think for yourself. With few features, they're also reliable. Consider one as a back-up.

Build it yourself

You don't have to buy a flight instrument straight off the shelf. If you have the know-how and the patience, you can build your own. Just be honest about your skills. Making your own instrument is one thing; being able to rely on it is quite another.

And finally...

You have reached the end of this book – but not the adventure! Learning to fly well and achieve your goals and ambitions can be a life-long journey. As a pilot you will never stop learning. We hope you have enjoyed what you have read, and that this finds its way onto your bookshelf. See you in the sky!

▶**LEARN MORE**

- **International Civil Aviation Organisation (ICAO)**, icao.int

- **How to read ICAO maps** tinyurl.com/natgeo-airmaps

- **Lat/Long and GPS coordinates finder**, latlong.net

- **GPS & barometric altitude explained** tinyurl.com/flying-gps

- **iPhone apps**, FlySkyHy, SeeYou Navigator

- **Android apps**, XCSoar, XCTrack , SeeYou Navigator

► **ENJOY THE RIDE**
Ed Ewing enjoys early spring thermals in the Stubai Valley, Austria
Photo: Marcus King

ALPHA Series

ADVANCE

SUCCESS Series

The perfect Start

Coordinated equipment from a single source

Spread your wings like a bird, step into the air and simply fly. As one of the leading premium brands we offer perfectly coordinated equipment for the first steps. Latest technology combined with the highest quality materials ensure your pleasure and safety while you learn, and for long afterwards.

www.advance.ch

Index

ALL OF THE FUN, NONE OF THE STRESS

The Atlas 2 is an easy intermediate wing for beginning and leisure pilots who want a confidence-inspiring wing that still offers great XC possibilities.

Using technology developed for our competition wings, we have further optimised the sail tension and 3D shaping. The result is a smoother take-off, better pitch damping, lighter handling and a useful "thermal sniffing" ability.

EN B // 6 sizes // 55-125 kg

independence

•• paragliding

Pioneer³
LTF/EN A

fly it your way

30 years airborne experience

www.independence.aero

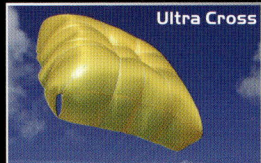
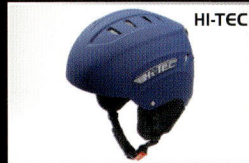

FUN IS WHAT YOU MAKE OF IT ...!

PURE PASSION FOR FLYING

SKYWALK

f skywalk.paragliders ⃝ skywalkparagliders www.skywalk.info

Photo: Tristan SM.

UNITS

1m = 3.28ft	1m/s = 197 ft per minute	1km/h = 0.54 knots =
100m = 328ft	2m/s = 394 ft per minute	0.62mph
1,000m = 1,093 yards	3m/s = 591 ft per minute	1 knot = 1.15mph = 1.85km/h
1km = 0.62 miles	5m/s = 984 ft per minute	1mph = 0.87 knots = 1.61km/h
100km = 62.14 miles	10m/s = 1,969 ft per minute	
10ft = 3.05m		
1,000ft = 304.8m		10km/h = 5.4knots = 6.2mph
1 mile = 1,609m (1.6km)		15km/h = 8.1 knots = 9.32mph
100 miles = 160.94km		32km/h = 17.3 knots = 20mph
0.5m/s = 98.5 ft per minute		50km/h = 27 knots = 31.07mph

WELCOME TO EARTH'S GREATEST PLAYGROUND

At SWING we are convinced that paragliding is the most awesome thing in the world. This is why we have been living and loving this wonderful sport as pioneers for more than 30 years. Whether you are attempting your first take-offs or you are an experienced XC pilot looking for the perfect line - Our mission is to bring you the best possible flying experience through reliable paragliding equipment and our patented RAST technology.

RAST
Rock solid flight
by SWING

SWING

MEET THE TEAM

Sauerland, Germany, 2001

Ölüdeniz, Turkey, 2008

Pedra Bonita, Brazil, 2009

Netherlands, 2014

Stubai, Austria, 2018

Coupe Icare, France, 2019

Australia, 1999

Panchgani, India, 2002

Spanish Open, 2005

Rio de Janeiro, 2006

Owens Valley, USA, 2016

Tandem SIV, Austria, 2017

Bastienne Wentzel, lead author

Bastienne learned to fly paragliders in 2008, around the famous site of St. Vincent-les-Forts in France. Ever since, she spends a big chunk of her free time flying. She enjoys flying acro, coastal soaring, hike-and-fly and quietly floating around in beautiful places such as Europe, Turkey, Morocco, Brazil, South Africa and Kyrgyzstan.

A professional science writer she is an assistant instructor, teaches paragliding theory courses, and edits the Dutch paragliding magazine Lift.

Ed Ewing, author and editor

Ed first flew a paraglider aged 18 in the hills near Edinburgh, Scotland. Like many of us, he quickly became obsessed with paragliding, and worked as a trainee instructor in Scotland and Spain while learning to fly XC. He has flown the flatlands in Australia, mountains in India, and XC in South America. A journalist, he has written about free flight for the Guardian and the FT, and worked on events like the FAI World Air Games, Red Bull Air Race and Red Bull X-Alps. He has edited Cross Country since 2013.

316

Westbury, UK, 1994   Coastal soaring, UK 1999

Wiltshire, UK, 1994   Chamonix, France, 1998

North Wales, 2001   Florida, 2009

Lauterbrunnen, CH, 2005   Mont Blanc, France, 2011

Annecy, France, 2010   France, 2020

Kilimanjaro, 2017   France, 2020

Marcus King, designer

Inspired by seeing paragliders flying from Planpraz, Chamonix while on a climbing trip, Marcus learned to fly in 1991 on the UK's Wiltshire Downs. He moved to France to join Ozone in 2001 before becoming Cross Country magazine's designer in 2004. A keen photographer since childhood, his twin loves of photography and paragliding have taken him all over the world. His passion for cross-country flying is as strong as ever, and he also enjoys flying tandem, sharing his love for free flight with others.

Charlie King, illustrator

Charlie's first flight was a 21st birthday gift from now-husband Marcus, a tow-launch taster day on a ram-air parachute from a field in Cheltenham, UK. She learned to hill-fly in south-east Wales in 1994-5 and enjoyed the laid-back British scene and its endless weekends with paragliders, campervans and friends. On moving to the mountains in France in 2002 she discovered the pleasures of hike-and-fly, and agrees with the 1978 folks from Mieussy who first found that mountains and paragliders do go very well together.

►THANK YOU, CONTRIBUTORS

This book would not have been possible without the help of many people. Thank you all for your support, time, feedback, contributions and enthusiasm!

Advance Paragliders, AirDesign, Jorge Atramiz, Tex Beck, Ronald ten Berge, Leonard Bik, Gareth Bird, André Bizot, Peter Blokker, Charles Blonk, Laurent Boninfante, Chris Borra, Nanny Bosch, Martin Bucknall, Jeroen Buis, Kieran Campbell, Brett Coupland, Jess Cox, Andrew Craig, Gerald van Dalen, Suzanne van Engelshoven, Adi Geisegger, Peter van Gemert, Martijn Geurts, Jeff Goin, Till Gottbrath, Ant Green, Joanna Di Grigoli, Steve Ham, Roland ter Harkel, Prof. Dr. Jacco Hoekstra, Independence Paragliding, Ayke Jager, KNMI, Leontien Kragten, Fons de Leeuw, Hans ter Maat, Mac Para, Burkhard Martens, Jérôme Maupoint, Gavin McClurg, Philipp Medicus, Geert Mesander, Hugh Miller, Lea Montforts, Margit Nance, Lucas ten Napel, Frank van den Nieuwenhoff, Paul Nylander, Russell Ogden, Ozone Gliders, Georgeana Parsons, Tom Prideaux-Brune, Peter Rehorst, Honza Rejmanek, Jocky Sanderson, Jan Sikking, Skywalk, Brian Steele, Verity Sowden-Green, Ernst Strobl, Rob Sporrer, Swing Paragliders, Vera Valkestijn, Vincent Verbon, Erwin Voogt, Matt Warren, Eric Wierenga, Dr Matt Wilkes, Rogier Wolff and Barry Zeldenrust. Particular thanks to instructor Chris White for invaluable feedback on several early drafts.

▲ **NEVER STOP LEARNING**
The fun only increases as you get better
Photo: Adi Geisegger

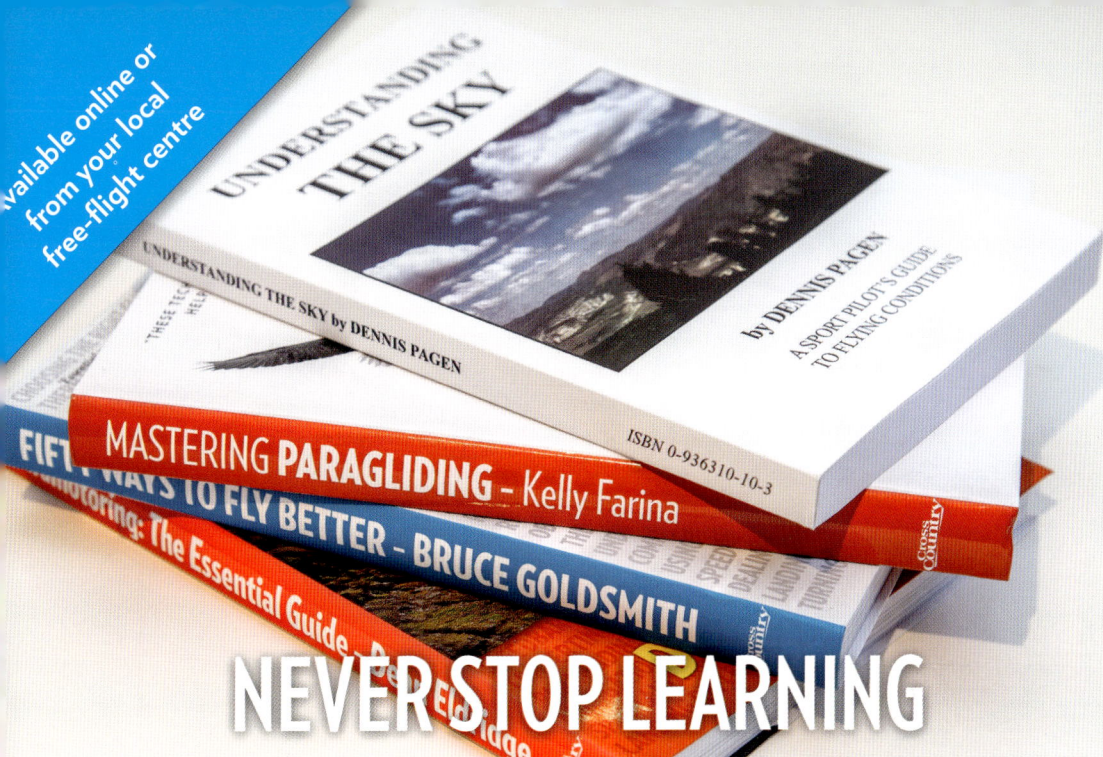

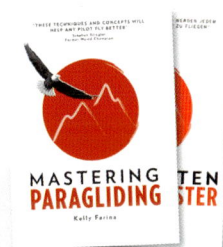

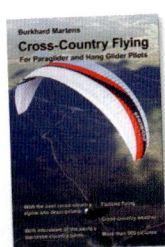

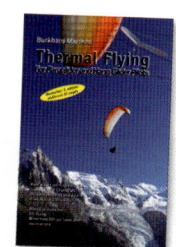

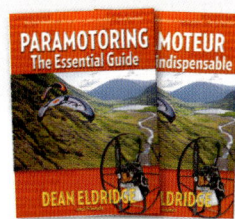

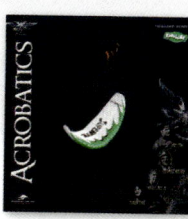

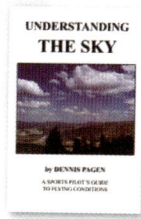

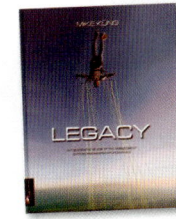

Cross Country

In the core, since 1988

STAY CONNECTED

More journal than magazine, Cross Country has kept pilots stoked with inspiration and information since 1988. Learn to fly better with technique, weather and safety articles, read the latest glider and gear reviews, and be inspired with adventure and flying stories in every one of the ten issues you'll receive throughout the year. Respected as independent and authoritative, Cross Country is a reader-supported publication read in over 100 countries.

+ Ten issues per year delivered in high quality print, Zinio digital - or both

+ Includes a free 100+ page Travel Guide to the world's most exciting flying destinations

+ Beautiful photography, simple design and the highest production values from our passionate editors - we've all been flying for 20+ years!

+ Subscriber Prize Draws: twice a year, a lucky subscriber wins a new paraglider of their choice

Every issue is packed with insight, inspiration and education

Advice to help you fly better

Glider, harness and instrument reviews

Insightful columns

Inspirational photography

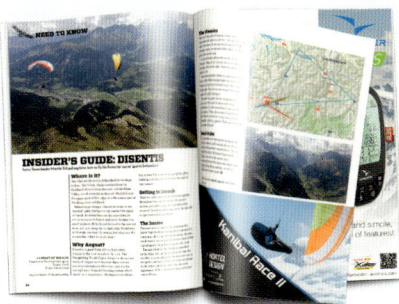

Travel, new destinations and sites

New equipment and gear news

"I just subscribed, the first copy arrived yesterday and I immediately fell in love with it."
Massimo Gulli, new paraglider pilot, Italy

Subscribe today at *xcmag.com*. Find us on social media #xcmag